A. Lincoln

From the original negative taken from life by Brady, in 1864, now in the
private collection of Frederick H. Meserve, New York City

REMINISCENCES OF
ABRAHAM LINCOLN

BY DISTINGUISHED MEN OF HIS TIME

COLLECTED AND EDITED BY
ALLEN THORNDIKE RICE

NEW AND REVISED EDITION

HARPER & BROTHERS PUBLISHERS
NEW YORK AND LONDON
MCMIX

CONTENTS

PUBLISHER'S NOTE

WITH the passage of time personal recollections of Lincoln acquire a superlative value. Historians and biographers must often write at second hand, but the personal quality of testimony given by associates and friends supplies the intimate touch and inner glimpse which make the real man live before us.

In the present edition of this book, revised from the original volume prepared by the late Allen Thorndike Rice, the publishers have aimed to keep everything that contributes to a knowledge of Lincoln's personality. There are the recollections of lawyers who rode the circuit with Lincoln in Illinois, who heard from his lips the story of his life and listened to his tales before the fires of wayside taverns. There are descriptions of his early political campaigns by men who listened to his speeches, and there are vivid pictures of Lincoln the President, Lincoln in the Cabinet, Lincoln in the dark days of the Civil War, Lincoln at Gettysburg, Lincoln the liberator of the slaves, and Lincoln the friend of the soldiers, — pictures sketched by friends, members of his administration, high officers of the Union Army, and others who were brought into close contact with Lincoln the man.

It is the personal Lincoln, therefore, who lives before us in these pages. Critical history is not attempted, and there is relatively little formal eulogy save for the tributes of poet and orator which close the book.

I

INTRODUCTORY

IT was mainly with the view of accumulating a mass of trustworthy evidence concerning the personal traits and private utterances of Abraham Lincoln that I conceived the plan and approached the task of uniting in one or more volumes the opinions of the most distinguished characters, still surviving, of the great war which produced them. The result has been gratifying beyond expectation, furnishing—I think it is not too much to say—a remarkable book about a remarkable man.

Most men who visited Washington during the civil war met Abraham Lincoln. Amid the clash of armed strife and the din of party struggle, he never denied to the humblest citizen a willing ear and a cheering word. Although not "all things to all men," in the common acceptation of the phrase, there was rarely an hour too crowded for him to utter a memorable word or to tell an apt story to the passing visitor. By degrees and by accretion, these utterances and stories, or rather these parables, have grown in number with the growth of a great reputa-

tion.   Story after story and trait after trait, as varying in value as in authenticity, has been added to the
Lincolniana, until at last the name of the great war
President has come to be a biographic lodestone, at-
tracting without distinction or discrimination both the
true and the false.   Talleyrand himself was not made
sponsor for so many historic sayings as have fallen
to the heritage of Abraham Lincoln.   It may, indeed, be doubted whether his entire presidential term
would have sufficed to utter the number attributed
to him.   Yet it is certain that he rarely failed to
seize an opportunity to illustrate the situation by a
homely parable, which substituted a story for an argument and left the argument to the listener's own
deductive powers.   He rarely refused audience to
any one.   He rarely declined to face any person or
any situation, however annoying the interview or
the occasion.   He felt himself capable of confronting
all the difficulties of his high place, and this faith in
his own strength sufficed to guide him through some
of the severest trials that have ever fallen to the
lot of a public man.   His many-sided nature enabled him to excel in most of the tasks that he attempted, and the triumphant power he showed on
most occasions was one of the essential characteristics of his nature.   From a local politician and an
obscure member of Congress, he suddenly arose to
be one of the world's most influential statesmen.

From a volunteer against Indian insurgents, he became the mover of vast armies, and met with firmness, patience and skill the most harassing exigencies
of a great civil war. Beginning as a stump speaker
and corner-grocery debater, he lived to take his place
in the front rank of immortal orators. It was this
power of compassing the most trying situations that
made the brief and crowded space of four years suf-
fice for him to accomplish a task that generations
had been preparing, and which, to use his own words,
before assuming the presidency, "offered more difficulties than had devolved upon Washington."

But, to struggle was not new to him. His whole
life had been a series of obscure but heroic struggles,
and it may safely be said that no man of Lincoln's
historical stature ever passed through a more checkered or more varied career. It fills one with astonishment to follow the vocations that successively fell
to the lot of this extraordinary man, since, as a boy,
in 1826, he left the school (to reach which he
walked nine miles every day), to the sad hour when,
in 1865, he perished, as President of the United
States. Beginning as a farm laborer, studying at
night by the light of the fire, he was the hostler, he
ground corn, he built fires and he cooked—all for
thirty-one cents a day. In 1827, he is recorded as an
athlete of local renown, while, at the same time, he
was a writer on temperance and a champion of the

integrity of the American Union. In 1830, we are told that he undertook "to split for Mrs. Nancy Miller four hundred rails for every yard of brown jean, dyed with walnut bark, that would be required to make him a pair of trousers." He next turned his attention to public speaking—beginning his career as orator standing on an empty keg at Decatur. Next we find him, in turn, a Mississippi boatman, a clerk at the polls, a salesman, a debater in frontier debating clubs, a militia captain in the Black Hawk War, a private for a month in a volunteer spy company, and an unsuccessful candidate for the Legislature. In 1832, he seriously thought of becoming a blacksmith, but he changed his views, and bought a country store on credit. Ruined by a drunken partner, he failed, but, as money came to him, he paid his honest debts—discharging the last note in 1849. We next find him qualifying as a land surveyor, after six weeks' study. In 1833, he is appointed postmaster at New Salem, using his hat as a post-office. He was also, as occasion called, a referee and umpire, the unquestioned judge in all local disputes, wagers and horse races. Having read law, he became a lawyer. In 1834, he was a successful candidate for the Legislature of Illinois, and, as a member of it, protested against slavery. Challenged about this time to fight a duel, he became reconciled with his adversary and married Miss Mary Todd, after constituting himself her champion. Defeated as candidate for Congress, in 1843, he was returned in 1846. About this time he patented a novel steamboat. In 1854, he sought without success to be appointed General Land Commissioner. Subsequently, he is seen engaged vigorously in State politics, opposing Judge Douglas in a debate that attracted national attention, and that gave him the nomination for the Presidency of the United States.

The face of Lincoln told the story of his life—a life of sorrow and struggle, of deep-seated sadness, of ceaseless endeavor. It would have taken no Lavater to interpret the rugged energy stamped on that un-comely plebeian face, with its great crag-like brows and bones, or to read there the deep melancholy that overshadowed every feature of it.

Even as President of the United States, at a period when the nation's peril invested the holder of the office with almost despotic power, there seems to have been in Lincoln's nature a modesty and lack of desire to rule which nothing could lessen or efface. Wielding the power of a king, he retained the modesty of a commoner.

And, surely, it is not among the least remarkable of her achievements, that American Democracy should have produced great statesmen and great soldiers, when called for by great events, who, as a rule, have been free from that dangerous ambition which has tainted the fairest names of European history. If we have not had our age of Pericles, of Augustus or of Leo, we can boast of a history that has given us, within the period of a century, the patriotism of a Washington, a Lincoln and a Grant.

If we may believe tradition, Lincoln came from a stock which proves the hereditary source of his chief characteristics. His humor, his melancholy, his strange mingling of energy and indolence, his generosity, his unconventional character, his frugality, his tenderness, his courage, all are traceable to his ancestry as well as to the strange society which molded the boy and nerved the man to face without fear every danger that beset his path. He revealed to the old world a new type of man, of the Anglo-Saxon race, it is true, but modified by circumstances so novel and potent, and even dominating in their influence, as to mark a new departure in human character. Lincoln was the type and representative of the " Western man "—an evolution of family isolation, of battles with primeval forces and the most savage races of men, of the loneliness of untrodden forests, of the absence of a potent public opinion, of a state of society in which only inherent greatness of human character was respected; in which tradition and authority went for naught, and courage and will were alone recognized as having rightful domination. The peculiarities of this society were not less reflected in its character than in its tastes. Thus, in Lincoln, for example, Rabelais and Machiavelli, coarse wit and political cunning, were quite as conspicuous as that tenderness and self-abnegation which recall the early history of the Christian Church. The Western man, the American of the Western prairies and forests, could in no sense be termed a colonial Englishman, as a large class of cultivated Eastern Americans might not unjustly be described. England had no mortgage on the mind or character or manners of these children of the West. The Western settlers had no respect for English traditions or teachings, whether of Church or of State. Accustomed all their lives to grapple with nature face to face, they thought and they spoke, with all the boldness of unrestrained sincerity, on every topic of human interest or of sacred memory, without the slightest recognition of any right of external authority to impose restrictions, or even to be heard in protest against their intellectual independence. As their life developed the utmost independence of creed and individuality, he whose originality was the most fearless and self-contained was chief among them. Among such a people, blood of their blood and bone of their bone, differing from them only in stature, Abraham Lincoln arose to rule the American people with a more than kingly power, and received from them a more than feudal loyalty.

Those who follow his life must be impressed with the equal serenity of Lincoln's temper, in moments of the darkest adversity as in the hours of his greatest triumphs. It has been said that it is easier to stand adversity than prosperity, but, however true this may be of private life, it is hardly applicable to times of stress in public affairs. I was struck with the remark of a great captain, when, in returning some compliment about America, I referred to the feats of the armies under his command. " I accept your praise of our victories," he rejoined, " but what our armies would have been in defeat I cannot say."

Lincoln's character was weighed in both balances; and it was not found wanting. No man could have borne more nobly than he the sternest test of defeat. At these moments of extreme tension, his character alone came to his rescue.

He was melancholy without being morbid—a leading characteristic of men of genuine humor; and it was this sense of humor that often enabled him to endure the most cruel strokes, that called for his sense of pity and cast a gloom over his official life. On these occasions he would relieve himself by comparing trifles with great things and great things with trifles. No story was too trivial or even too coarse for his purpose; provided that it aptly illustrated his ideas or served his policy. To this peculiar tendency of mind we owe the many stories and quaint sayings which lend to every recollection of Lincoln a strange and uncommon interest.

I know no better illustration of the peculiar rapidity with which he would pass from one side of his nature to the other than a reminiscence for which I am indebted to Governor Curtin of Pennsylvania, who, at the time, was one of the leading "War Governors." He was summoned to see Lincoln, at the White House, on arriving after midnight from the battle-field of Fredericksburg, where he had been inspecting the wounded and surveying this field of national disaster. Lincoln showed much anxiety about the wounded, and asked many questions about the battle.

Governor Curtin replied, "Mr. President, it was not a battle, it was a butchery," and proceeded to give a graphic description of the scenes he had witnessed. Lincoln was heart-broken at the recital, and soon reached a state of nervous excitement bordering on insanity.

Finally, as the Governor was leaving the room, he went forward, and, taking the President by the hand, tenderly expressed his sympathy for his sorrow. He said, "Mr. President, I am deeply touched by your sorrow, and at the distress I have caused you.

I have only answered your questions. No doubt my impressions have been colored by the sufferings I have seen. I trust matters will look brighter when the official reports come in. I would give all I possess to know how to rescue you from this terrible war."

Lincoln's whole aspect suddenly changed, and he relieved his mind by telling a story.

"This reminds me, Governor," he said, "of an old farmer out in Illinois that I used to know. He took it into his head to go into hog raising. He sent out to Europe and imported the finest breed of hogs he could buy. The prize hog was put in a pen, and the farmer's two mischievous boys— James and John—were told to be sure not to let him out. But James, the worst of the two, let the brute out next day. The hog went straight for the boys, and drove John up a tree. Then the hog went for the seat of James's trousers, and the only way the boy could save himself was by holding on to the hog's tail. The hog would not give up his hunt nor the boy his hold! After they had made a good many circles around the tree, the boy's courage began to give out, and he shouted to his brother, 'I say, John, come down, quick, and help me *let this hog go!*' Now, Governor, that is exactly my case. I wish some one would come and help me let this hog go!"

This was a striking illustration of the sudden transitions to which Lincoln's nature was prone. It sought relief in the most trying situations by recalling some parallel incident of a humorous character. His sense of humor never flagged. Even in his telegraphic correspondence with his generals we have instances of it which reflect his peculiar vein.

General Sherman, who, like Cæsar in this as in other respects, enjoys a joke even at his own expense, relates a story that illustrates this peculiarity. Soon after the battle of Shiloh the President promoted two officers to Major-Generalships. A good deal of dissatisfaction was expressed at this act. Among other critics of the President was General Sherman himself, who telegraphed to Washington, that, if such ill-advised promotions continued, the best chance for officers would be to be transferred from the front to the rear. This telegram was shown to the President. He immediately replied by telegraph to the General that, in the matter of appointments, he was necessarily guided by officers whose opinions and knowledge he valued and respected.

"The two appointments," he added, "referred to by you in your dispatch to a gentleman in Washington were made at the suggestion of two men whose advice and character I prize most highly:

I refer to Generals Grant and Sherman." General Sherman then recalled the fact that, in the flush of victory, General Grant and himself had both recommended these promotions, but that it had escaped his memory at the time of writing his telegraphic dispatch.

The oddity of Lincoln's reply is characteristic. He subsequently sent to General Sherman the right to promote, at his own choice, eight colonels under his command.

His feeling toward Sherman and Grant, at the close of the war, as well as his extreme sensitiveness to rebuke on the part of those he esteemed, is well illustrated by another incident, for which, also, I am indebted to General Sherman. In conversation with him—I think at Richmond—the President asked the General whether he could guess what had always attracted him to Grant and Sherman and led to a friendlier feeling for them than he had for others. " It was because," he said, " you never found fault with me, from the days of Vicksburg down."

There is a sermon in these words which suggests many reflections. The responsibility of office weighed heavily upon the President, but never overwhelmed him; yet the rebuke of a friend caused him the keenest pangs.

General Schenck once told me of being with

Lincoln on the occasion of his receiving bad news from the army. Placing his hands upon the General's knee and speaking with much emotion, he said, "You have little idea of the terrible weight of care and sense of responsibility of this office of mine. Schenck, if to be at the head of Hell is as hard as what I have to undergo here, I could find it in my heart to pity Satan himself."

It will be seen from this remark that Lincoln was sometimes weary of the great burden that had fallen on him, and that he would gladly have resigned it to others had this seemed possible without imperilling the national interests he had so close at heart.

The following war episode, related to me by Mr. W. H. Croffut, who has given much attention to the subject, will help to illustrate the willingness of Lincoln to put into other hands, and even to surrender to another political party, the administration of the Government, provided that the act could contribute toward the great end of peace and reunion. Mr. Croffut says:

I have forgotten the exact month to which the beginning of this narrative refers; indeed, I am not quite certain about the year, but it was winter time —probably the dawn of 1880. I had called at Thurlow Weed's, to inquire after the health of that aged man, then fourscore, and to enjoy hearing him talk about the by-gone times in which he bore a distinguished part. His tall form reclined upon a lounge wheeled in front of a hearth blazing with cannel coal. As I casually mentioned General McClellan in the conversation, he raised himself on his elbow and said, " He might have been President as well as not." Responding to my expression of surprise and interest, he went on :

"I'll tell you what led up to it. About the middle of December, 1862, Seward telegraphed me to come to Washington. It had happened before that I had been summoned in the same way. I took it as a matter of course and caught the first train South. I got to Washington, and, after breakfast, went straight to the State Department. Mr. Seward was waiting for me. He took me right over to the White House, saying, 'The President wants to see you.'

"We found the President deeply depressed and distressed. I had never seen him in such a mood. 'Everything goes wrong,' he broke out. 'The rebel armies hold their own ; Grant is wandering around in Mississippi ; Burnside manages to keep ahead of Lee ; Seymour has carried New York, and, if his party carries and holds many of the Northern States, we shall have to give up the fight, for we can never conquer three-quarters of our countrymen, scattered in front, flank, and rear. What shall we do ?'

"I suggested that we could continue to wait, and that the man capable of leading our splendid armies would come in time.

"'That's what I've been saying,' said Seward, who didn't believe, even then, that the war was going to be a long one.

"Mr. Lincoln did not seem to heed the remark, but he said:

"'Governor Seymour could do more for our cause than any other man living. He has been elected Governor of our largest State. If he would come to the front he could control his partisans, and give a new impetus to the war. I have sent for you, Mr. Weed, to ask you to go to Governor Seymour and tell him what I say. Tell him, now is his time. Tell him, I do not wish to be President again, and that the leader of the other party, provided it is in favor of a vigorous war against the rebellion, should have my place. Entreat him to give the true ring to his annual message; and if he will, as he easily can, place himself at the head of a great Union party, I will gladly stand aside and help to put him in the Executive Chair. All we want is to have the rebellion put down.'

"I was not greatly surprised, for I knew before that such was the President's view. I had before heard him say, 'If there is a man who can push our armies forward one mile further or one hour faster than I can, he is the man that ought to be in my place.'

"I visited Governor Seymour at Albany, and delivered my commission from Lincoln. It was received most favorably. Seymour's feeling was always right, but his head was generally wrong. When I left him it was understood that his message to the Legislature would breathe an earnest Union spirit, praising the soldiers and calling for more, and omitting the usual criticisms of the President. I forwarded this expectation to Lincoln.

"Judge of my disappointment and chagrin when Seymour's message came out—a document calculated to aid the enemy. It demanded that the war should be prosecuted 'on constitutional grounds' —as if any war ever was or ever could be—and denounced the administration for the arbitrary arrest of Vallandigham and the enforcement of the draft.

"This attempt to enlist the leader of the Democratic party having failed, Lincoln authorized me to make the same overture to McClellan.

"'Tell the General,' he said, 'that we have no wish to injure or humiliate him; that we wish only for the success of our armies; that if he will come forward and put himself at the head of a Union-Democratic party, and, through that means, push forward the Union cause, I will gladly step aside and do all I can to secure his election in 1864.'

" I opened negotiations through S. L. M. Barlow, McClellan's next friend. Mr. Barlow called. I told him the scheme to bring McClellan forward. He approved of it, and agreed to see the General. He shortly afterward told me he had seen him and secured his acquiescence; 'for,' he added, 'Mac is eager to do all he can do to put down the rebellion.' I suggested a great Union-Democratic meeting in Union Square, at which McClellan should preside and set forth his policy, and this was agreed to by both Mr. Barlow and McClellan. At the suggestion of Mr. Barlow, I drew up some memoranda of principles which it seemed to me desirable to set forth on that occasion, and these Mr. Barlow agreed to deliver to McClellan. The time set for the mass meeting was Monday, June 16th. Once more there seemed a promise of breaking the Northern hostility and ending the war, by organizing a great independent Union party under McClellan. But this hope failed us, too. For, on the very eve of the meeting, I received a formal letter from McClellan declining to preside, without giving reasons. If he had presided at that war-meeting, and had persistently followed it up, nothing but death could have kept him from being elected President of the United States in 1864."

This narrative, continues Mr. Croffut, seemed to me so extraordinary that I called on General McClellan, who resided on Gramercy Park, and told him the story, with the purpose of ascertaining why he did not preside at the meeting after agreeing to do so.

"You amaze me!" he said. "No such events ever occurred. Mr. Weed is a good old man, and he has forgotten. Mr. Lincoln never offered me the Presidency in any contingency. I never declined to preside at a war-meeting. How could I, when I was a Union soldier, and the only criticism I ever made on the Administration was that it did not push the armies fast enough? There never was a time when I would have refused to preside at any meeting that could help the Union cause. I remember nothing about any such memoranda, and am sure I never wrote to Thurlow Weed in my life."

I asked the General if no such overture was ever made by Mr. Weed.

"Not as I remember," he said. "I recollect his once speaking to me about the desirableness of taking the leadership of a War-Democratic party, but I do not remember the purport of this proposition."

At General McClellan's suggestion I called on Mr. Barlow, who also had forgotten all about it.

Returning to Mr. Weed's, I asked if he could find the letter received from General McClellan, in which he declined to preside at a war-meeting. He doubted if he had kept it, but Miss Harriet Weed, his faithful daughter and invaluable secretary, going in search of it, returned in an hour, bringing it from an upper room. It ran as follows:

(Private)

OAKLANDS, N. J., *June* 13, 1863.

My Dear Sir:

Your kind note is received.

For what I cannot doubt that you would consider good reasons, I have determined to decline the compliment of presiding over the proposed meeting of Monday next.

I fully concur with you in the conviction that an honorable peace is not now possible, and that the war must be prosecuted to save the Union and the Government, at whatever cost of time and treasure and blood.

I am clear, also, in the conclusion that the policy governing the conduct of the war should be one looking not only to military success, but also to ultimate re-union, and that it should consequently be such as to preserve the rights of all Union-loving citizens, wherever they may be, as far as compatible with military security. My views as to the prosecution of the war remain, substantially, as they have been from the beginning of the contest; these views I have made known officially.

I will endeavor to write you more fully before Monday.

In the meantime believe me to be, in great haste, truly your friend,

GEORGE B. McCLELLAN.

Hon. THURLOW WEED, New York.

"The General has forgotten that formal letter, has he?" said Mr. Weed, smiling. "If he had presided at that meeting, and rallied his party to the support of the war, he would have been President. I never heard what his reasons were, either 'before Monday' or any other day. Just see what an embarrassing time it was to refuse to preside at a war-meeting. Grant seemed to be stalled in front of Vicksburg, and that very morning came a report that he was going to raise the siege. Banks was defeated, the day before, at Port Hudson, and, two days earlier, a rebel privateer had captured six of our vessels off the Chesapeake. The very day that McClellan wrote the letter, Lee was rapidly marching through Maryland into Pennsylvania, and the North was in a panic. There couldn't have been a worse time to decline to preside at a Union meeting, and I am sorry that the General has forgotten what prevented his doing so."

I took the letter and returned to General McClellan with it.

"Well!" he exclaimed, as he took it and inspected it, "that is my writing. I wrote that, and had forgotten about it. I don't know why I declined to preside; but it was probably because I am shy in the presence of multitudes, am not in the habit of speech-making, and should be certain to preside awkwardly. But why should anybody suppose me indifferent to the prosecution of the war?"

"Because," I said, "a year later they found you standing as a candidate for President on a platform which declared the war up to that time a failure, and seemed to disparage the services of our soldiers in the field."

"I never stood on that platform a day!" he exclaimed. "Everybody knows I did not. I repudiated it in my letter, and made my repudiation of it the only condition of accepting the nomination. I told all my friends so!"

"Mr. Weed thinks," I added, "that if you had presided instead of refusing to preside, and had followed it up with corresponding action, it would have united the North, finished the war a year sooner, saved thousands of lives, and made you President."

"Oh, well," he said, laughing, "that's an interesting speculation. Nobody can tell. At any rate I didn't, and it's all over now."

Shortly afterward, I mentioned these facts to Frederick W. Seward.

"Yes," he said, "I have often heard Mr. Weed

tell the story. The fact is that neither Lincoln nor my father expected that the Administration would be re-elected. Their only hope was to have the war carried on vigorously. The President used to say, ' I am sure there are men who could do more for the success of our armies in my place than I am doing; I would gladly stand aside and let such a one take my place, any day.' Looking back at the Mexican and other wars, we thought some general would succeed Lincoln in 1864, and McClellan evidently thought so too. We did not foresee the tremendous victories and the splendid wave of patriotic feeling that carried Lincoln in again."

Colonel John Hay tells me that he is acquainted with Lincoln's effort to stir up McClellan and Seymour, heard, I suppose, when he was in the White House. And Roscoe Conkling tells me that it is not news to him.

One morning, a year before he died, Mr. Weed said to me:

"Governor Seymour was here yesterday. He stayed to dinner, and we had a good talk about old times. I spoke of the scheme to make him President, and he remembered the details as I did. But he said that his reason for his action was that he 'wanted to carry on the war legally.' He said he couldn't have carried his party with him to approve of the arbitrary arrest by Stanton of the Northern opponents of the war. When Seymour was sitting here I told him that he would have been President, certain, if he had come out heartily and unreservedly for the war in 1863; and he said, 'Well, it isn't much matter. I was not in good health at the time, and it might have killed me. It is a hard, laborious, thankless office—it is just as well as it is."

No act or utterance of General McClellan should be interpreted to convey any feeling of resentment toward Lincoln. In a conversation, not over two months before his death, General McClellan affirmed to me his belief that Lincoln intended to give him all the time for preparation that he required and demanded. The conversation turned upon the battle of Antietam, when some reference to the President's visit to the field occasioned the remark.

General McClellan had fought the battle without a commission. The victory proclaimed, the President at once visited the scene of conflict.

"I remember well," said General McClellan, "our sitting on the hillside together, Lincoln, in his own ungainly way, propped up by his long legs, with his knees almost under his chin.

"'General,' said he to me, 'you have saved the country. You must remain in command and carry us through to the end.'

"'That will be impossible,' replied McClellan. 'We need time. The influences at Washington will be too strong for you, Mr. President. I will not be allowed the required time for preparation.'"

General McClellan then recalled the exact words of Lincoln in reply:

"General, I pledge myself to stand between you and harm."

"And I honestly believe," said General McClellan, "that the President meant every word he said, but that the influences at Washington were, as I predicted, too strong for him or for any living man."

In a conversation with General Sherman, I once asked him if he had ever heard the story that General Grant, at one important crisis, cut the telegraph wires between Washington and his headquarters in order to get rid of civil interference with his military operations.

"Did he?" said the General, laughing, "why, I did that! I never heard before that Grant did it!"

He spoke for some time of the serious obstacles to the prosecution of the war caused by political interferences, and added, "I could do more with one hundred thousand men free from political control, than with three hundred thousand near Washington."

In the better sense, Lincoln was, perhaps, somewhat of a casuist in believing that the end some-times sanctifies the means; but his masterly com-mon sense was the guiding beacon in every stress and storm of events. He was so great in all the larger attributes of statesmanship that few, aside from those intimately associated with him, recog-nized his genius as a practical politician. He was ambitious, not merely because he knew his own great resources and aptitudes, but because he pro-foundly believed himself to be necessary to the country in the dire exigencies of the period. He alone had complete grasp of a situation unparalleled in our history; and this was the general conviction of the large majority of the loyal men of the North. There is no cause, then, to marvel that he should have greatly desired a re-election in 1864, because his second term would not only cover the close of the war drama which, for four years, had absorbed the attention of a watchful world, but also the still greater responsibilities of reconstructing the shat-tered Union.

Recognizing the fact that the anxiety of Lin-coln for a second term was a far nobler passion than anything rooted in mere personal pride or ambition, and remembering his offer to Governor Seymour, we can easily understand how he could justify him-self in bringing all his skill in practical politics to bear on the problem of re-election.

An incident, hitherto unpublished, will illustrate this trait.

During the fall of 1864 it became evident that Pennsylvania was a "doubtful State." General Mc-Clellan, the candidate of the Democratic party, was not only popular there as a native Pennsylvanian, but, even among those loyal to the administration, he had a strong following and great sympathy, from the belief that he had been a much abused man. Lincoln was advised by the Republican State Committee of Pennsylvania that the prospect was very uncertain. It was felt that, on the result in the Keystone State, hinged the fate of the national election. A gentleman belonging to the Republican Committee, then, as now, one of the leading politicians of the State, had a consultation with the President on the situation. He thus relates the interview :

"Mr. President," I said, " the only sure way to organize victory in this contest, is to have some fifteen thousand, or more, Pennsylvania soldiers furloughed and sent home to vote. While their votes in the field would count man for man, their presence at the polls at home would exert an influence not easily to be estimated, by exciting enthusiasm and building up party *morale*. I would advise you to send a private message to General Grant, to be given in an unofficial way, asking for such an issu·

ance of furloughs to Pennsylvania soldiers in the field."

Lincoln was silent for some moments and seemed to be pondering. Then he answered :

" I have never had any intimation from General Grant as to his feeling for me. I don't know how far he would be disposed to be my friend in the matter, nor do I think it would be safe to trust him."

The President's interlocutor responded with some heat, " And do you mean to say that the man at whose back you stood, in defiance of the clamor of the country, for whom you fought through thick and thin, would not stand by you now ? "

" I don't know that General Grant would be my friend in this matter," reiterated the President.

" Then, let it be done through General Meade, the direct commander of the Army of the Potomac— and General Sheridan, how about him ? "

At this question, Lincoln's face grew sunny and bright. " I can trust Phil," he said; " he's all right ! "

As a result of this conference, one of the assistant secretaries of war was sent to Petersburg with a strictly unofficial message to General Meade, and another agent was deputed to visit General Sheridan. Some 10,000 or more Pennsylvania soldiers went home to vote when the time came, and Pennsylvania was carried by a handsome majority for the administration.

If statesmanship is a practical science, to be tested by the touch-stone of enduring success, then is Lincoln entitled to a place among the world's great statesmen. He was not of the rulers who seek only to impress their own will on the nation. He was not of the rulers who play for mere place in the great game of politics.

As, in the first instance, tyrants are the selfish masters, so, in the other, demagogues are the selfish servants. But, above them, stand the men who have sought power to hold it as a sacred trust, and whose ambition and conduct are regulated by an ardent purpose to serve great national interests. It seems not too much to say that among these was Lincoln.

He was pre-eminently a democratic ruler. Profoundly believing in a government of the people, by the people and for the people, however earnest his wish, as a man, to promote and enact justice between classes and races, he never went faster nor further than to enforce the will of the people that elected him. His strength as a President lay in his deep sympathy with the people, "the plain folks," as he loved to call them, and his intuitive knowledge of all their thoughts and aims, their prejudices and preferences, equally and alike. He was elected to save the Union, not to destroy slavery; and he did not aid, directly or indirectly, the movement to abolish slavery, until the voice of the people was heard demanding it in order that the Union might be saved. He did not free the negro for the sake of the slave, but for the sake of the Union. It is an error to class him with the noble band of abolitionists to whom neither Church nor State was sacred when it sheltered slavery. He signed the proclamation of emancipation solely because it had become impossible to restore the Union *with* slavery.

Like the nation itself, Lincoln, although personally opposed to slavery, was but slowly educated into the belief that no republican civilization could endure with slavery as a corner-stone, or even as one of the pillars, of the Temple of Democracy. He believed that the spread of slavery should be resisted; for the Constitution did not contemplate its extension. He believed at one time that slavery should not be interfered with in the States that sustained it; for the Constitution, in fact, although not in words, had recognized its legality. It was not until slavery *or* the Union must be sacrificed that he became the emancipator of the negro race in America.

The Constitution, indeed, was the fetich of the pre-rebellion period of our history, and it commanded the loyal worship of nearly all the earlier statesmen of the republic.

It was not until the Southern politicians, growing more and more arrogant, passed, with the aid of their Northern allies, the Fugitive Slave Law, that the conscience of the North made itself felt as a political force; for, hitherto, it had been satisfied with moral and religious protests, or with silent lamentations over the impossibility of abolishing slavery under the Federal Constitution.

That act gave the death-blow to the Whig party. Out of its ashes arose the Republican party, which was organized solely to prevent the extension of slavery into virgin territory, but which was destined to destroy it and subsequently to enfranchise the slaves whom it had emancipated.

Yet the Fugitive Slave Law did not arouse in Abraham Lincoln the profound indignation that he was afterward to transmute into emancipation.

The Fugitive Slave Law, by some oversight, had omitted the District of Columbia from its operations. On the 10th of January, 1849, in the 30th Congress, Abraham Lincoln offered a resolution to extend the Fugitive Slave Law over the District of Columbia!

It was for this act, when the news of his nomination for the presidency reached Massachusetts, that he was denounced by the greatest of American anti-slavery orators, Wendell Phillips, as "the Slave Hound of Illinois."

This proposition, however, was not presented in what might otherwise have well been regarded as its naked deformity. It was part of a bill, offered by the obscure congressman from Illinois, to provide for the gradual extinction of slavery in the District.

As this incident in the public life of Lincoln has been but slightly noticed, it may be well to put the entire record before the reader :

" *January* 8, 1849. At Second Session, 30th Congress, Mr. Lincoln voted against a motion to suspend the rules and take up the following :

" *Resolved :* That the Committee on the Judiciary is hereby instructed to report a bill to the House, providing effectually for the apprehension and delivery of fugitives from Iowa who have escaped, or who may escape, from one State into another."

" *January* 13, 1849. Mr. Lincoln gave notice of a motion for leave to introduce a bill abolishing slavery in the District of Columbia by consent of the free white people of the District of Columbia, with compensation to owners.

" At Second Session, 30th Congress, January 10th, 1849, John Wentworth, of Illinois, introduced the following :

" *Whereas,* The traffic now prosecuted in this metropolis of the Republic in human beings as chattels is contrary to natural justice and the fundamental principles of our political system, and is notoriously a reproach to our country throughout Christendom, and a serious hinderance to the progress of republican liberty among the nations of the earth ; therefore,

" *Resolved*, That the Committee for the District of Columbia be instructed to report a bill, as soon as practicable, prohibiting the slave trade in said District."

" Mr. Lincoln thereupon read an amendment which he intended to offer, if he could obtain the opportunity, as follows :

" That the Committee on the District of Columbia be instructed to report a bill in substance as follows :

" SEC. 1. *Be it enacted, etc.*, That no person not now within the District of Columbia, nor now owned by any person or persons now resident within it, nor hereafter born within it, shall ever be held in slavery within said District.

" SEC. 2. That no person now within said District, or now owned by any person or persons now resident within the same, or hereafter born within it, shall ever be held in slavery within the limits of said District.

" *Provided*, That officers of the Government of

the United States, being citizens of the slave-holding States, coming into said District on public business, and remaining only so long as may be reasonably necessary for that object, may be attended into and out of said District, and while there, by the necessary servants of themselves and their families, without their rights to hold such servants in service being thereby impaired.

" Sec. 3. That all children born of slave mothers within said District on or after the first day of January, in the year of our Lord one thousand eight hundred and fifty, shall be free ; but shall be reasonably supported and educated by the respective owners of their mothers, or by their heirs or representatives, and shall serve reasonable service as apprentices to such owners, heirs and representatives, until they respectively arrive at the age of — years, when they shall be entirely free ; but the municipal authorities of Washington and Georgetown, within their respective jurisdictional limits, are hereby empowered and required to make all suitable and necessary provisions for enforcing obedience to this section, on the part of both masters and apprentices.

" Sec. 4. That all persons now within said District, lawfully held as slaves, or now owned by any person or persons now residents within said District, shall remain such at the will of their respective owners, their heirs and legal representatives ;

"Provided, That any such owner, or his legal representatives, may at any time receive from the Treasury of the United States the full value of his or her slave of the class in this section mentioned, upon which such slave shall be forthwith and forever free.

"And provided further, That the President of the United States, the Secretary of State, and the Secretary of the Treasury shall be a board for determining the value of such slaves as their owners may desire to emancipate under this section, and whose duty it shall be to hold a session for such purpose on the first Monday of each calendar month, to receive all applications, and, on satisfactory evidence in each case that the person presented for valuation is a slave and of the class in this section mentioned, and is owned by the applicant, shall value such slave at his or her full cash value, and give to the applicant an order on the Treasury for the amount, and also to such slave a certificate of freedom.

"Sec. 5. That the municipal authorities of Washington and Georgetown, within their respective jurisdictional limits, are hereby empowered and required to provide active and efficient means to arrest and deliver up to their owners all fugitive slaves escaping into said districts.

"Sec. 6. That the officers of elections within said District of Columbia are hereby empowered and required to open polls at all the usual places of holding elections on the first Monday of April next, and receive the vote of every free white male citizen above the age of twenty-one years, having resided within said District for the period of one year or more next preceding the time of such voting for or against this act, to proceed in taking such votes in all respects, not herein specified, as at elections under the municipal laws, and with as little delay as possible to transmit correct statements of the votes so cast to the President of the United States; and it shall be the duty of the President to canvass such votes immediately, and if a majority of them be found to be for this act, to forthwith issue his proclamation giving notice of the fact; and this act shall only be in full force and effect on and after the day of such proclamation.

"Sec. 7. That involuntary servitude for the punishment of crime whereof the party shall have been duly convicted shall in nowise be prohibited by this act.

"Sec. 8. That for all the purposes of this act, the jurisdictional limits of Washington are extended to all parts of the District of Columbia not now included within the present limits of Georgetown."

It was the 5th section of this bill that aroused Wendell Phillips's indignation. Both of these eminent men lived long enough to honor each other's services and complement each other's career—for, without the agitator, the emancipator would have had no public opinion to support him, and, without Mr. Lincoln's act, Mr. Phillips's oratory would have remained brilliant rhetoric only.

Growing, as the people grew, in moral conviction, sympathizing with them and aiming only to do their will, Abraham Lincoln may rightly be regarded as a model democratic statesman. Thus growing and thus acting, his official measures had all the force of a resistless fate. What he achieved endured, because it was founded on the rock of the people's will. It has been the destiny of many illustrious reformers to outlive the reforms for which they zealously strove, and history furnishes innumerable illustrations of the truth that reforms not based on public opinion rarely outlast the lifetime of their champions. What eager idealists, therefore, decried in Lincoln—his loyal deference to the will of the majority, his tardiness in adopting radical measures, and his reluctance to advance more rapidly than the "plain folks"— time has shown to be the highest wisdom in the ruler of a democracy.

Lincoln's deep-rooted faith in representative democracy was strikingly illustrated in his first public act—the appointment of his Cabinet. Believing in the rightfulness of party rule, that is to say, in the rule of the majority, instead of seeking to call as his councillors men who might serve his personal ends, he selected them from the most popular of his rivals —men who had competed with him for the Presidential nomination. His Cabinet thus represented not only every division of his party, but consisted of those whom these factions regarded as their ablest representatives. It was a Cabinet of "all the talents" and all the popularities ; and yet among these veteran statesmen, most of them long-trained and skillful in all the arts of statecraft, Lincoln was acknowledged the master spirit. This Cabinet numbered among its members men no less eminent than Seward, Chase and Stanton.

The question of ascendency in the Cabinet during the War of the Rebellion is still earnestly discussed by some. The names of Lincoln, Seward and Stanton have each advocates claiming unquestioned preeminence for one or the other of these great statesmen. Some, with greater zeal and fidelity than knowledge or justice, have sought to exalt the great Secretary of State or the great Secretary of War at the expense of the great War President. Surely no labor of love could be more futile. For history will place all of these illustrious Americans on the most honored pedestals in the nation's pantheon, and will add that each of them supplemented, not overshadowed, his associates. Yet no one who was familiar with the secrets of the administration could well doubt that in all critical issues the uncouth Western statesman, unused to power, asserted and maintained his inherent as well as his official supremacy. His common sense, his unselfish purpose, his keen perceptions, his unostentatious manners, his mental ubiquity, and his insight into men, soon made him as pre-eminent and as powerful with the leaders of the people as he had always been with the people themselves.

Stanton's iron will was felt at every important epoch of the war, but when his idea of policy conflicted with the purpose of his chief, the great War Minister was forced to yield. Seward, perhaps the ablest American diplomatist of the century, found also in the man of the people a master who knew when to exact implicit obedience. This fact is demonstrated by the State document herewith reproduced in *fac-simile* *—the dispatch conveying to Mr. Adams, our Minister at the Court of St. James's, Mr. Seward's first full instructions after the outbreak of the Rebellion. It was corrected by the President, as will now be seen, in words that testify to his statesmanship, as, without question, they saved the nation from a war with England, which, at that period, would probably have resulted in the establishment of the Southern Confederacy.

---

* This *fac-simile*, originally designed by me for this volume, was, for urgent reasons, unnecessary here to state, first published in the issue of the *North American Review* for April, 1886.

Lincoln, then, had been President for only three months. Certainly, when he came to the office, the farthest thing from the thought of the people was to credit him with diplomatic knowledge or skill. But this paper, by its erasures, its substitutions and its amendments, shows a nice sense of the shades of meaning in words, a comprehensive knowledge of the situation, and a thorough appreciation of the grave results which might follow the use of terms that he either modified or erased. These corrections of Mr. Seward's dispatch, by the " rail-splitter " of Illinois, form a most interesting addition to the history of Lincoln, and to that of our diplomacy.

The paper is one that needs few comments to bring its remarkable character before the reader. The burdens of home affairs, which then lay heavily on the new President, will readily recur to every student of our history. The countless demands upon his time gave little opportunity for reflection. Prompt action was required in all directions and in everything, small and great. But, as his handiwork shows, he turned with perfect composure from the home to the equally threatening foreign field, and revised, with a master-hand, the most important dispatch that had as yet been prepared by Mr. Seward. The work shows a freedom, an insight into foreign affairs, a skill in the use of language, a delicacy of criticism and a discrimination in methods of diplomatic dealing which entitle the President to the honors of an astute statesman.

The opening of the dispatch is Mr. Seward's first draft as corrected by himself. The President's revision begins with the direction to leave out the paragraph, "We intend to have a clear and simple record of whatever issue may arise between us and Great Britain." He seemed to see no reason for harshly reproving Mr. Dallas; and so he modified the expression, "The President is surprised and grieved," to the President "regrets." With the multiplicity of facts crowding his mind, he yet did not forget that no explanations had been demanded of Great Britain; and so he wrote in the margin: "Leave out, because it does not appear that such explanations were demanded." He did not care to reflect upon the body of our representatives abroad, and therefore he struck out the sentence on that subject, which is marked. He crossed out "wrongful" and wrote "hurtful," showing a knowledge of the exact value of words worthy of a Trench. A wrongful act implies intention to harm, but in the word "hurtful" the charge of intent is not found. In the unsettled condition of the question of recognizing the Southern Confederacy, he did not deem it best to threaten; and so, instead of "No one of these proceedings will be *borne* by the United States," he first substituted "will pass unnoticed," for "borne," and then, strengthening his own expression somewhat, he finally wrote "will pass unquestioned."

In discussing the question of privateers, Lincoln wrote "Omit" opposite another threat in the expression, "the laws of nations afford an adequate and proper remedy, and we shall avail ourselves of it." This last clause he struck out. An examination of the *fac-simile* will at once disclose the nature of the more extensive changes that were made. The close of the letter exhibits further examples of minor corrections which are of exceeding interest. The changes in one sentence are especially noteworthy. "If that nation will now repeat the same great crime," wrote Mr. Seward. "If that nation *shall* now repeat the same great *error*," amended Lincoln. "Social *calamities*" he changed to "social *convulsions*," as if he had in mind that, in the end, the results might not prove calamitous, however great the convulsions. The paper will bear long study, and no one can examine it without acquiring a new and more exalted estimate of Lincoln's many-sided powers.

Frequent efforts have been made to obtain a copy of the draft here published, but, even when backed by the authority of Congress, they have failed in securing it.

In the Forty-fourth Congress, first session, in the

Senate, on Tuesday, June 6, 1876, Senator Boutwell offered, for present consideration, this resolution, to which he said he supposed there would be no objection :

"*Resolved*, That the President be requested, if not in his opinion inconsistent with the public interests, to furnish the Senate with a *fac-simile* copy of the original draft of the letter of the Secretary of State to the Minister of the United States, at the Court of St. James's, in May, 1861, in relation to the proclamation of Her Majesty, the Queen of Great Britain, recognizing the belligerent character of the Confederate States."

There being now no valid objection to its publicity, I have availed myself of an opportunity of giving to the public the draft of this famous diplomatic dispatch ; and, in order to make the comparison less difficult, the dispatch also is given in full, as printed in the official correspondence, page by page, with notes of the corrections made in the draft as *addenda* to each page.

Of the value of this volume I may speak without vanity, as my function has been that of collector only. The contributors took an earnest and generally a conspicuous part, each in his own field, in the great American struggle for nationality and freedom. I have not sought to eliminate statements with which I disagree, nor to prevent the occasional conflict of testimony which results from that inherent fallibility of human evidence that sometimes troubles, however slightly, even the highest sources of authority. Each writer reports what he himself believes, or saw, or heard, and stands sponsor for his own contribution to these interesting memoirs.

It has been necessary to postpone the publication of many essays as interesting and as valuable as those embraced in this collection ; for, in my desire to secure the testimony of every eminent associate of Lincoln, I endeavored to leave no prominent American of the war period uninformed of the work in progress. These additional essays will appear at a later day.

The public, I venture to believe, will look with sincere satisfaction upon the result obtained through the prompt and able co-operation of the distinguished contributors to these reminiscences. For the time is fast coming when we shall seek in vain for survivors of the dark days that fashioned the career of Abraham Lincoln. Already, within the brief period of one year, death has stricken many names from the list—among them the historic ones of Grant, McClellan, Hancock, and McDowell. Yet a little while, and few witnesses will remain to tell the tale. And coming generations will remember with tenderness the recorded words of the great-hearted statesman to whom every sorrow of the nation was more than sorrow of his own. They will dwell fondly upon his pathetic simplicity, and with pride upon his rare and splendid gifts. With peculiar affection they will recall his every utterance, grave or humorous. They will recollect with gratitude the devoted patriotism which guided him through all, and they will remember with keen sorrow the calamity of his tragic end.

ALLEN THORNDIKE RICE.

THE DISPATCH AS PRINTED.

No. 10.]   DEPARTMENT OF STATE,
WASHINGTON, *May* 21, 1861.

SIR: This Government considers that our relations in Europe have reached a crisis in which it is necessary for it to take a decided stand, on which not only its immediate measures but its ultimate and permanent policy can be determined and defined. At the same time it neither means to menace Great Britain nor to wound the susceptibilities of that or any other European nation. That policy is developed in this paper.

The paper itself is not to be read or shown to the British Secretary of State, nor are any of its positions to be prematurely, unnecessarily, or indiscreetly made known. But its spirit will be your guide. You will keep back nothing when the time arrives for its being said with dignity, propriety, and effect, and you will all the while be careful to say nothing that will be incongruous or inconsistent with the views which it contains. [*See Page* 1 *of fac-simile copy.*

Mr. Dallas in a brief dispatch of May 2 (No. 333), tells us that Lord John Russell recently requested an interview with him on account of the solicitude which his lordship felt concerning the effect of certain measures represented as likely to be adopted by the President.   In that conversation the British Secretary told Mr. Dallas that the three representatives of the Southern Confederacy were then in London, that Lord John Russell had not yet seen them, but that he was not unwilling to see them, unofficially. He farther informed Mr. Dallas that an understanding exists between the British and French Governments which would lead both to take one and the same course as to recognition.   His lordship then referred to   [*Page* 2.

the rumor of a meditated blockade by us of Southern ports, and a discontinuance of them as ports of entry. Mr. Dallas answered that he knew nothing on those topics, and therefore could say nothing.   He added that you were expected to arrive in two weeks. Upon this statement Lord John Russell acquiesced in the expediency of waiting for the full knowledge you were expected to bring.

Mr. Dallas transmitted to us some newspaper reports of ministerial explanations made in Parliament.

You will base no proceedings on parliamentary debates farther than to seek explanations when necessary and communicate them to this department.

The President regrets   [*Page* 3.

On this page, after the word department, the President drew a line around the sentence " We intend to have a clear and simple record of whatever issue may arise between us and Great Britain," and wrote the words " Leave out." He also similarly encircled the words " is surprised and grieved," and rendered the phrase " The President regrets."

that Mr. Dallas did not protest against the proposed unofficial intercourse between the British Government and the missionaries of the insurgents.

It is due, however, to Mr. Dallas to say, that our instructions had been given only to you and not to him, and that his loyalty and fidelity, too rare in these times, are appreciated.

Intercourse of any kind with the so-called commissioners is liable to be construed as a recognition of the authority which appointed them. Such intercourse would be none the less hurtful to us for being called unofficial, and it might be even more injurious, because we should have no means of knowing what points might be resolved by it. Moreover,

[*Page* 4.

After the phrase " missionaries of the insurgents " the Secretary had added, " as well as against the demand for explanations made by the British Government ; " but the President wrote " Leave out, because it does not appear that explanations were demanded."

As the Secretary wrote the second sentence, it read : " It is due, however, to Mr. Dallas to say that our instructions had been given only to you, not to him, and that his loyalty and fidelity, too rare in these times *among our representatives abroad*, are *confessed and* appreciated." The President wrote " Leave out " against the words italicized.

In the last complete sentence on this page, also, the President substituted the word "hurtful" for "wrongful."

unofficial intercourse is useless and meaningless if it is not expected to ripen into official intercourse and direct recognition. It is left doubtful, here, whether the proposed unofficial intercourse has yet actually begun. Your own antecedent instructions are deemed explicit enough and it is hoped that you have not misunderstood them. You will, in any event, desist from all intercourse whatever, unofficial as well as official, with the British Government, so long as it shall continue intercourse of either kind with the domestic enemies of this country.

When intercourse shall have been arrested for this cause, you will communicate with this department and receive further directions.   [*Page* 5.

After the words "domestic enemies of this country" the Secretary had added "confining yourself simply to a delivery of a copy of this paper to the Secretary of State." "Leave out," wrote the President.

"After doing this, you will communicate with this department," was the language of Mr. Seward. "When communication shall have been arrested for this cause, you will communicate with this department," was the President's emendation.

Lord John Russell has informed us of an understanding between the British and French Governments that they will act together in regard to our affairs. This communication, however, loses something of its value from the circumstance that the communication was withheld until after knowledge of the fact had been acquired by us from other sources. We know, also, another fact that has not yet been officially communicated to us, namely, that other European States are apprised by France and England of their agreement, and are expected to concur with or follow them in whatever measures they adopt on the subject of recognition. The United States have been impartial and just in all their conduct towards the several nations of Europe. They will not complain, however, of the combination now announced by the two leading powers, although they think they had a right to expect a more independent if not a more   [Page 6.

friendly course from each of them. You will take no notice of that or any other alliance. Whenever the European governments shall see fit to communicate directly with us, we shall be, as heretofore, frank and explicit in our reply.

As to the blockade, you will say that, by our own laws, and the laws of nations, this Government has a clear right to suppress insurrection. An exclusion of commerce from national ports, which have been seized by the insurgents, in the equitable form of blockade, is a proper means to that end. You will not insist that our blockade is to be respected if it be not maintained by a competent force, but passing by that question as not now a practical, or at least an urgent one, you will add that the blockade is now and it will continue to be so maintained, and therefore we expect it to be respected by Great Britain. You will add that we have.

                                    [Page 7.

"As to the blockade," wrote the Secretary, "you will say that, by the laws of nature and the laws of nations, this Government has a clear right to suppress insurrections." For the phrase "the laws of nature," the President wrote "our own laws."

already revoked the *exequatur* of a Russian consul who had enlisted in the military service of the insurgents, and we shall dismiss or demand the recall of every foreign agent, consular or diplomatic, who shall either disobey the Federal laws or disown the Federal authority.

As to the recognition of the so-called Southern Confederacy it is not to be made a subject of technical definition. It is, of course, direct recognition to publish an acknowledgment of the sovereignty and independence of a new power. It is direct recognition to receive its ambassadors, ministers, agents, or commissioners officially. A concession of belligerent rights is liable to be construed as a recognition of them. No one of these proceedings will pass unquestioned by the United States in this case.

Hitherto recognition has been moved only on the assumption that the so-called Confederate States are *de facto* a self-sustaining power. Now, after long forbearance, designed to soothe discontent and avert the need of civil war, [*Page* 8.

"No one of these proceedings," wrote the Secretary, "will be borne by the United States in this case." The President first substituted "unnoticed" for "borne," and then corrected his own word by writing "will pass unquestioned."

the land and naval forces of the United States have been put in motion to repress the insurrection. The true character of the pretended new State is at once revealed. It is seen to be a power existing in pronunciamento only. It has never won a field. It has obtained no forts that were not virtually betrayed into its hands or seized in breach of trust. It commands not a single port on the coast nor any highway out from its pretended Capital by land. Under these circumstances, Great Britain is called upon to intervene and give it body and independence by resisting our measures of suppression. British recognition would be British inter-   [*Page* 9.

vention to create, within our territory, a hostile State by overthrowing this Republic itself. * * *
As to the treatment of privateers in the insurgent service you will say that this is a question exclusively our own. We treat them as pirates. They are our own citizens, or persons employed by our citizens, preying on the commerce of our country. If Great Britain shall choose to recognize them as lawful belligerents, and give them shelter from our pursuit and punishment, the laws of nations afford an adequate and proper remedy.   [*Page* 10.

After the words "overthrowing this Republic itself," Mr. Seward added this sentence, which Lincoln eliminated: "When this act of intervention is distinctly performed, we, from that hour, shall cease to be friends, and (*become once more as we have twice before been*), be forced to be enemies of Great Britain." Here the President seems at first to have decided to strike out only the words that are italicized, but subsequently he erased the entire sentence.

After the last sentence on the page, following the words "proper remedy," the Secretary had written " and we shall avail ourselves of it. And while you need not say this in advance, be sure that you say nothing inconsistent with it." " *Out*," wrote the President.

Happily, however, her Britannic Majesty's Government can avoid all these difficulties. It invited us, in 1856, to accede to the declaration of the Congress of Paris, of which body Great Britain was herself a member, abolishing privateering everywhere, in all cases and forever. You already have our authority to propose to her our accession to that declaration. If she refuse to receive it, it can only be because she is willing to become the patron of privateering when aimed at our devastation.

These positions are not elaborately defended now, because to vindicate them would imply a possibility of our waiving them. * * *

We are not insensible of the grave importance of this occasion. We see how, upon the result of the debate in which we are engaged, a war may

[*Page* 11.

After the second paragraph on this page the President wrote : "Drop all from this line to the end, and in lieu of it write ' This paper is for your own guidance only, and not to be read or shown to any one.'"

ensue between the United States and one, two, or even more, European nations. War in any case is as exceptionable from the habits, as it is revolting from the sentiments, of the American people. But if it come, it will be fully seen that it results from the action of Great Britain, not our own; that Great Britain will have decided to fraternize with our domestic enemy either without waiting to hear, from you, our remonstrances and our warnings, or after having heard them. War in defence of national life is not immoral, and war in defence of independence is an inevitable part of the discipline of nations.

The dispute will be between the European and the American branches of the British race. All who belong to that race will especially deprecate it, as they ought. It may well be believed that men of every race and kindred will deplore it. A war not unlike it, between the same parties, occurred at the close of the last century. Europe atoned by forty years of suffering for the error that Great Britain committed in provoking that contest.   [*Page* 12.

For our "remonstrances and wrongs," on this page, the President substituted "our remonstrances and our warnings."

"Europe atoned by forty years of suffering for the crime," wrote Mr. Seward; "forty years of suffering for the error," wrote Lincoln.

If that nation shall now repeat the same great error, the social convulsions which will follow may not be so long, but they will be more general. When they shall have ceased it will, we think, be seen, whatever may have been the fortunes of other nations, that it is not the United States that will have come out of them with its precious constitution altered, or its honestly obtained dominion in any way abridged. Great Britain has but to wait a few months and all her present inconveniences will cease with all our own troubles. If she take a different course, she will calculate for herself the ultimate as well as the immediate consequences, and will consider what position she will hold when she shall have forever lost the sympathies and the affections of the only nation on whose sympathies and affections she has a natural claim. In making that calculation, she will do well to remember that, in the controversy she proposes to open, we shall be actuated by neither pride, nor passion, nor cupidity, nor ambition, but we shall stand simply on the principle of self-preservation, and that our cause will involve the independence of nations, and the rights of human nature.

I am, sir, respectfully, your obedient servant,

WILLIAM H. SEWARD.

CHARLES FRANCIS ADAMS, ESQ., &c., &c., &c.

[*Page* 13.

The subtile corrections on this page have already been noted.

Mr Dallas in a brief dispatch
of May. 2ᵈ (No 333) tells us that Lord
John Russell recently requested an in-
-terview with him on account of the solici-
-tude which His Lordship felt concerning
the effect of certain measures represented
as likely to be adopted by the President.
In that conversation the British Secretary
told Mr Dallas that the three Representatives
of the Southern Confederacy were then in
London, that Lord John Russell had not
yet seen them, but that he was not unwilling to see them unofficially. He farther
informs Mr Dallas that an understanding
exists between the British and French
Governments which would lead both to
take one and the same course as to recog-
-nition. His Lordship then referred to
                                          the

C. F. Adams Esqr
     &c   &c   &c

the rumor of a meditated blockade by us of Southern ports and a discontinuance of them as ports of entry. Mr. Dallas answered that he knew nothing on those topics and therefore could say nothing. He added that you were expected to arrive in two weeks. Upon this statement Lord John Russell acquiesced in the expediency of waiting for the fuller knowledge you were expected to bring.

Mr. Dallas transmitted to us some newspaper reports of Ministerial explanations made in Parliament.

You will base no proceedings on parliamentary debates farther than to seek explanations when necessary and communicate them to this Department. We intend to have a clear and simple record of whatever issues may arise between us and Great Britain.

The President regrets is Surprised and grieved

[56]

grieved that Mr. Dallas did not
protest against the proposed unofficial intercourse between the
British Government and the emissaries
of the insurgents, as well ~~passable~~ as
against the demand for explanations
made by the British Government.
It is due however to Mr. Dallas to
say that our instructions had been
given only to you and not to him,
and that his loyalty and fidelity,
too rare in these times ~~are proposed~~
~~are~~ appreciated.

[Intercourse of any kind
with the so-called Commissioners
is liable to be construed as a recognition of the authority which
appointed them. Such intercourse
would be none the less ~~wrongful~~ hurtful
to us, for being called unofficial,
and it might be even more injurious,
because we should have no means
of knowing what point might
be resolved by it. disavow,
                              unofficial

[57]

unofficial intercourse is useless and meaningless, if it is not expected to ripen into official intercourse and direct recognition. It is left doubtful here whether the proposed unofficial intercourse has yet actually begun. Your own ~~statement~~ present instructions are deemed explicit enough, and it is hoped that you have not misunderstood them. You will, in any event desist from all intercourse whatever, unofficial as well as official with the British Government, so long as it shall continue intercourse of either kind with the domestic enemies of this country; confining yourself simply to a delivery of a copy of this paper to the Secretary of State. After doing this you will communicate with this Department and receive farther directions.

[58]

Lord John Russell has informed us of an understanding between the British and French Governments that they will act together in regard to our affairs. This communication however loses something of its value from the circumstance that the communication was withheld until after knowledge of the fact had been acquired by us from other sources We know also another fact that has not yet been officially communicated to us namely that other European States are apprized by France and England of their agreement and are expected to concur with or follow them in whatever measures they adopt on the subject of recognition. The United States have been impartial and just in all their conduct towards the several nations of Europe. They will not complain however of the combination now announced by these two leading powers, although they think they had a right to expect a more independent if not a more

friendly course from each of them.
You will take no notice of that or
any other alliance Whenever the
European governments shall see
fit to communicate directly with
us we shall be as heretofore
frank and explicit in our reply

As to the blockade; you will
say that by ~~the~~ our own laws ~~of nature~~
~~the laws of nature of the law~~
and of nations this government has
a clear right to suppress insurrection.
An ~~exclusion~~ of commerce from national
ports which have been seized by the
insurgents, in the equitable form of
blockade, is a proper means to that
end. You will ~~admit~~ not omit that our
blockade is ~~not~~ to be respected
if it be not maintained by a
competent force — but you will
add that it the blockade is now and it will
continue to be so maintained,
and therefore we expect it to
be respected by Great Britain.
You will add that we have

that question as not
now a practical one
or at least an
urgent or

already revoked the exequatur of a Russian
Consul who had enlisted in the Military
service of the insurgents and we shall dismiss or demand the recall of every foreign
agent, Consular or Diplomatic who shall
either disobey the Federal laws or disown
the Federal authority

As to the recognition of the so called
Southern Confederacy it is not to be made
a subject of technical definition. It is of course
recognition to publish an acknowledgment
of the Sovereignty and independence of
a new power. It is recognition to receive
its ambassadors Ministers agents or
commissioners officially. A concession
of belligerent rights is liable to be con
strued as a recognition of them. No one of
these proceedings will imprudent be by the
United States in this case

Hitherto recognition has been
moved only on the assumption that the so-
called Confederate States are de facto a
self sustaining power. Now after long
forbearance, designed to soothe discontent and avert the need of civil war,

the

the land and naval forces of the
United States have been put
in motion to repress the insurrection
The true character of the pretended
new State is at once revealed
It is seen to be a Power existing
in pronunciamentos only. It has
never won a field. It has obtained
no forts that were not virtually
betrayed into its hands or seized
in breach of trust. It commands
not a single port on the coast
nor any highway out from its
pretended Capital by land. Under
these circumstances Great Britain
is called upon to intervene and give
it body and independence resisting by counting
our measures of suppression.
British recognition would be British intervention

[62]

vention to create within our own
territory a hostile state by overthrowing this Republic itself. When this
act of intervention is distinctly
performed, we from that hour
shall cease to be friends and (become once more, as we have
twice before been) forced to become enemies of Great Britain

As to the treatment of privateers in the insurgent service
you will say that this is a
question exclusively our own.
We treat them as pirates. They
are our own citizens, or persons
employed by our citizens, preying on the commerce of our country: If Great Britain shall
choose to recognise them as
lawful belligerents, and give
them shelter from our pursuit
and punishment the laws
of nations afford an ade-
quate and proper remedy,
(and we shall avail ourselves
of it. And while you need not to
say this in advance be sure that you
say nothing inconsistent with it-

[63]

Happily, however Her Britannic Majesty's Government can
avoid all these difficulties
It invited us in 1856 to accede
to the declaration of the Congress of Paris, of which body
Great Britain was herself a
member, abolishing privatee-
ing everywhere in all cases
and for ever. You always have our
authority to propose to her our
accession to that declaration
If she refuse to receive it it
can only be because she is
willing to become the patron
of privateering when aimed at
our devastation

These positions are not elaborately defended now, because to
vindicate them would imply a
possibility of our waiving them.

We are not insensible of the
grave importance of this occasion.
We see how upon the result of the
debate in which we are engaged, a war may

This paper is for your own guidance only, and is
to remain, or shown to any one.

[64]

ensue, between the United States and one, two, or even more European nations War in any case is as exceptionable from the habits as it is revolting from the sentiments of the American people. But if it come it will be fully seen that it results from the action of Great Britain, not our own, that Great Britain will have decided to fraternize with our domestic enemy either without waiting to hear from you our remonstrances and our warning or after having heard them. War in defence of national life is not immoral, and war in defence of independence is an inevitable part of the discipline of nations.

The dispute will be between the European and the American branches of the British race. All who belong to that race will especially deprecate it, as they ought. It may well be believed that men of every race and kindred will deplore it. A war not unlike it occurred between the same parties occurred at the close of the last century Europe atoned by forty years of suffering for the error that Great Britain committed in provoking that contest

[65]

If that nation shall now repeat the same great error the social controversy which will follow may not be so long but they will be more general. When they shall have ceased it will, we think, be seen, whatever may have been the fortunes of other nations that it will be the United States that will have come out of them with its precious Constitution altered or its honestly obtained dominion in any degree abridged Great Britain has but to wait a few months and all her present inconveniences will cease with all our own troubles If she take a different course she will calculate for herself the ultimate as well as the immediate consequences, and will consider what position she will hold when she shall have forever lost the sympathies and the affections of the only nation on whose sympathies and affections she has a natural claim. In making that calculation she will do well to remember that in the controversy she proposes to open we shall be actuated by neither pride, nor passion, nor cupidity, nor ambition; but we shall stand simply on the principle of self preservation and that our cause will involve the independence of nations and the rights of human nature

I am, Sir, respectfully your obedient servant

W. H. S.

II

LINCOLN'S STORY OF HIS OWN LIFE

IN the autumn of 1849, I was sitting with Judge David Davis in a small country hotel in Mt. Pulaski, Illinois, when a tall man, with a circular blue cloak thrown over his shoulders, entered one door of the room, and passing through without speaking, went out another. I was struck by his appearance. It was the first time I had ever seen him, and I said to Judge Davis, when he had gone, "Who is that?" "Why, don't you know him? That is Lincoln." In a few moments he returned, and, for the first time, I shook the hand and made the acquaintance of that man who since then has so wonderfully impressed himself upon the hearts and affections of mankind.

The State of Illinois contained at that time in round numbers about 500,000 souls, and Chicago about 28,000 instead of 700,000 as now. The county seats of the State, now containing 5,000 and 20,000 as a general rule, then contained 500 to 1,000, with a log court house and a log jail. The settlements in the country skirted along the timber, the streams were without bridges, and the prairies were wholly unsettled. Dim roads or trails extended from one county seat to another, and the ordinary mode of travel was on horseback or, occasionally, in a buggy.

We were then attending the circuit court, which circuit embraced fourteen counties. These courts commenced about the first of September and closed about Christmas, and commenced again about February and closed about June. The time allotted for holding court was from two to three days to a week at a place.* Mr. Lincoln had, just before that time, closed his only term in Congress, and had, when I met him, returned to his former life as a lawyer upon this, the Eighth Judicial Circuit. For eleven years thereafter we traversed this circuit together, the size of the circuit being diminished by the Legislature as the country increased in settlement; staying at the same little country hotel, riding and driving together over the country, and trying suits together, or, more frequently, opposed to each other.

In the fall of 1853, as I was riding with him in a buggy from De Witt County to Champaign, a distance of about fifty miles, upon the business of attending this court, and as we were traversing a prairie some twelve or fifteen miles in width, and nearing Champaign, I said to Mr. Lincoln, " I have heard a great many curious incidents of your early

---

* See Note, p. 80.

life, and I would be obliged if you would begin at your earliest recollection and tell me the story of it continuously." The season and the surroundings seemed adapted to lazy story telling. The weather was the perfection of Indian summer time, and the tall grasses covered the prairie everywhere like ripened grain. Occasionally, a distant prairie fire filled the air with hazy smoke, the quail whistled to his mate, and, at times, the red deer started from the tall grasses of the dell as we passed along. I give this story as nearly as I can in the substance of his own language:

"I can remember," he said, "our life in Kentucky; the cabin, the stinted living, the sale of our possessions, and the journey with my father and mother to Southern Indiana."

I think he said he was then about six years old. Shortly after his arrival in Indiana his mother died.

"It was pretty pinching times," he said, "at first in Indiana, getting the cabin built, and the clearing for the crops; but presently we got reasonably comfortable, and my father married again."

He had very faint recollections of his own mother, he was so young when she died, but he spoke most kindly of her and of his step-mother, and of her care for him in providing for his wants.

He told me of earning his first half dollar. Standing upon the shore of a river a steamboat was passing along in the middle of the stream. Some one on board the boat called to him to come with a small boat. He went, took off a passenger, and was paid the half dollar. Afterwards, playing upon a flat-boat which was fastened so as to reach out into the stream, he dropped his half dollar from the farthest end of the boat.

Said he, " I can see the quivering and shining of that half dollar yet, as in the quick current it went down the stream and sunk from my sight forever."

" My father," he said, " had suffered greatly for the want of an education, and he determined at an early day that I should be well educated. And what do you think he said his ideas of a good education were ? We had an old dog-eared arithmetic in our house, and father determined that somehow, or some-how else, I should cipher clear through that book."

With this standard of an education, he started to a school in a log-house in the neighborhood, and began his educational career. He had attended this school but about six weeks, however, when a calam-ity befell the father. He had endorsed some man's note in the neighborhood, for a considerable amount, and the prospect was he would have it to pay, and that would sweep away all their little possessions. His father, therefore, explained to him that he wanted to hire him out and receive the fruits of his labor, and his aid in averting this calamity. Accordingly, at the expiration of six weeks, he left school, and never returned to it again. These six weeks, therefore, constitute the entire sum of his education in school. From this time until he was about nineteen, he lived in Southern Indiana. He was a strong, athletic boy, good-natured, and ready to out-run, out-jump and out-wrestle or out-lift anybody in the neighborhood. There were in that vicinity a few books which he literally devoured—the Bible, *Shakespeare*, Bunyan's *Pilgrim's Progress*, Weems' *Life of Washington*, Weems' *Life of Marion*, etc. He said to me that he had got hold of and read through every book he ever heard of in that country for a circuit of about fifty miles.

At the age of nineteen his father sold out his possessions in Indiana, and loaded all their movable goods upon a wagon, and Lincoln drove the oxen that hauled them upon this new migration westward. They arrived in Coles County, Illinois, about the month of August, and that fall built a cabin for the coming winter and broke land for a crop the next year. Lincoln's father gave him his time in the autumn of the next year, he coming of age the following February. It was a few months before he would be entitled to it by operation of law, and he started off into the world to seek his fortune. His step-mother tied up all his earthly possessions in a bundle, and Lincoln, running a stick through it where the knot was tied, threw it over his shoulder, and started, with his father's and mother's blessing, upon a wonderful journey of life.

It commenced along an old Indian trail from Coles to Macon County. See him, as he goes on foot through the grasses of the prairie—a tall, lithe, young man, a stick and a pack upon his back, starting out on that unknown journey which took him, first to be a rail-splitter, then to the captaincy of a flat-boat, then to the life of a little merchant, then to a captaincy in the Black Hawk War, to the county surveyorship of Sangamon County, to a membership in the legislature of the State, to the electorship at large for the State, to the championship of oratory for Henry Clay in 1844, to a membership in Congress, in 1846 to 1848, to a conceded position of leadership as a member of the bar in the State of Illinois, and, lastly, to the presidency and to martyrdom in the country upon which he was then so humbly walking.

Arriving at Macon County he found some cousins by the name of Hanks, and in connection with one of these young men, that winter took the job of splitting rails, at a fixed price per hundred. He worked about in this manner, for a year or more, when he drifted over the line of Macon into Sangamon County, and worked for some prominent farmer, whose name I have forgotten.

It was an easy task in those days, in Illinois, to raise products, but corn was worth only ten cents a bushel, and was sometimes used for fuel. If the products could only be marketed, liberal profits would arise. Hence Lincoln, while working there, conceived the idea of building a flat-boat upon the Sangamon River, running it down the Sangamon into the Illinois, down the Illinois to the Mississippi, and thence to New Orleans. This had never been done, and the apparent obstacle was a dam across the Sangamon River near Springfield. Lincoln had some device by which he thought this obstacle could be overcome.

The enterprise being agreed upon, Mr. Lincoln felled, in the forest, the timber, and hewed the beams, built the boat, loaded it with provisions, and was then elected to his first office, which was the captaincy of that flat-boat. The crew consisted of Lincoln, himself the Captain, and one or two other men. The dam was successfully passed at high water by some device I have forgotten, and Lincoln passed down the Illinois and the Mississippi to New Orleans, sold his cargo there, and worked his passage back by assisting in firing on a steamboat. Since his assassination I have seen and conversed with one of the captains of a boat upon which he thus worked his passage coming back.

On the occasion of one of these passages, in the

vicinity of Natchez, a negro came very near smash-
ing the head of the future emancipator of his race.
The boat one night was tied up to the shore and
the crew asleep below. A noise being heard Captain Lincoln came up, and just as his head emerged
through the hatchway, a negro, who was pilfering,
struck him a blow with a heavy stick, but the point
of the stick reached over his head, and struck the
floor beyond, at the same time, thus lightening the
blow on his head, but making a scar which he wore
always, and which he showed me at the time of
telling this story.

After his experience in flat-boating, which lasted
two or three years, Lincoln resided for awhile in the
town of New Salem, in Sangamon County. Here
he was employed as a clerk in a store, and afterward became a partner. I remember well his expression in describing that little store, which contained a very few goods of various kinds. Turning
to me he said, " I reckon that was *the* store-keep-
ing." A difference, however, soon arose between
him and the old proprietor, the present partner of
Lincoln, in reference to the introduction of whiskey
into the establishment. The partner insisted that,
on the principle that honey catches flies, a barrel of
whiskey in the store would invite custom, and their
sales would increase, while Lincoln, who never liked
liquor, opposed this innovation. He told me, not

more than a year before he was elected President, that he had never tasted liquor in his life. "What!" I said, "do you mean to say you never tasted it?" "Yes, I never tasted it." The result was that a bargain was made by which Lincoln should retire from his partnership in the store. He was to step out as he stepped in. He had nothing when he stepped in, and he had nothing when he stepped out. But the partner took all the goods, and agreed to pay all the debts, for a part of which Mr. Lincoln had become jointly liable.

About this time, the Black Hawk War broke out. Black Hawk, an Indian chief near Rock Island, had committed some depredations upon the whites, and the inhabitants of the State becoming exasperated, formed companies and joined the nucleus of officers and soldiers of the regular army, and marched together to Rock Island, and then marched back again. This was about all there was to the war. A company was raised and organized at New Salem.

During Lincoln's youth he had everywhere been distinguished as the crowning athlete of the neighborhood in which he lived. Everywhere along the frontier, since that frontier has marched from the east westward, some fellow in every neighborhood had been "cock of the walk," who could out-wrestle, out-run, and out-jump everybody. Lincoln was that person wherever he lived in early life. He was that boy when young in Indiana, and afterward in New Salem he made a hero of himself by wrestling, running, jumping, lifting, and other innocent amusements of that character. He was six feet three and a-half inches tall, long-armed, long-limbed, brawny-handed, with no superfluous flesh, toughened by labor in the open air, of perfect health, and his grip was like the grip of Hercules.

Together with the talk of organizing a company in New Salem, began the talk of making Lincoln captain of it. His characteristics as an athlete had made something of a hero of him. Turning to me with a smile at the time, he said, " I cannot tell you how much the idea of being the captain of that company pleased me."

But when the day of organization arrived, a man who had been captain of a real company arrived in his uniform, and assumed the organization of the company. The mode of it was as follows : A line of two was formed by the company, with the parties who intended to be candidates for officers standing in front. The candidate for captain then made a speech to the men, telling them what a gallant man he was, in what wars he had fought, bled and died, and how he was ready again, for the glory of his country, to lead them. Then another candidate ; and when the speech-making was ended, they commanded those who would vote for this man, or that, to form a line behind their favorite. Thus there were one, two or three lines behind the different men, as there were different candidates, and then they counted back, and the fellow who had the longest tail to his kite, was the real captain. It was a good way. There was no chance for ballot-box stuffing or a false count.

When the real captain with his regimentals came and assumed the control, Lincoln's heart failed him. He formed in the line with the boys, and after the speech was made they began to form behind the old captain, but the boys seized Lincoln, and pushed him out of the line, and began to form behind him, and cried form behind " Abe," and in a moment of irresolution he marched ahead, and when they counted back he had two more than the other captain, and he became real captain.

Whatever was to be done in this war, Lincoln did well, as we may infer from the facts which succeeded his return. As he returned home, he found his old partner had been his own best customer at that whiskey barrel, and that all the goods were gone, but having failed to pay the debts, there were eleven hundred dollars for which Lincoln was jointly liable. I cannot forget his face of seriousness as he turned to me and said, " That debt was the greatest obstacle I have ever met in life ; I had no way of speculating, and could not earn money

6

except by labor, and to earn by labor eleven hundred dollars, besides my living, seemed the work of a lifetime. There was, however, but one way. I went to the creditors and told them that if they would let me alone, I would give them all I could earn, over my living, as fast as I could earn it."

Providence is often kinder than our fears. About this time events of this character occurred in Lincoln's life. He had previously borrowed some books and learned something of surveying, and upon his return from the war, was employed in the County Surveyor's office of the County of Sangamon, and for four years thereafter was elected member of the State legislature.

" At that time," said he, " members of the legislature got four dollars a day, and four dollars a day was more than I had ever earned in my life."

With an economical mode of life which he knew so well, he succeeded, with what he saved in winter, at the legislature, and what he earned in the summer as surveyor, in paying what he called " the national debt."

The life, in the legislature, with politicians developed the natural gift he had for public speaking, and that legislature, in which he was celebrated, is to-day remembered in Illinois as the legislature of the " long nine," of which Lincoln was one, each of the nine being more than six feet tall.

Although deficient in education acquired at school, life was to him a school, and he was always studying and mastering every subject which came before him. He knew how to dig out any question from its very roots, and when his own children began to go to school, he studied with them, and acquired in mature life the elements of an education. I have seen him myself, upon the circuit, with "a geometry," or "an astronomy," or some book of that kind, working out propositions in moments of leisure, or acquiring the information that is generally acquired in boyhood. He is the only man I have ever known to bridge back thoroughly in the matter of spelling. There are but very few college graduates who spell as well as Mr. Lincoln spelled.

At the close of his term in the legislature he was persuaded to move to Springfield and study law. John T. Stuart, a most eminent lawyer in the State, loaned him books, and William Butler, still remembered as State Treasurer of the State, loaned him money and board, and he immediately commenced studying and practicing law. He rose in his profession with great rapidity, and soon became distinguished as a leader in it. He was also a leader of the Whig party in the State, and canvassed it in 1840. Again, with distinguished ability, he was the champion of Henry Clay in 1844, was elevated to Congress in

1846, and in 1848, having made a canvass for President Taylor, returned upon the circuit, to the practice of the law, where I first met him, as described.

Mr. Lincoln told this story as the story of a happy childhood. There was nothing sad nor pinched, and nothing of want, and no allusions to want, in any part of it. His own description of his youth was that of a joyous, happy boyhood. It was told with mirth and glee, and illustrated by pointed anecdote, often interrupted by his jocund laugh which echoed over the prairies. His biographers have given to his early life the spirit of suffering and want, and as one reads them, he feels like tossing him pennies for his relief. Mr. Lincoln gave no such description, nor is such description true. His was just such life as has always existed and now exists in the frontier States, and such boys are *not* suffering, but are rather like Whittier's "Barefoot boy with cheeks of tan," and I doubt not Mr. Lincoln in after-life would gladly have exchanged the pleasures of gratified ambition and of power for those hours of happy contentment and rest.

LEONARD SWETT.

NOTE.—The courts referred to, on page 68, were presided over by David Davis, who was the judge from 1849 until 1862, when he left the bench for the Supreme Court of the United States, to which post Mr. Lincoln had appointment. Ward W. Lamar was the prosecuting attorney for the last five or six years, and also travelled the circuit.

III

POLITICAL LIFE IN ILLINOIS

M R. LINCOLN was nearly eight years my
senior, and settled in Illinois ten years before
I did.   We first find him in the State splitting rails
with Thomas Hanks, in Macon County, in 1830.   Not
long afterward he made his way to New Salem, an
unimportant and insignificant village on the Sangamon River, in the northern part of Sangamon
County, fourteen miles from Springfield.   In 1839
a new county was laid off, named " Ménard," in honor
of the first lieutenant-governor of the State, a French
Canadian, an early settler of the State and a man
whose memory is held in reverence by the people of
Illinois, for his enterprise, benevolence and the admirable personal traits which adorned his character.
A distinguished and wealthy citizen of St. Louis,
allied to him by marriage, Mr. Charles Pierre Chou-
teau, is now erecting a monument to him, to be
placed in the State-house grounds at Springfield.
The settlement of New Salem, now immortalized
as the early home of Lincoln, fell within the new
county of " Ménard."   Remaining there " as a sort

of clerk in a store," to use his own language, he then went into the Black Hawk war and was elected captain of a company of mounted volunteers. In one of the great debates between Lincoln and Douglas, at Ottawa, in 1858, he, in a somewhat patronizing manner and in a spirit of badinage, spoke of having known Lincoln for "twenty-four years" and when a "flourishing grocery-keeper" at New Salem. The occasion was too good a one not to furnish a repartee, and the people insisted that while Lincoln denied that he had been a flourishing "grocery-keeper" as stated, yet added that, if he had been, it was "certain that his friend, Judge Douglas, would have been his best customer." The Black Hawk war over, Mr. Lincoln returned to New Salem to eke out a scanty existence by doing small jobs of surveying and by drawing up deeds and legal instruments for his neighbors. In 1834, still living in New Salem, he was one of nine members elected from Sangamon County to the lower house of the Legislature.

I landed at Galena by a Mississippi River steamboat, on the first day of April, 1840, ten years after Hanks and Lincoln were splitting rails in Macon County.

The country was then fairly entered on that marvelous Presidential campaign between Van Buren and Harrison, by far the most exciting election the country has ever seen, and which, in my judgment,

will never have a parallel, should the country have
an existence for a thousand years. Illinois was one
of the seven States that voted for Van Buren, but
the Whigs contested the election with great zeal and
most desperate energy. Galena, theretofore better
known as the Fevre River Lead Mines, still held its
importance as the center of the lead mining region,
and was regarded as one of the principal towns in
the State in point of population, wealth and enterprise. But the bulk of population of the State at
that time, as well as the weight of political influence,
was south of Springfield.

Mr. Lincoln was first elected to the lower branch of
the Legislature (then sitting at Vandalia), from Sangamon County, in 1834; and that was his first appearance in public life. He was re-elected in 1836, 1838
and 1840, having served in all four terms—eight years.
He then peremptorily declined a further election.

Before his election to the Legislature, Mr. Lincoln
had read law in a fugitive way at New Salem, but
arriving at Vandalia, as a member of the Legislature,
a new field was open to him in the State law library,
as well as in the miscellaneous library at the capital.
He then devoted himself most diligently not only to
the study of law, but to miscellaneous reading. He
always read understandingly, and there was no principle of law but what he mastered, and such was the
way in which he always impressed his miscellaneous

readings on his mind, that people in his later life were amazed at his wonderful familiarity with books, even those so little known by the great mass of readers. The seat of government of Illinois having been removed from Vandalia to Springfield, in 1839, the latter place then became the center of political influence in the State.

Mr. Lincoln was not particularly distinguished in his legislative service. He participated in the discussion of the ordinary subjects of legislation, and was regarded as a man of good sense, and a wise and practical legislator. His uniform fairness was proverbial. But he never gave any special evidence of that masterly ability for which he was afterward distinguished, and which stamped him, as by common consent, the foremost man of all the century. He was a prominent Whig in politics, and took a leading part in all political discussions. There were many men of both political parties in the lower house of Legislature during the service of Mr. Lincoln, who became afterward distinguished in the political history of the State, and among them might be mentioned Orlando B. Ficklin, John T. Stuart, William A. Richardson, John A. McClernand, Edward D. Baker, Lewis W. Ross, Samuel D. Marshall, Robert Smith, William H. Bissell, and John J. Hardin, all subsequently members of Congress, and James Semple, James Shields, and Lyman

Trumbull, United States Senators. There were also many men of talent and local reputation, who held an honorable place in the public estimation and made their mark in the history of the State. Springfield was the political center for the Whigs of Illinois in 1840.

Lincoln had already acquired a high reputation as a popular speaker, and he was put on the Harrison electoral ticket with the understanding he should canvass the State.

Edward D. Baker was also entered as a campaign orator, and wherever he spoke he carried his audiences captive by the power of his eloquence and the strength of his arguments. He was one of the most effective stump speakers I ever listened to. It was his wonderful eloquence and his power as a stump speaker that elected him to Congress from Illinois in a district to which he did not belong, and made him a United States Senator from Oregon when he was a citizen of California.

John T. Stuart was already known by his successful canvass with Douglas, in 1838, as an able speaker and a popular man; and John J. Hardin, of Jacksonville, (killed at Buena Vista) was widely known as a popular and successful orator. These Springfield Whigs led off in canvassing the State for Harrison in 1840.

Lincoln and Baker were assigned to the " Wabash

Country," where, as Baker once told me, they would make speeches one day and shake with the ague the next. It is hard to realize at this day what it was to make a political canvass in Illinois half a century gone by. There were no railroads and but few stage lines. The speakers were obliged to travel on horse-back, carrying their saddle-bags filled with "hickory" shirts and woolen socks. They were frequently obliged to travel long distances, through swamps and over prairies, to meet their appointments. The accommodations were invariably wretched, and no matter how tired, jaded and worn the speaker might be, he was obliged to respond to the call of the wait-ing and eager audiences.

In 1840, Stephen T. Logan, then a resident of Springfield, was one of the best known and most prominent men in the State. Though a Whig, he was not so much a politician as a lawyer. In 1841, he and Mr. Lincoln formed a law partnership which continued until 1843, and there was never a stronger law firm in the State. Like Lincoln, Logan was a Kentuckian, and a self-made man. Though a nat-ural born lawyer, he had yet studied profoundly the principles of the common law. He was elected a circuit judge in 1835, and held the office until 1837. He displayed extraordinary qualities as a *nisi prius* judge. In 1842 he consented to serve in the lower branch of the Legislature from Sangamon County.

He had even more simplicity of character, and was more careless in his dress than Mr. Lincoln. I shall never forget the first time I ever saw him. It was in the Hall of the House of Representatives, on February 10, 1843, and when he was a member of that body. He had a reputation at that time as a man of ability and a lawyer second to no man in the State. I was curious to see the man of whom I had heard so much, and I shall never forget the impression he made on me. He was a small, thin man, with a little wrinkled and weazened face, set off by an immense head of hair, which might be called "frowzy." He was dressed in linsey-woolsey, and wore very heavy shoes. His shirt was of unbleached cotton, and unstarched, and he never encumbered himself with a cravat or other neck wear. His voice was shrill, sharp and unpleasant, and he had not a single grace of oratory—but yet, when he spoke, he always had interested and attentive listeners. Underneath this curious and grotesque exterior there was a gigantic intellect. When he addressed himself to a jury or to a question of law before the courts, or made a speech in the Legislature or at the hustings, people looked upon him and listened with amazement. His last appearance in any public position was as a delegate to the " Peace Convention " at Washington, in the spring of 1861. In his later years he lived the life of a retired gentleman in his beautiful home in the environs of Springfield. His memory has been honored by placing his portrait, one of the most admirable ever painted by Healy, in the magnificent room of the Supreme Court at Springfield.

I never met Mr. Lincoln till the first time I attended the Supreme Court at Springfield, in the winter of 1843 and 1844. He had already achieved a certain reputation as a public speaker, and was rapidly gaining distinction as a lawyer. He had already become widely known as a Whig politician, and his advice and counsel were much sought for by members of the party all over the State. One of the great features in Illinois, nearly half a century gone by, was the meeting of the Supreme Court of the State. There was but one term of the court a year, and that was held first at Vandalia and then at Springfield. The lawyers from every part of the State had to follow their cases there for final adjudication, and they gathered there from all the principal towns of the State. The occasion served as a reunion of a large number of the ablest men in the State. Many of them had been dragged for hundreds of miles over horrible roads in stage-coaches or by private conveyance. For many years I traveled from Galena, one of the most remote parts of the State, to Springfield, in a stage-coach, occupying usually three days and four nights, traveling incessantly, and arriving at the end of the journey

more dead than alive. The Supreme Court library
was in the court-room, and there the lawyers would
gather to look up their authorities and prepare their
cases. In the evening it was a sort of rendezvous
for general conversation, and I hardly ever knew of
an evening to pass without Mr. Lincoln putting in
his appearance. He was a man of the most social
disposition and was never so happy as when surrounded by congenial friends. His penchant for
story-telling is well known, and he was more happy
in that line than any man I ever knew. But many
stories have been invented and attributed to him that
he never heard of. Never shall I forget him as he
appeared almost every evening in the court-room,
sitting in a cane-bottom chair leaning up against the
partition, his feet on a round of the chair, and surrounded by many listeners. But there was one thing,
he never pressed his stories on unwilling ears nor
endeavored to absorb all attention to himself. But
his anecdotes were all so droll, so original, so appropriate and so illustrative of passing incidents that
one never wearied. He never repeated a story or an
anecdote, nor vexed the dull ears of a drowsy man
by thrice-told tales; and he enjoyed a good story
from another as much as any person.

There were many good story-tellers in that group
of lawyers that assembled evenings in that Supreme
Court-room, and among them was the Hon. Thomp-

son Campbell, Secretary of State under Gov. Ford
from 1843 to 1846. Mr. Campbell was a brilliant
man and a celebrated wit. Though differing in politics, until the repeal of the Missouri Compromise, he
and Mr. Lincoln were strong personal friends, and
many of his stories, like those of Mr. Lincoln, have
gone into the traditions of the State. They were
never so happy as when together and listening to the
stories of each other. Mr. Campbell was elected to
Congress from the Galena district in 1850, and served
one term. In 1853 President Pierce appointed him
a judge of the United States Land Court of California.

Mr. Lincoln was universally popular with his associates. Of an even temper, he had a simplicity
and charm of manner which took hold, at once, on
all persons with whom he came in contact. He was
of the most amiable disposition, and not given to
speak unkindly of any person, but quick to discover
any weak points that person might have. He was
always the center of attraction in the court-room at
the evening gatherings, and all felt there was a great
void when, for any reason, he was kept away.

The associates of Mr. Lincoln at the bar, at this
time, were, most of them, men of ability, who gave
promise of future distinction both at the bar and in
the field of politics. The lawyers of that day were
brought much closer together than they ever have

been since, and the "*esprit du corps*" was much more marked. Coming from long distances and suffering great privations in their journeys, they usually remained a considerable time in attendance upon the court.

Among the noted lawyers at this time, the friends and associates of Mr. Lincoln, who subsequently reached high political distinction, were John J. Hardin, falling bravely at the head of his regiment at Buena Vista; Lyman Trumbull, for eighteen years United States Senator from Illinois; James A. McDougall, Attorney-General of Illinois, and subsequently member of Congress and United States Senator from California; Stephen A. Douglas, Edward D. Baker, Thompson Campbell, Joseph Gillespie, O. B. Ficklin, Archibald Williams, James Shields, Isaac N. Arnold (who was to become Mr. Lincoln's biographer); Norman H. Purple, O. H. Browning, subsequently United States Senator and Secretary of the Interior, Judge Thomas Drummond, of the United States Circuit Court, and many others, all the contemporaries of Mr. Lincoln, and always holding with him the most cordial and friendly relations.

In the Presidential campaign of 1844, Mr. Lincoln canvassed the State very thoroughly for Mr. Clay, and added much to his already well-established reputation as a stump speaker. His reputation also as a lawyer had steadily increased. In August, 1846, he was elected to Congress as a Whig from the Springfield district.

Ceasing to attend the courts at Springfield, I saw but little of Mr. Lincoln for a few years. We met at the celebrated River and Harbor Convention at Chicago, held July 5, 6 and 7, 1847. He was simply a looker on, and took no leading part in the convention. His dress and personal appearance on that occasion could not well be forgotten. It was then for the first time I heard him called " *Old* Abe." Old Abe, as applied to him, seems strange enough, as he was then a young man, only thirty-six years of age. One afternoon, several of us sat on the sidewalk under the balcony in front of the Sherman House, and among the number the accomplished scholar and unrivaled orator, Lisle Smith. He suddenly interrupted the conversation by exclaiming, " There is Lincoln on the other side of the street. Just look at 'Old Abe,'" and from that time we all called him " Old Abe." No one who saw him can forget his personal appearance at that time. Tall, angular and awkward, he had on a short-waisted, thin swallow-tail coat, a short vest of same material, thin pantaloons, scarcely coming down to his ankles, a straw hat and a pair of brogans with woolen socks.

Mr. Lincoln was always a great favorite with young men, particularly with the younger members of the bar. It was a popularity not run after, but which followed. He never used the arts of the demagogue to ingratiate himself with any person. Beneath his ungainly exterior he wore a golden heart. He was ever ready to do an act of kindness whenever in his power, particularly to the poor and lowly.

Mr. Lincoln took his seat in Congress on the first Monday in December, 1847. I was in attendance on the Supreme Court of the United States at Washington that winter, and as he was the only member of Congress from the State who was in harmony with my own political sentiments, I saw much of him and passed a good deal of time in his room. He belonged to a mess that boarded at Mrs. Spriggs, in "Duff Green's Row" on Capitol Hill. At the first session, the mess was composed of John Blanchard, John Dickey, A. R. McIlvaine, James Pollock, John Strohm, of Pennsylvania; Elisha Embree, of Indiana; Joshua R. Giddings, of Ohio; A. Lincoln, of Illinois, and P. W. Tompkins, of Mississippi. The same members composed the mess at Mrs. Spriggs' the short session, with the exception of Judge Embree and Mr. Tompkins. Without exception, these gentlemen are all dead. He sat in the old hall of the House of Representatives, and for the long session was so unfortunate as to draw one of the most undesirable seats in the hall. He par-

7

ticipated but little in the active business of the House, and made the personal acquaintance of but few members. He was attentive and conscientious in the discharge of his duties, and followed the course of legislation closely. When he took his seat in the House, the campaign of 1848 for President was just opening. Out of the small number of Whig members of Congress who were favorable to the nomination of General Taylor by the Whig Convention, he was one of the most ardent and outspoken. The following letter addressed to me on the subject will indicate the warmth of his support of General Taylor's nomination :

WASHINGTON, *April* 30, 1848.

DEAR WASHBURNE :

I have this moment received your very short note asking me if old Taylor is to be used up, and who will be the nominee. My hope of Taylor's nomination is as high—a little higher than when you left. Still the case is by no means out of doubt. Mr. Clay's letter has not advanced his interests any here. Several who were against Taylor, but not for anybody particularly before, are since taking ground, some for Scott and some for McLean. Who will be nominated, neither I nor any one else can tell. Now, let me pray to you in turn. My prayer is, that you let nothing discourage or baffle you, but that in spite

POLITICAL LIFE IN ILLINOIS

of every difficulty you send us a good Taylor delegate from your circuit. Make Baker, who is now
with you I suppose, help about it. He is a good
hand to raise a breeze. General Ashley, in the Senate from Arkansas, died yesterday. Nothing else
new, beyond what you see in the papers.

Yours truly,

A. LINCOLN.

I was again in Washington part of the winter of
1849 (after the election of General Taylor), and saw
much of Mr. Lincoln. A small number of mutual
friends—including Mr. Lincoln—made up a party to
attend the inauguration ball together. It was by far
the most brilliant inauguration ball ever given. Of
course Mr. Lincoln had never seen anything of the
kind before. One of the most modest and unpre-
tending persons present—he could not have dreamed
that like honors were to come to him, almost within
a little more than a decade. He was greatly interested in all that was to be seen, and we did not take
our departure until three or four o'clock in the morning. When we went to the cloak and hat room, Mr.
Lincoln had no trouble in finding his short cloak,
which little more than covered his shoulders, but,
after a long search, was unable to find his hat. After
an hour he gave up all idea of finding it. Taking
his cloak on his arm, he walked out into Judiciary

Square, deliberately adjusting it on his shoulders, and started off bareheaded for his lodgings. It would be hard to forget the sight of that tall and slim man, with his short cloak thrown over his shoulders, starting for his long walk home on Capitol Hill, at four o'clock in the morning, without any hat on.

And this incident is akin to one related to me by the librarian of the Supreme Court of the United States. Mr. Lincoln came to the library one day for the purpose of procuring some law books which he wanted to take to his room for examination. Getting together all the books he wanted, he placed them in a pile on a table. Taking a large bandana handkerchief from his pocket, he tied them up, and putting a stick which he had brought with him through a knot he had made in the handkerchief, adjusting the package of books to his stick he shouldered it, and marched off from the library to his room. In a few days he returned the books in the same way.

Mr. Lincoln declined to run for Congress for a second term, 1848. His old partner and friend, Judge Stephen T. Logan, was the Whig candidate, and, to the amazement of every one, was defeated by a Democrat, Colonel Thomas L. Harris, of "Ménard" County.

From 1849, on returning from Congress, until 1854, he practiced law more assiduously than ever before. In respect to that period of his life he once wrote to a friend :

" I was losing interest in politics when the repeal of the Missouri Compromise aroused me again."

There was a great upturning in the political situation in Illinois, brought about by the repeal of the Missouri Compromise in 1854. In the fall of that year an election was to be held in Illinois for members of Congress and for members of the Legislature which was to elect a successor to General Shields, who had committed what was to the people of Illinois, the unpardonable sin of voting for the repeal of the Missouri Compromise. There was something in that legislation which was particularly revolting to Mr. Lincoln, as it outraged all his ideas of political honesty and fair dealing.

There was an exciting canvass in the State, and Mr. Lincoln entered into it with great spirit, and accomplished great results by his powerful speeches. From his standing in the State and from the great service he had rendered in the campaign, it was agreed that if the Republicans and anti-Nebraska men should carry the Legislature, Mr. Lincoln would succeed General Shields. I know that he himself expected it. There is a long and painful history of that Senatorial contest yet to be written, and when the whole truth is disclosed it will throw a flood of new light on the character of Mr. Lincoln, and will add new luster to his greatness, his generosity, his magnanimity and his patriotism.   There is no event in Mr. Lincoln's entire political career that brought to him so much disappointment and chagrin as his defeat for United States Senator in 1855, but he accepted the situation uncomplainingly, and never indulged in reproaches or criticism upon any one; but, on the other hand, he always formed excuses for those who had been charged with not acting in good faith toward him and to those with whom he was associated.   He never forgot the obligations he was under to those who had faithfully stood by him in his contest, through good and evil report.

Allied to him by the strongest ties of personal and political friendship, I did all in my power to secure for him, which I did, the support of the members of the Legislature from my Congressional District. The day after the election for Senator he addressed to me a long letter, several pages of letter-paper, giving a detailed account of the contest and the reasons of his action in persuading his friends to vote for and elect Judge Trumbull, and expressing the opinion that I would have acted in the same way if I had been in his place.   He then says:

"I regret my defeat moderately, but am not nervous about it.   * * * Perhaps it is as well for our grand cause that Trumbull is elected."

He then closes his letter as follows:

"With my grateful acknowledgments for the kind, active, and continual interest you have taken for me in this matter, allow me to subscribe myself,

"Yours, forever,

"A. LINCOLN."

On the last day of the balloting in the Legislature, it seemed inevitable that a Nebraska Democrat would be elected United States Senator. Judge Trumbull had the votes of five anti-Nebraska Democrats. And of this crisis Mr. Lincoln writes to me:

"So I determined to strike at once, and accordingly advising my friends to go for him, which they did, and elected him on that, the 10th ballot."

Though the failure to elect Mr. Lincoln brought grief to many hearts, yet the election of Judge Trumbull was well received by the entire anti-Nebraska party in the State. He proved himself an able, true and loyal Senator, rendered great services to the Union cause, and proved himself a worthy representative of a great, loyal and patriotic State.

Notwithstanding the great satisfaction with which Judge Trumbull's election had been received, there was a deep and profound feeling among the old Whigs, the Republicans and many anti-Nebraska Democrats, that Mr. Lincoln should have had the position, and that he had not been fairly treated. But never a complaint or a suggestion of that kind escaped the lips of Mr. Lincoln. Cheerily and bravely and contentedly he went back to his law office, and business poured in upon him more than ever.

In stepping one side and securing the election of Judge Trumbull, he " builded better than he knew." Had Mr. Lincoln been elected Senator at that time, he would never have had the canvass with Judge Douglas in 1858, never been elected President in 1860, to leave a name that will never die.

From 1855 to 1858, Mr. Lincoln was absorbed in the practice of his profession, though he took an active part in the canvass of 1856, when the gallant Colonel Bissell was elected Governor. But what was somewhat remarkable, in all this time, without the least personal effort, and without any resort to the usual devices of politicians, Mr. Lincoln's popularity continued to increase in every portion of the State.

In the fall of 1858, there was to be an election of a Legislature which would choose a successor to Judge Douglas, whose term of service was to expire March 3, 1859. The Republican party by this time, had become completely organized and solidified, and in Illinois the Republican and Democratic parties squarely confronted each other. Everywhere, by common consent, no Republican candidate for Senator was spoken of except Mr.

Lincoln. In the Republican State Convention in the summer of 1858, a resolution was unanimously passed designating Mr. Lincoln as the unanimous choice of the Republicans of the State, as the candidate for United States Senator, to succeed Judge Douglas. That action is without precedent in the State, and shows the deep hold Mr. Lincoln had on his party.

Without being designated by any authorized body of Democrats, yet by common consent of the party, Judge Douglas became the candidate of the Democratic party. No other candidates were mentioned on either side, either directly or indirectly.

The seven joint discussions which the candidates had in different parts of the State have become a part of the political history of the country. It was a battle of the giants. The parties were rallied, as one man, to the enthusiastic support of their respective candidates, and it is hard for any one not in the State at the time to measure the excitement which everywhere prevailed. There was little talk about Republicanism and Democracy, but it was all " Lincoln and Douglas," or " Douglas and Lincoln." I attended only one of these joint discussions. It was at Freeport, in my Congressional District, which was the bulwark of Republicanism in the State. Two years later it gave Mr. Lincoln a majority for President of nearly fourteen thousand, and my own

majority for member of Congress was about the
same.   The Freeport discussion was held in August.
The day was bright, but the wind sweeping down
the prairies gave us a chilly afternoon for an out-of-
door gathering.   In company with a large number
of Galena people, we reached Freeport by train,
about ten o'clock in the morning.   Mr. Lincoln had
come in from the south the same morning, and we
found him at the Brewster House, which was a
sort of rallying-point for the Republicans.   He had
stood his campaign well, and was in splendid condition.   He was surrounded all the forenoon by
sturdy Republicans, who had come long distances,
not only to hear him speak, but to see him, and it
was esteemed the greatest privilege to shake hands
with " Honest Old Abe."   He had a kind word or
some droll remark for every one, and it is safe to
say that no one who spoke to him that day will ever
have the interview effaced from memory.   The
meeting was held on a vacant piece of ground, not
far from the center of the town.   The crowd was
immense and the enthusiasm great.   Each party
tried to outdo the other in the applause for its
own candidate.   The speaking commenced, but the
chilly air dampened the ardor of the audience.   Mr.
Lincoln spoke deliberately, and apparently under a
deep sense of the responsibility which rested upon
him.   The questions he propounded to Mr. Douglas

he had put in writing (and the answers to which sounded the political death-knell of Mr. Douglas); he read slowly, and with great distinctness. The speech of Mr. Douglas was not up to his usual standard. He was evidently embarrassed by the questions, and floundered in his replies. The crowd was large, the wind was chilly, and there was necessarily much " noise and confusion," and the audience did not take in the vast importance of the debate. On the whole, it may be said that neither party was fully satisfied with the speeches, and the meeting broke up without any display of enthusiasm.

It is not my purpose in this essay to follow the incidents of the Presidential campaign of 1860. The great event in Illinois was the monster Republican mass meeting held at Springfield during the canvass. It was a meeting for the whole State, and more in the nature of a personal ovation to Mr. Lincoln than merely a political gathering. It was one of the most enormous and impressive gatherings I had ever witnessed.

Mr. Lincoln, surrounded by some intimate friends, sat on the balcony of his humble home. It took hours for all the delegations to file before him, and there was no token of enthusiasm wanting. He was deeply touched by the manifestations of personal and political friendship, and returned all his salutations in that off-hand and kindly manner which belonged to him. I know of no demonstration of a similar character that can compare with it except the review by Napoleon of his army for the invasion of Russia, about the same season of the year in 1812.

Mr. Lincoln remained quietly at his own home in Springfield during the Presidential canvass of 1860, but he watched narrowly all the incidents of the campaign. On the 26th of May he wrote me as follows:

"* * * I have your letters written since the nominations, but till now I have found no moment to say a word by way of answer. Of course I am glad that the nomination is well received by our friends, and I sincerely thank you for so informing me. So far as I can learn, the nominations take well everywhere, and if we get no back-set, it would seem as if they were going through.

"I hope you will write often; and as you write more rapidly than I do, don't make your letters so short as mine.

"Yours, very truly,

"A. LINCOLN."

Mr. Lincoln had his periods of anxiety and deep concern during the canvass. As chairman of the House Congressional (Republican) Committee, I was engaged at Washington during the campaign. On the 9th of September Mr. Lincoln wrote me as follows from Springfield:

"Yours of the 5th was received last evening. I was right glad to get it. It contains the latest 'posting' which I now have. It relieves me some from a little anxiety I had about Maine. Jo. Medill, on August 30th, wrote me that Colfax had a letter from Mr. Hamlin, saying we were in great danger of losing two members of Congress in Maine, and that your brother would not have exceeding six thousand majority for Governor. I addressed you at once, at Galena, asking for your latest information. As you are at Washington, that letter you will receive some time after the Maine election.

"Yours, very truly,
"A. LINCOLN."

Though the election was over there came gloomy days for Mr. Lincoln, but he pondered well on the great problem before him. He had weighed well all the important questions which had arisen, and in him there was neither change nor shadow of turning. On the 13th day of December he wrote to me as follows :

"HON. E. B. WASHBURNE :

"*My dear Sir :*—Your long letter received. Prevent as far as possible any of our friends from demoralizing themselves and our cause by entertaining propositions for compromise of any sort on slavery extension. There is no possible compromise

upon it, but which puts us under again, and all our
work to do over again.   Whether it be a Missouri
line or Eli Thayer's Popular Sovereignty, it is all
the same.—Let either be done, and immediately
filibustering and extending slavery recommences.
On that point hold firm as a chain of steel.

"Yours, as ever,

"A. LINCOLN."

As the time of inauguration drew near there was
an intense anxiety, not unmingled with trepidation,
all over the loyal North as to how Mr. Lincoln
might meet the approaching crisis.   Many and
varied were the speculations as to what course he
would take.   Looking at his character and life, many
feared he had not fully comprehended the gravity
of the situation.   On the contrary, Mr. Lincoln had
weighed the whole matter and fully determined in
his own mind what course he would pursue.   In
December, 1860, he wrote me the following letter:

"*Confidential.*

"SPRINGFIELD, *Dec.* 21, 1860.

"HON. E. B. WASHBURNE:

"*My dear Sir :*—Last night I received your letter,
giving an account of your interview with General
Scott, and for which I thank you.   Please present
my respects to the General and tell him confidentially

I shall be obliged to him to be as well prepared as he can to either *hold*, or retake, the forts, as the case may require, at and after the inauguration.

"Yours, as ever,

"A. LINCOLN."

On the 13th of February, 1861, the two Houses of Congress met in joint session to count and declare the electoral vote. As in all times of great excitement, the air was filled with numberless and absurd rumors; a few were in fear that in some unforeseen way the ceremony of the count might be interrupted and the result not declared. And hence all Washington was on the *qui vive*. The joint meeting was to take place in the Hall of the House of Representatives at high noon. An immense throng filled the House end of the Capitol. All the gilded corridors leading to the Hall of the House were crowded, and the galleries packed. Beautiful and gorgeously dressed ladies entered the Hall, found their way into the cloak rooms, and many of them occupied the seats of the members, who gallantly surrendered them for the occasion.

At twenty minutes after twelve, the door-keeper announced the Senate of the United States. The Senators entered, headed by their President, Hon. John C. Breckenridge, the members of the House rising to receive them. The Vice-President took his seat on the right of the Speaker of the House of Representatives (the Hon. William Pennington, of New Jersey). The joint convention of the two Houses was presided over by Mr. Breckenridge, who served out his term of Vice-President, till March 4, 1861. The Hon. Lyman Trumbull was appointed teller on the part of the Senate, and Messrs. Phelps, of Missouri, and Washburne, of Illinois, on the part of the House. The count proceeded without incident, and the Vice-President announced the election of Lincoln and Hamlin. Mr. Sherman, of Ohio, then offered the ordinary resolution of notification to the President elect, by a committee of two members from the House, to be joined by one member from the Senate. Mr. Hindman, of Arkansas, one of the most violent and vindictive secessionists, insisted that the same committee "inform General Scott that there was no more use for his janizaries about the Capitol, the votes being counted and the result proclaimed." Mr. Grow, of Pennsylvania, responded that gentlemen seemed to trouble themselves a good deal about General Scott on all occasions.

There was a certain feeling of relief among the loyal people of the country that Mr. Lincoln had been declared to be duly elected President, without the least pretense of illegality or irregularity.

The second session of the Thirty-seventh Congress convened on the first Monday of December, 1861.

The Senators and Representatives of the rebellious States were no longer with us. The rumblings of treason, deep and significant, were everywhere heard. What was to be the outcome no one could tell. Anxiety and sadness sat enthroned in both Houses, but there was faith unshaken and courage unsubdued. A state of things existed well calculated to shake the stoutest hearts.

The loyal members of both Senate and House were closely organized to concert measures to meet the appalling emergencies that confronted them. It was determined that each House should appoint one of its members to form a committee to watch the current of events and discover as far as possible the intentions and acts of the rebels. This committee of "Public Safety," as it might be called, was a small one, only two members, Governor Grimes, the Senator from Iowa, on the part of the Senate, and myself on the part of the House. Clothed with full powers, we at once put ourselves in communication with General Scott, the head of the army, with headquarters at Washington, and Chief of Police Kennedy, of New York City, a loyal and true man with a skill unsurpassed by a Fouché or a Vidocq. He at once sent us some of his most skillful and trusted detectives; and earnestly, loyally, and courageously they went to work to unravel the plots and schemes set on foot to destroy us. And never was detective

8

work more skillfully and faithfully done, not only in Washington, but in Baltimore and Richmond and Alexandria. They were all good rebels ; they had long beards and wore slouched hats and seedy coats ; they chewed tobacco and smoked cheap cigars ; damned the Yankees and drank bad whisky; and they obtained a great deal of valuable information in respect to hostile plans and schemes.

As the 4th of March drew near, what occupied our most anxious thought was, how Mr. Lincoln could get to Washington and be inaugurated. Another committee was formed, one from each House, to look after that matter. Governor Seward was the Senate member, and I was put on on the part of the House, for the reason, perhaps, that I was from Illinois, a known personal friend of the President who had been in close correspondence with him all winter. Associating ourselves together, we came to the conclusion that everything must be done with the most profound secrecy. Governor Seward, his son Frederic W. Seward, subsequently his Assistant Secretary of State, and myself were the only persons in Washington who had any knowledge whatever of Mr. Lincoln's proposed movements. That there was a conspiracy in Baltimore to assassinate him as he should pass through, there can be no reasonable doubt. We hoped he might be able to come through in the day-time from Philadelphia, taking a train secretly and cutting the wires, so that his departure could not be known. But General Scott's detectives in Baltimore had developed such a condition of things, that Governor Seward thought that the President-elect and his friends in Philadelphia should be advised in regard thereto, and on the night of the 22d of February he sent his son, Frederic W., over to Philadelphia to consult with them. Till now we had believed the President would come over from Philadelphia on the train leaving there at noon of the 23d. In the mean time the President had promised to run up to Harrisburg to attend a reception of the Pennsylvania Legislature at twelve o'clock on that day. Up to this time the situation had been fully discussed by the friends of Mr. Lincoln in the light of all the information received, but no particular programme agreed upon. It was not until the party started for Harrisburg the next morning that the best method of getting to Washington was finally talked over. Mr. Lincoln had previously had a conversation with the detective Pinkerton and Mr. Frederic W. Seward in regard to the condition of things at Baltimore. The Hon. Norman B. Judd, of Chicago, one of the most conspicuous and trusted friends of Mr. Lincoln, who had accompanied the party from Springfield, suggested a plan which, after full discussion by Mr. Lincoln and all his friends present, was agreed upon and successfully carried out. This plan, as is generally known, was that after the dinner which Governor Curtin had tendered to him had been finished, at six o'clock in the afternoon, he should take a special car and train from Harrisburg for Philadelphia to intercept the night train from New York to Washington. The telegraph wires from Harrisburg were all cut, so there could be no possible telegraphic connection with the outside world.

The connection was made at Philadelphia. Mr. Lincoln was transferred to the Washington train without observation, to arrive at his destination on time the next morning without the least miscarriage, as will be stated hereafter. On the afternoon of the 23d, Mr. Seward came to my seat in the House of Representatives, and told me he had no information from his son nor any one else in respect of Mr. Lincoln's movements, and that he could have none, as the wires were all cut, but he thought it very probable he would arrive in the regular train from Philadelphia, and he suggested that we would meet at the depot to receive him. We were promptly on hand; the train arrived in time, and with strained eyes we watched the descent of the passengers. But there was no Mr. Lincoln among them; though his arrival was by no means certain, yet we were much disappointed. But as there was no telegraphic connection, it was impossible for us to have any information. It was no use to speculate—sad, disappointed, and under the empire of conflicting emotions we separated to go to our respective homes, but agreeing to be at the depot on the arrival of the New York train the next morning before daylight, hoping either to meet the President or get some information as to his movements. I was on hand in season, but to my great disappointment Governor Seward did not appear. I planted myself behind one of the great pillars in the old Washington and Baltimore depot, where I could see and not be observed. Presently the train came rumbling in on time. It was a moment of great anxiety to me.

There has been a great deal printed in the newspapers about Mr. Lincoln's arrival in Washington and about the "Scotch cap" and "big shawl" he wore through Baltimore, etc., etc., most of which is mere stuff. I propose now to tell about his arrival at Washington, from my own personal knowledge— what I saw with my own eyes and what I heard with my own ears, not the eyes and ears of some one else.

As I have stated, I stood behind the pillar awaiting the arrival of the train. When it came to a stop I watched with fear and trembling to see the passengers descend. I saw every car emptied, and there was no Mr. Lincoln. I was well-nigh in despair, and when about to leave I saw slowly emerge from the last sleeping car three persons. I could not mistake the long, lank form of Mr. Lincoln, and my heart bounded with joy and gratitude. He had on a soft low-crowned hat, a muffler around his neck, and a short bob-tailed overcoat. Any one who knew him at that time could not have failed to recognize him at once, but, I must confess, he looked more like a well-to-do farmer from one of the back towns of Jo Daviess County coming to Washington to see the city, take out his land warrant and get the patent for his farm, than the President of the United States.

The only persons that accompanied Mr. Lincoln were Pinkerton, the well-known detective, recently deceased, and Ward H. Lamon. When they were fairly on the platform and a short distance from the car, I stepped forward and accosted the President: " How are you, Lincoln?"

At this unexpected and rather familiar salutation the gentlemen were apparently somewhat startled, but Mr. Lincoln, who had recognized me, relieved them at once by remarking in his peculiar voice :

" This is only Washburne !"

Then we all exchanged congratulations and walked out to the front of the depot, where I had a carriage in waiting. Entering the carriage (all four of us) we drove rapidly to Willard's Hotel, entering on Fourteenth Street, before it was fairly daylight. The porter showed us into the little receiving room at the head of the stairs, and at my direction went to the office to have Mr. Lincoln assigned a room.

We had not been in the hotel more than two minutes before Governor Seward hurriedly entered, much out of breath and somewhat chagrined to think he had not been up in season to be at the depot on the arrival of the train. The meeting of those two great men under the extraordinary circumstances which surrounded them was full of emotion and thankfulness. I soon took my leave, but not before promising Governor Seward that I would take breakfast with him at eight o'clock ; and as I passed out the outside door the Irish porter said to me with a smiling face :

"And by faith it is you who have brought us a Prisidint."

At eight the Governor and I sat down to a simple and relishing breakfast. We had been relieved of a load of anxiety almost too great to bear. The President had reached Washington safely and our spirits were exalted, and with a sense of great satisfaction we sipped our delicious coffee and loaded our plates with the first run of Potomac shad.

Mr. Blaine, in his *Twenty Years of Congress*, has been led into an error in speaking of the manner in which Lincoln reached Washington. He says :

"He reached Washington by a night journey taken secretly, much against his own will and to his subsequent chagrin and mortification, but urged upon him by the advice of those in whose advice and wisdom he was forced to confide."

The only truth in the statement is that he "reached Washington by a night journey taken secretly."

I was the first man to see him after his arrival in Washington and talk with him of the incidents of his journey, and I know he was neither "mortified" nor "chagrined" at the manner in which he reached Washington. He expressed to me in the warmest terms his satisfaction at the complete success of his journey; and I have it from persons who were about him in Philadelphia and Harrisburg that the plan agreed upon met his hearty approval, and he expressed a cheerful willingness to adapt himself to the novel circumstances. I do not believe that Mr. Lincoln ever expressed a regret that he had not, "according to his own desire, gone through Baltimore in open day," etc. It is safe to say he never had any such "desire." His own detective, Pinkerton, a man who had his entire confidence, had been some time in Baltimore, with several members of his force, in unraveling rebel plots, produced to him the most conclusive evidence of a conspiracy to assassinate him. General Scott's detectives had discovered the same thing, and there was a great deal of individual testimony tending to establish the same fact. While Mr. Lincoln would have confronted any danger in the performance of duty, he was not a man given to bravado and quixotic schemes, and what he subsequently stated touching this matter comprises really all there is in it. He declared :

"I did not believe then, nor do I now believe I should have been assassinated had I gone through Baltimore as first contemplated, but *I thought it wise to run no risk where no risk was necessary.*" *

In the same paragraph Mr. Blaine says, that "it must be creditable to the administration of Mr. Buchanan that ample provision had been made for the protection of the rightful ruler of the nation" (p. 240). If Mr. Blaine means by this that Mr. Buchanan, driven by public indignation, had ordered a few straggling companies of regular infantry to Washington, that is one thing ; but if he referred to the protection of the "rightful ruler" of the nation in getting to Washington, his good faith was imposed upon. I was in a position to know all that was going on in relation to Mr. Lincoln's journey to Washington, and I never heard it suggested or hinted that Mr. Buchanan occupied himself with that matter. I am satisfied he had no more knowledge of Mr. Lincoln's movements than those of "the man in the moon."

I cannot here recount all Mr. Lincoln's acts of kindness to me while President. He always seemed anxious to gratify me, and I can recollect of no

---

* Lossing's *Pictorial History of the Rebellion*, vol. i., p. 279.

single favor that I asked of him that he did not cheerfully accord. I will mention a simple incident. In the fall of 1863, my brother, Gen. Washburne, of Wisconsin, was stationed at a most unhealthy camp at Helena, Arkansas. He was taken dangerously sick with malarial dysentery, and there was little prospect of his recovery unless he could be removed to some healthier location. I wrote to Mr. Lincoln, briefly, asking for a leave of absence for him for cause of health, and in due time I received the following reply :

" *Private and Confidential.*

EXECUTIVE MANSION, }
WASHINGTON, *Oct.* 26, 1863. }

" HON. E. B. WASHBURNE :

"*My dear Sir :*—Yours of the 12th has been in my hands several days. Inclosed I send a leave of absence for your brother, in as good form as I think I can safely put it. Without knowing whether he would accept it, I have tendered the collectorship of Portland, Maine, to your other brother, the Governor.

"Thanks to both you and our friend Campbell for your kind words and intentions. A second term would be a great honor, and a great labor, which together, perhaps, I would not decline, if tendered.

" Yours truly,

" A. LINCOLN."

This last paragraph refers to a letter of the Hon. Thompson Campbell, whom I have before referred to in this essay, and in which we asked permission to bring him forward as a candidate for a re-election.

But I must bring my contribution to a close. The rebellion, in April, 1865, was fast approaching an end. Having expressed a desire to be at the front, wherever that might be, when the hour of its final collapse might come finally to strike, General Grant had given me a pass of the broadest character, to go anywhere in the Union lines.

The news of the fall of Richmond reached Galena at eleven o'clock Monday morning, April 3, 1865. I took the train "for the front" at five P.M., and arrived in Washington Thursday morning, April 6th. I found that the President, Mrs. Lincoln, and a party of friends had left on an excursion for Fortress Monroe, City Point, and Richmond. Mr. Blaine joined me, and we made the trip together to City Point. On arriving there, late Friday afternoon, we found the President and party had returned from Richmond, and were on their steamer, the *River Queen*, which was to remain at City Point over night. In the evening Mr. Blaine and myself went on board the steamer to pay our respects to the President. I never passed a more delightful evening. Mr. Lincoln was in perfect health and in exuberant spirits. His relation of his experiences

and of all he saw at Richmond had all of that quaint-
ness and originality for which he was distinguished.
Full of anecdote and reminiscence, he never flagged
during the whole evening.   His son Robert was in
the military service and with the advancing army,
and knowing that I was bound for the " front " the
next morning, he said to me :

" I believe I will drop Robert a line if you will
take it.   I will hand it to you in the morning before
you start."

I went to the wharf the next morning, and soon
Mr. Lincoln came ashore from his steamer, with the
letter in his hand.   He was erect and buoyant, and
it seemed to me that I had never seen him look so
great and grand.   After a few words of conversation,
he handed me the letter, and I bid him what proved
to be, alas ! a *final adieu*.   I made my way with all
diligence and through much tribulation to the
" front," and arrived at Appomattox in season to see
the final surrender of the Army of Northern Virginia, and General Lee and his associate generals
prisoners of war.

Returning to City Point, I found awaiting me
there a small Government steamer which was to take
me to Washington.   On arriving there I met the
most terrible news that had ever shocked the civilized
world : *Mr. Lincoln had been assassinated*.   That was
Saturday night, April 15, 1865.   I gave directions

to have the steamer proceed directly to Washington, where I arrived early Monday morning, April 17th, and in season to participate in the stupendous preparations to do honor to the memory of the dead President.

I was on the Congressional Committee to escort his remains to Springfield, Illinois, where I followed his colossal hearse to the grave.

E. B. WASHBURNE.

IV

LEADER OF THE ILLINOIS BAR

IN the summer of 1854 I became a citizen of De
Witt County, Illinois, having emigrated from
Ohio for the purpose of practicing law. At that time
I knew something of Mr. Lincoln's history, having
known of him while he was a member of Congress
a few years before. I found he had a very strong
hold upon popular affection, and stood high in the
confidence of the people of the State. He was the
leader of the bar, Judge Logan having substantially retired from the active practice; and although
he was but forty-five, he was alluded to in popular
parlance as "old Mr. Lincoln;" and in that connection I recall an incident occurring while he was a
candidate for the Senate against Judge Douglas in
1858. He delivered a speech at Clinton, and as we
were riding in the "inevitable procession" of American politics, the "small boy" of the period said to
one of his companions: "There! there goes old Mr.
Lincoln!" This was said in a tone to be heard by
the immediate company, and Mr. Lincoln was asked
how long they had been calling him old. Said he:

"Oh, they have been at that trick many years. They commenced it when I was scarcely thirty."

It seemed to amuse him; he was not old enough to be sensitive about his age.

The first time I met him was in September, 1854, at Bloomington; and I was introduced to him by Judge Douglas, who was then making a campaign in defense of the Kansas-Nebraska bill. Mr. Lincoln was attending court, and called to see the Judge. They talked very pleasantly about old times and things, and during the conversation the Judge broadened the hospitalities of the occasion by asking him to drink something. Mr. Lincoln declined very politely, when the Judge said: "Why, do you belong to the temperance society?" He said:

"I do *not* in theory, but I do in fact, belong to the temperance society, in this, to wit, that I do not drink anything, and have not done so for a very many years."

Shortly after he retired, Mr. J. W. Fell, then and now a leading citizen of Illinois, came into the room, with a proposition that Mr. Lincoln and Mr. Douglas have a discussion, remarking that there were a great many people in the city, that the question was of great public importance, and that it would afford the crowd the luxury of listening to the acknowledged champions of both sides. As soon as the proposition was made it could be seen that the

Judge was irritated. He inquired of Mr. Fell, with some majesty of manner: "Whom does Mr. Lincoln represent in this campaign—is he an Abolitionist or an Old Line Whig?"

Mr. Fell replied that he was an Old Line Whig.

"Yes," said Douglas, "I am now in the region of the Old Line Whig. When I am in Northern Illinois I am assailed by an Abolitionist, when I get to the center I am attacked by an Old Line Whig, and when I go to Southern Illinois I am beset by an Anti-Nebraska Democrat. I can't hold the Whig responsible for anything the Abolitionist says, and can't hold the Anti-Nebraska Democrat responsible for the positions of either. It looks to me like dogging a man all over the State. If Mr. Lincoln wants to make a speech he had better get a crowd of his own ; for I most respectfully decline to hold a discussion with him."

Mr. Lincoln had nothing to do with the challenge except perhaps to say he would discuss the question with Judge Douglas. He was not aggressive in the defense of his doctrines or enunciation of his opinions, but he was brave and fearless in the protection of what he believed to be the right. The impression he made when I was introduced was as to his unaffected and sincere manner, and the precise, cautious, and accurate mode in which he stated his thoughts even when talking about commonplace things.

9

In 1854 and down to the commencement of the war the circuit practice in Illinois was still in vogue, and the itinerant lawyer was as sure to come as the trees to bud or the leaves to fall.   In and among these Mr. Lincoln was the star ; he stood above and beyond them all.   He traveled the circuit attending the courts of Judge David Davis's district, extending from the center to the eastern boundary of the State, until he was nominated for the Presidency. He liked the atmosphere of a court-house, and seemed to be contented and happy when Judge Davis was on the bench and he had before him the "twelve good and lawful men" who had been called from the body of the county to "well and truly try the issue."   In every county in which he practiced he was among his friends and acquaintances ; he usually knew the most, and always the leading men on the jury.   He was not what might be called an industrious lawyer, and when his adversary presented a reasonably good affidavit for a continuance, he was willing that the case should go over until the next term.   He was particularly kind to young lawyers, and I remember with what confidence I always went to him, because I was certain that he knew all about the matter, and would most cheerfully tell me.   I can see him now through the decaying memories of thirty years, standing in the corner of the old court-room, and as I approached him with a paper I did not understand, he said:

"Wait until I fix this plug for my 'gallis,' and I will pitch into that like a dog at a root."

While speaking, he was busily engaged in trying to connect his suspender with his pants by making a "plug" perform the function of a button. Mr. Lincoln used old-fashioned words, and never failed to use them if they could be sustained as proper. He was probably taught to say "gallows," and he never adopted the modern "suspender."

In the convulsions of nations, how rapidly history makes itself! Mr. Lincoln was the attorney of the Illinois Central Railroad Company, to assist the local counsel in the different counties of the circuit, and in De Witt County, in connection with the Hon. C. H. Moore, attended to the litigation of the company. In '58 or '59 he appeared in a case which they did not want to try at that term, and Mr. Lincoln remarked to the court:

"We are not ready for trial."

Judge Davis said: "Why is not the company ready to go to trial?"

Mr. Lincoln replied: "We are embarrassed by the absence or rather want of information from Captain McClellan."

The Judge said: "Who is Captain McClellan, and why is he not here?"

Mr. Lincoln said: "All I know of him is that he is the engineer of the railroad, and why he is not here this deponent saith not."

In consequence of the absence of Captain McClellan the case was continued. Lincoln and McClellan had perhaps never met up to that time, and the most they knew of each other was that one was the attorney and the other the engineer of the Illinois Central Railroad Company. In less than two years from that time the fame of both had spread as broad as civilization, and each held in his grasp the fate of a nation. The lawyer was directing councils and cabinets, and the engineer, in subordination to the lawyer as commander-in-chief, was directing armies greater and grander than the combined forces of Wellington and Napoleon at Waterloo.

Mr. Lincoln did not make a specialty of criminal cases, but was engaged frequently in them. He could not be called a great lawyer, measured by the extent of his acquirement of legal knowledge; he was not an encyclopedia of cases, but in the text-books of the profession and in the clear perception of legal principles, with natural capacity to apply them, he had great ability. He was not a case lawyer, but a lawyer who dealt in the deep philosophy of the law. He always knew the cases which might be quoted as absolute authority, but beyond that he contented himself in the application and discussion of general principles. In the trial of a case he moved cautiously, and never examined, or cross-examined a witness to the detriment of his side.

If the witness told the truth he was safe from his attacks, but woe betide the unlucky and dishonest individual who suppressed the truth, or colored it against Mr. Lincoln's side. His speeches to the jury were very effective specimens of forensic oratory. He talked the vocabulary of the people, and the jury understood every point he made and every thought he uttered. I never saw him when I thought he was trying to make a display for mere display; but his imagination was simple and pure in the richest gems of true eloquence. He constructed short sentences of small words, and never wearied the mind of the jury by mazes of elaboration.

The Kansas-Nebraska bill having been passed in May, 1854, great political excitement prevailed in Illinois because of the connection of Senator Douglas with that measure. Mr. Douglas and Mr. Lincoln had been political antagonists as Whigs and Democrats, and when the Republican Party was formed in 1854 that antagonism continued, Mr. Douglas adhering to the Democratic Party and Mr. Lincoln becoming the leader of the Republican Party in Illinois. In 1858, during the campaign preceding the election of Senator, Mr. Lincoln made a speech at Springfield, on the 17th of June, in which he charged a purpose on the part of Mr. Douglas, Mr. Buchanan, and Judge Taney to nationalize slavery. That speech is one of the most remarkable that he ever delivered, and the one in which he used the expression, " a house divided against itself cannot stand." Mr. Douglas came to Illinois upon the adjournment of the Senate and made a speech in Chicago, in which he did not take occasion to contradict the charge made in Mr. Lincoln's Springfield speech. Mr. Lincoln then made another speech at Springfield, in which he noticed the fact that he made the charge referred to on the 17th of June; that Mr. Douglas had since then made a speech in Chicago, and did not deny it ; and, said he, in his second Springfield speech : "I am entitled to what the lawyers call a default, and I here take the default on him on that charge, he having refused and failed to answer."

Some time in the latter part of July Mr. Douglas began his regular campaign in De Witt, that being a strong Buchanan county, Colonel Thomas Snell having organized the Danite party there in opposition to Mr. Douglas. We wrote Mr. Lincoln that, inasmuch as Mr. Douglas was to begin his regular campaign there, he had better come and hear him ; and on the morning of the day the meeting was held Mr. Lincoln came to Clinton. There was an immense crowd for a country town, and the people were very much excited upon the subject of politics.

On the way to the grove, Mr. Lincoln said : " I have challenged Judge Douglas for a discussion;

what do you think of it?" I said: "The question is already settled; but I approve your judgment in whatever you may do." Mr. Douglas spoke to an immense audience, and made one of the most forcible political speeches I ever heard. He spoke over three hours, in the course of which he took occasion to reply to Mr. Lincoln's Springfield speech, with reference to the "default" which he said Mr. Lincoln in his second speech had sought to make against him. As he progressed in his argument he became very personal, and I said to Mr. Lincoln: "Do you suppose Douglas knows you are here?"

"Well," said he, "I don't know whether he does or not, he has not looked around in this direction; but I reckon the boys have told him I am here."

When Judge Douglas finished there was a great shout for Mr. Lincoln. He stepped on the seat very much excited, and said:

"This is Judge Douglas's meeting. I have no right and therefore no disposition to interfere, but if you ladies and gentlemen desire to hear what I have to say on these questions, and will meet me to-night at the Court-house yard, *I will try* and answer the gentleman."

Mr. Douglas was in the act of putting on his cravat, and turned in the direction of Mr. Lincoln. Both became poised in a tableau of majestic power. The scene exhibited a meeting of giants—a contest of great men—and the situation was dramatic in the extreme.

Lincoln made a speech that night which in volume and force did not equal the speech of Judge Douglas ; but for sound and cogent argument it was superior. Negro equality was then the bugbear of politics, and the Republican Party was defending itself against these slanderous charges of the Democracy. Mr. Lincoln said in his speech :

"Judge Douglas charges me with being in favor of negro equality, and to the extent that he charges I am not guilty. *I am guilty* of hating servitude and loving freedom ; and while I would not carry the equality of the races to the extent charged by my adversary, I am happy to confess before you that in some things the black man is the equal of the white man. In the right to eat the bread his own hands have earned he is the equal of Judge Douglas or any other living man."

When he spoke the last sentence he had stretched himself to his full height, and as he reached his hands toward the stars of that still night, then and there fell from his lips one of the grandest expressions of American statesmanship.

After the meeting his friends congratulated him especially on the beauty of the thought in the last sentence of the quotation.

He said : " Do you think that is fine ?" and when

assured that it was, he laughingly said : "If you think so, I will get that off again." Mr. Douglas, having received a challenge from Mr. Lincoln, replied to him in a few days, and the memorable discussion was the result.

Mr. Lincoln's resources as a story-teller were inexhaustible, and no condition could arise in a case beyond his capacity to furnish an illustration with an appropriate anecdote. Judge Davis was always willing that he should tell a story in court, even if the gravity of the situation was for the time being suspended, and no one enjoyed the mirth of the occasion more than his honor on the bench ; but while that was true, the distinguished barrister was always deferential and respectful toward the court, and never forgot the professional amenities of the bar.

In the debate with Judge Douglas "he builded better than he knew." He was preparing, as he thought, a stepping-stone to the Senate, but what was rejected then became the corner-stone in that fortune that raised him to the Presidency. When he was invited to deliver a speech at Cooper Institute, in February, 1860, he hesitated about accepting. He said to his friends : "I don't know whether I shall be adequate to the situation ; I have never appeared before such an audience as may possibly assemble to hear me. I am appalled by the magnitude of the undertaking." He was, however, relieved of his fear before he went by having, as he said, formulated a line of thought which would prevent a failure.

In May, 1860, a State Convention was held at Decatur to appoint delegates to Chicago. Mr. Lincoln was there, and at that convention the rail movement was inaugurated by Governor Oglesby. He had formerly lived in that county, and had worked on a farm with Mr. John Hanks, who was still living, and it occurred to the Governor, in conversation with Mr. Hanks, that if they could get some of the rails that Lincoln and Hanks split it would be a good thing for the campaign ; and so on the day of the convention Oglesby arranged that just at the close of the business of the convention Mr. Hanks should march in with one of these rails on his shoulder, which he did ; and as Mr. Lincoln rose to speak, his attention was called to the rail. He said :

" Fellow-citizens, it is true that many, many years ago John Hanks and I made rails down on the Sangamon. We made good, big, honest rails, but whether that is one of the rails, I am not, at this distant period of time, able to say."

That inaugurated the rail movement. He closed his reference to the rails with a eulogy on free labor embracing the finest thought of his theory upon that subject. At that convention the question was asked him whether he would attend the Chicago Convention, and he replied: "I am a little too much of a candidate to go, and not quite enough of a candidate to stay away; but upon the whole I believe I will not go."

Mr. Lincoln took no public part in the campaign of 1860. He attended one political meeting, but declined to speak. On the day appointed by law the Republican electors met at Springfield and were entertained at dinner by Mr. J. C. Conkling, the elector for that district. Mr. Lincoln was there as one of the guests, and talked freely but sadly as to the condition of things incident to his election. Governor Yates, who had been elected Governor, was of the party, and expressed to him the necessity of being firm and determined. He replied that he hoped he would be adequate to the responsibility of the situation; and that in his hands, as President, the Republic of Washington would not perish. How much work he did, at Springfield, in the preparation of his inaugural was not known by his most intimate friends. He may have consulted some of the members of his Cabinet who visited him before he left for Washington, but beyond them he kept his own counsel. That fact illustrates one of the distinguishing features of his character. As to the ordinary affairs of life he was indifferent—he listened to anybody; but when the highest and most important functions of duty were called into requisition he was one of the

most self-reliant men of history.   As President of the
United States he was indifferent as to who was Minister to the Court of St. James or Postmaster at New
York—councils and cabinets might decide such
questions ; but when the question arose whether liberty was to be given to all, in the solitude of his un-
measured genius the problem was solved.   He was
advised long before 1860, by some of his more intimate friends, that his positions on the subject of
slavery and human rights would be prejudicial to his
party and to himself personally.   He paid no attention to such admonitions.   The question with him
was whether the thing was right, and not what his
friends may have thought about the expediency of it.

In almost all the situations of life, public or private, Mr. Lincoln had some anecdote to illustrate
the situation.

During the war there was a contest between the
military and civil authorities as to the policy of
bringing out cotton from a certain insurrectionary
district.   The civil authorities having granted permission to do so were in favor of bringing it out,
and the military authorities in carrying out their
belligerent operations were opposed to it.   In that
condition of things I was requested by some gentlemen in Washington that I find out from him what
would be the probable result of the contest then existing between the civil and military authorities as

to the policy of bringing cotton out of the seceded States. The permits that were issued by the Treasury Department were nullified by the military authorities, and the matter was brought before the President as to what should be done. After having talked for a considerable time with him about other matters, I referred to the subject, and said that a number of gentlemen who were then in the city had requested me to ask him what would probably be the result of the contest. As soon as I made the inquiry a pleasant smile came over his face, the memory of other days was with him, and he said: "By the way, what has become of our friend, Robert Lewis?" Mr. Lewis had for a number of years been clerk of the Circuit Court of De Witt County, and was a great personal friend of Mr. Lincoln's. He was a great wit, and was very much enjoyed in his association by Mr. Lincoln. I remarked to the President that Mr. Lewis was still in his old home, and he then said: "Do you remember a story that Bob used to tell us about his going to Missouri to look up some Mormon lands that belong to his father?" I said: "Mr. President, I have forgotten the details of that story, and I wish you would tell it." He then said that when Robert became of age he found among the papers of his father's a number of warrants and patents for lands in North-east Missouri, and he concluded the best thing he could do was to go to Missouri and investigate the condition of things. It being before the days of railroads, he started on horseback with a pair of old-fashioned saddle-bags. When he arrived where he supposed his land was situated, he stopped, hitched his horse, and went into a cabin standing close by the roadside. He found the proprietor, a lean, lanky, leathery-looking man, engaged in the pioneer business of making bullets preparatory to a hunt. Mr. Lewis observed, on entering, a rifle suspended on a couple of buck horns above the fire. He said to the man: "I am looking up some lands that I think belong to my father," and inquired of the man in what section he lived. Without having ascertained the section, Mr. Lewis proceeded to exhibit his title papers in evidence, and having established a good title as he thought, said to the man: "Now, that is my title, what is yours?" The pioneer, who had by this time become somewhat interested in the proceeding, pointed his long finger toward the rifle, and said: "Young man, do you see that gun?" Mr. Lewis frankly admitted that he did. "Well," said he, "that is my title, and if you don't get out of here pretty damned quick you will feel the force of it." Mr. Lewis very hurriedly put his title papers in his saddle-bags, mounted his pony, and galloped down the road, and, as Bob says, the old pioneer snapped his gun twice at him before he could turn the corner. Lewis said that he had never been back to disturb that man's title since. "Now," said Mr. Lincoln, the "military authorities have the same title against the civil authorities that closed out Bob's Mormon title in Missouri. You may judge what may be the result in this case."

When I returned to the hotel I told the story to the anxious cotton speculators, and they all understood what would be the policy of the administration as well as if a proclamation had been issued. Mr. Lincoln was not in the habit of injecting his stories into an occasion, but told them as they were suggested by the incident of the conversation; and the happy faculty of always being ready with one assisted and relieved him in the discharge of duties, from the humblest walks of life to the complex and complicated responsibilities of President of the United States.

With all the jollity of his every-day life, in all but the surface indications of his character, he was sad and serious. The poem which he so often quoted, "Oh, why should the spirit of mortal be proud?" was a reflex in poetic form of the deep melancholy of his soul. I have heard him, as he sat by the decaying embers of an old-fashioned fire-place, when the day's merriment and business were over and the night's stillness had assumed dominion, quote at length his favorite poem.

Another story is told illustrative of Mr. Lincoln's ability to relieve the embarrassment of his situation as President by a master-stroke of wit. In 1862 the people of New York City were apprehensive of a bombardment by some of the Confederate cruisers; public meetings were held to express the gravity of the situation, and to induce the Government to do something by way of permanently protecting the city. In consummation of that purpose a delegation of fifty gentlemen, representing in their own right $100,000,000, was selected to visit Washington and have an interview with the President, and induce him to detail a gun-boat to protect the city. The committee requested a gentleman then staying at Washington to arrange with the President a time when he could see them. Mr. Lincoln seemed to be much puzzled what to say or do, and remarked to the gentleman who was arranging as to the interview:

"I have no gun-boats or ships of war that can be spared from active service; but, inasmuch as they have come to see me, I shall have to see them and get along as best I can."

The committee called at the appointed time, and were introduced as gentlemen "representing $100,-000,000 in their own right." The chairman of the delegation made a very earnest appeal to the President for protection, and remarked that they represented the wealth of the city—"one hundred millions in their own right." Mr. Lincoln heard them attentively, evidently impressed with the " hundred millions," and replied as follows :

" Gentlemen, I am, by the Constitution, commander-in-chief of the army and navy of the United States, and, as a matter of law, I can order anything done that is practicable to be done ; but, as a matter of fact, I am not in command of the gun-boats or ships of war—as a matter of fact, I do not know exactly where they are, but presume they are actively engaged. It is impossible for me, in the condition of things, to furnish you a gun-boat. The credit of the Government is at a very low ebb. Greenbacks are not worth more than 40 or 50 cents on the dollar, and in this condition of things, if I was worth half as much as you gentlemen are represented to be, and as badly frightened as you seem to be, I would build a gun-boat and give it to the Government."

The gentleman who accompanied the delegation says he never saw one hundred millions sink to such insignificant proportions as it did when that committee recrossed the threshold of the White House, sadder but wiser men. They had learned that money as well as muscle was a factor of war.

10

LAWRENCE WELDON.

V

THE LINCOLN-DOUGLAS
DEBATES AND THE GETTYSBURG ORATION

THE history of Mr. Lincoln's life is an exceedingly interesting one—more interesting in many
respects than that of any other man which our country has produced.

Of humble parentage, without opportunities for
mental culture in early life, he became an able lawyer,
a forcible writer, a captivating and instructive speaker,
an executive officer of singular foresight and wisdom
in the most trying period of our nation's history.
Before his joint debate with Mr. Douglas in 1858, he
was little known outside of his own State. The
ability which he displayed in that debate gave him a
national reputation. He and Mr. Douglas were the
rival candidates for a seat in the United States Senate, of which Mr. Douglas was a prominent member,
but whose term of office was about to expire. They
had frequently met as opposing counsel in important
suits. They were therefore well known to each
other, and by their public speeches they were well
known to the people of Illinois. They had, in one or
two instances, addressed the same audiences upon po-

litical subjects, but they had never met by agreement, at that time a common occurrence in the West, in public debate. The question which then was exciting the greatest interest throughout the Union was slavery—not (with the exception of a comparatively few ultra-antislavery men in the Northern States) whether it should be abolished in the States where it existed, but whether it should be extended into the Territories.

Mr. Douglas, as a United States Senator, had been largely instrumental in effecting a repeal of the compromise by which Missouri had been admitted into the Union and the extension of slavery into other Territories prohibited. He was the leading advocate, in fact the father, of the doctrine of popular sovereignty—the right of the people of the Territories, in preparing constitutions for admission into the Union as sovereign States, to determine for themselves whether they should be slave States or free.

Mr. Lincoln, although a hater of slavery, was not an Abolitionist. He had a profound reverence for the Constitution upon which the Union was founded, which recognized slavery as a local institution, but he was firm and unyielding in his opposition to its extension.

Thus they stood before the people of Illinois the acknowledged representatives of their respective parties—one, the advocate of the nationalization of slavery ; the other, the advocate of freedom for all, and everywhere except in those States in which slavery had a constitutional existence. Neither was an extremist ; neither was the exponent of ultra doctrines on either side. Mr. Lincoln did not go far enough, in merely opposing the extension of slavery, to satisfy the Abolitionists of the North, who demanded the extirpation of slavery, root and branch, without regard to the sanctions of the Constitution. Mr. Douglas, who was neither an advocate nor an opponent of slavery, did not go far enough to satisfy the pro-slavery leaders of the South, who contended for the right of slave-holders to take their slaves into the Territories and hold them there, in perpetual servitude, regardless of what he called popular, and they denounced as squatter, sovereignty. While, therefore, neither of them came up to the high standard of either Abolitionists on the one hand or pro-slavery men on the other, the difference between them was decided and irreconcilable ; and in order that the difference might be fairly and thoroughly discussed before the same audiences, Mr. Lincoln invited Mr. Douglas to meet him in a joint debate in some of the most populous counties of the State. The invitation was promptly accepted. The debate began on the 21st of August and closed on the 15th of October. They spoke in the open air, and their speeches were listened to with the deepest interest by the many thousands who thronged to hear them. They were fully and carefully reported, and were published in the leading journals North and South. No speeches ever made in the United States commanded so great attention or made so deep an impression upon the public mind. It was, indeed, the opening of the "irrepressible conflict" which Mr. Seward had predicted.

Mr. Lincoln, in a speech which he made a short time before, had avowed the sentiment that the United States could not permanently continue to be "part slave and part free;" that freedom or slavery sooner or later must become dominant in all the States; that slavery was local; that there was no warrant under the Constitution for its extension; and that its extension could rightfully be prevented by Congress. On the contrary, Mr. Douglas was committed to the doctrine that slavery was nationalized by the Constitution; that Congress had no authority to prevent its introduction to the Territories; that the people of each Territory and each State could alone decide whether they should be slave States or free. In a word, he was committed to the doctrine of popular sovereignty in its widest sense.

This really was the question to be discussed, but the discussion was not confined to it. In the course of the debate, slavery, its inhumanity, its influence upon the white population, its inconsistency with republicanism, were freely considered.

At the beginning of the debate the advantages seemed to be on the side of Mr. Douglas. The anti-slavery sentiment had not taken root in Illinois. Washed by the Ohio on the south, and the Wabash on the west, by which the largest part of her surplus productions were sent to the Southern markets, her pecuniary interests bound her to the South. From her earliest settlement the slave-owners had been her best, almost her only reliable customers. Nor was this all. Illinois had been largely settled by immigrants from the slave States, so that she was connected with the South by social as well as pecuniary ties. For more than half a century the Union had existed and rapidly grown in wealth and population, part slave and part free. Why might it not remain so, and still continue to thrive and prosper? Besides, there was something captivating in the doctrine of popular sovereignty—the right of the people to govern themselves according to their own good pleasure. Nor were these the only advantages possessed by Mr. Douglas. He was one of the ablest debaters in the country. To an almost un-limited command of language were added audacity and tact, which made him a formidable opponent in the United States Senate, filled as the Senate then was with very able and accomplished men. Upon the stump he had no equal. His voice was sonorous and flexible. Thoroughly versed in the political history of the country—bold, dashing, self-confident, and self-possessed—he was one whom very few men would have dared to encounter in a public debate. All this Mr. Lincoln perfectly understood, but he knew himself, and he was thoroughly convinced of the justice of his cause. He carried his conscience with him into the discussion. He made no statement which he did not believe to be true, took no position which he was not able to defend. Less gifted in language, he was clearer in statement, more persuasive and simple in style, stronger in his convictions, more earnest in presenting them, and more familiar with the character of those whom he was wont to call plain people, than his opponent.

It can hardly be said that he was a victor in the debate, but it cannot be denied that when it closed the advantage was not on the side of Mr. Douglas.

Like everybody else, I was greatly interested in the debate. Mr. Lincoln's speeches were not only very able, but they left the impression upon my mind that he possessed the elements of great personal popularity. So strong was this impression that, happening to be in Chicago in 1860, when the Republican Convention was in session, and being asked by some of the delegates (when it was certain that either Mr. Seward or Mr. Lincoln would be nominated) to which I thought their votes should be given, I did not hesitate to say "that that depended upon what they

wanted to do—if they wanted to vindicate the principles of the party, they should vote for Mr. Seward;
if they wanted to elect a President, they should vote
for Mr. Lincoln." Mr. Seward had rendered great
service to his party, of which he stood at the head ;
his ability was undoubted, and he was the decided
choice of the delegates from the Eastern States, but
I doubted that enough of the Western States could
be carried to secure his election.

Mr. Lincoln's election precipitated the rebellion,
but the time had come, sooner than had been expected and in a different way, for the settlement of
the question whether the United States were a Nation, to which allegiance was due by the people, or
a confederation of States, from which any State or
number of States might withdraw by their own independent action ; and of the equally important
question whether slavery or freedom should dom-
inate throughout the Union. These questions were
settled by war, and it is now quite certain that they
could not have been settled by any other means.
The cost of this settlement in treasure and blood
was enormous, but it was incomparably less than
would have been the evils which would have resulted from the nationalization of slavery or the perpetual strife which must have occurred between the
sections if the Union had been disrupted. That the
election of Mr. Lincoln was fortunate for the coun-

try, and the whole country, is generally admitted. It would have been quite impossible for either of the other distinguished men whose names were before the convention for nomination for the Presidency to have retained the confidence of the people through the protracted struggle to the same extent that he did.

Mr. Lincoln's character it is difficult to analyze, so rare and seemingly incongruous were its combinations. Instead, therefore, of attempting an analysis, I must confine my remarks to a description of his appearance, and of his prominent and singular, if not inconsistent, characteristics.

In form, Mr. Lincoln was tall and angular, lacking in compactness, but strong and sturdy, with great capacity for work and power of endurance. His features were coarse, and to strangers uncomely, but prepossessing to those who became his friends. His face, dull and heavy when in repose, was all alight with intelligence when in conversation. "I thought," said a lady, "when I first saw him that he was one of the ugliest of men. Now that I know him well, he seems to me to be perfectly charming." Grave and sedate in manner, he was full of kind and gentle emotions. He was fond of poetry. Shakespeare was his delight. Few men could read with equal expression the plays of the great dramatist.

The theater had great attractions for him, but it

was comedy, not tragedy, he went to hear. He had great enjoyment of the plays that made him laugh, no matter how absurd and grotesque, and he gave expression to his enjoyment by hearty and noisy applause. He was a man of strong religious convictions, but he cared nothing for the dogmas of the churches, and had little respect for their creeds. As a lawyer and advocate, Mr. Lincoln had no superior in Illinois and few superiors in the older States. His practice was not broad or varied enough to require constant study of authorities, but his mind was keen, clear, discriminating, and he was well grounded in the elementary principles of the law. His arguments before the court were always carefully prepared, pointed, and cogent. Before a jury he was especially effective. One of his most distinguished characteristics as an advocate was the suppression of himself in his arguments to the jurors. It was his aim to fix the facts, and the facts only, upon their minds. Comprehending perfectly the points upon which the case depended, to them he directed the attention of the jury, wasting no words upon unimportant matters; never wearisome by long speeches, with great aptitude discovering the characters of jurors, always intelligible and earnest, he never failed to interest and rarely to convince. The same qualities were displayed in his public speeches—models they were of clear, simple, and consequently of forcible speaking.

The first time I saw and heard him was at Indianapolis, shortly after the conclusion of his debate with Mr. Douglas. Careless of his attire, ungraceful in his movements, I thought as he came forward to address the audience that his was the most ungainly figure I had ever seen upon a platform. Could this be Abraham Lincoln whose speeches I had read with so much interest and admiration—this plain, dull-looking man the one who had successfully encountered in debate one of the most gifted speakers of his time? The question was speedily answered by the speech. The subject was slavery—its character, its incompatibility with Republican institutions, its demoralizing influences upon society, its aggressiveness, its rights as limited by the Constitution; all of which were discussed with such clearness, simplicity, earnestness, and force as to carry me with him to the conclusion that the country could not long continue part slave and part free—that freedom must prevail throughout the length and breadth of the land, or that the great Republic, instead of being the home of the free and the hope of the oppressed, would become a by-word and a reproach among the nations.

Mr. Lincoln was not a polished writer, but he wrote correctly and with great precision. In clearness of expression, in conciseness, in the use of apt and appropriate language, which everybody could understand, it would be difficult to find his superior. His letters in explanation and defense of his hesitation to proclaim freedom to the slaves, especially his reply to Mr. Greeley, are masterpieces of clear and forcible writing. The concluding paragraph of his first inaugural—"The mystic chords of memory, stretching from every battle-field and patriot grave to every living heart and hearth-stone all over this broad land, will yet swell the chorus of the Union, when again touched, as surely they will be, by the better angels of our nature"—is as happy in expression as it is touching and beautiful in thought.

Mr. Lincoln was not an orator, and yet where in the English language can be found eloquence of higher tone or more magnetic power than was exhibited in his little speech at the consecration of the battle-field cemetery near Gettysburg?—

"Four-score and seven years ago, our fathers brought forth on this continent a new nation, conceived in liberty, and dedicated to the proposition that all men are created equal. Now we are engaged in a great civil war, testing whether that nation, or any nation so conceived and so dedicated, can long endure. We are met on a great battle-field of that war. We have come to dedicate a portion of that field as a final resting-place for those who here gave their lives that that nation might live. It is altogether fitting and proper that we should do this.

" But, in a larger sense, we cannot dedicate—we cannot consecrate—we cannot hallow this ground. The brave men who struggled here have consecrated it far above our poor power to add or detract. The world will little note nor long remember what we *say* here, but it can never forget what they *did* here. It is for us, the living, rather to be dedicated here to the unfinished work which they who fought here have thus far so nobly advanced. It is, rather, for us to be here dedicated to the great task remaining before us, that from these honored dead we take increased devotion to that cause for which they gave the last full measure of devotion ; that we here highly resolve that these dead shall not have died in vain ; that this nation, under God, shall have a new birth of freedom ; and that government of the people, by the people, for the people, shall not perish from the earth."

He followed Edward Everett, whose speech was worthy of his reputation as one of the most accomplished orators of the age, and when he concluded, it is said that Mr. Everett, taking Mr. Lincoln's hand, remarked : " My speech will soon be forgotten ; yours never will be. How gladly would I exchange my hundred pages for your twenty lines !"

Mr. Lincoln excelled as a story-teller. The habit

of story-telling was formed in his early professional
life, when in company with a few other prominent
members of the bar, he visited counties, at long distances from his own, to try important cases. The
journeys from county to county were long and protracted, and as there were no newspapers nor books
in the cabins where they spent the nights, these
lawyer circuit-riders, as they were called, killed the
time, as the saying was, by telling stories, in which
invention as well as memory was brought into play.
In inventing stories and skill in telling them Mr.
Lincoln was the acknowledged leader. The habit
of story-telling, thus formed, became part of his nature, and he gave free rein to it, even when the fate
of the nation seemed to be trembling in the balance.
Some eight or ten days after the first battle of
Bull Run, when Washington was utterly demoralized
by its result, I called upon him at the White House,
in company with a few friends, and was amazed
when, referring to something which had been said
by one of the company about the battle which was
so disastrous to the Union forces, he remarked, in his
usual quiet manner, " That reminds me of a story,"
which he told in a manner so humorous as to indicate that he was free from care and apprehension.
This to me was surprising. I could not then understand how the President could feel like telling a
story when Washington was in danger of being capt-

ured, and the whole North was dismayed ; and I left the White House with the feeling that I had been mistaken in Mr. Lincoln's character, and that his election might prove to have been a fatal mistake. This feeling was changed from day to day as the war went on; but it was not entirely overcome until I went to Washington in the spring of 1863, and as an officer of the government was permitted to have free intercourse with him. I then perceived that my estimate of him before his election was well grounded, and that he possessed even higher qualities than I had given him credit for; that he was a man of sound judgment, great singleness and tenacity of purpose, and extraordinary sagacity; that story-telling was to him a safety-valve, and that he indulged in it, not only for the pleasure it afforded him, but for a temporary relief from oppressing cares ; that the habit had been so cultivated that he could make a story illustrate a sentiment and give point to an argument. Many of his stories were as apt and instructive as the best of Æsop's fables. All of his stories, however, were not of this character. Next to the theater he liked to tell stories and to listen to them. The evening of the day on which the reports of Sheridan's great victory in the Valley of Virginia were received I spent with him, in company with Mr. Randall, Postmaster-General, and a few of Mr. Lincoln's personal friends, at the Soldiers' Home. Mr. Lincoln was in the best of spirits, and Randall was also a good story-teller. For two hours there was a constant run of story-telling—Lincoln leading and Randall following—a contest between them as to which should tell the best story and provoke the heartiest laughter. The stories were not such as would be listened to with pleasure by very refined ears, but they were exceedingly funny. The verdict of the listeners was that, while the stories were equally good, Mr. Lincoln had displayed the most humor and skill.

Mr. Lincoln was severely denounced not only by the out-and-out Abolitionists, but by men less pronounced in their antislavery views, such as Mr. Wade and Mr. Greeley, for his delay in emancipating the slaves, under his war power, as it was called. This delay was caused by his doubts as to whether the public sentiment of the North, with which he always kept abreast, was prepared for a measure so momentous and far-reaching; by his profound respect for the Constitution which he had sworn to maintain; and especially by his fears that emancipation would retard, if it did not prevent, the restoration of the Union. In his letter to Mr. Greeley, on the 22d of August, 1862, he said:

"My paramount object is to save the Union, and not either to save or destroy slavery. If I could

11

save the Union without freeing any slaves, I would do it; if I could save it by freeing all the slaves, I would do it; and if I could save it by freeing some and leaving others alone, I would do it."

It must be admitted that this language was hardly consistent with the opinion he had so frequently expressed before his election, that the United States could not continue to be part slave, part free, or with his well-known abhorrence of slavery; but it was in perfect harmony with his utterances after he became President, and with the avowed purpose of the government in prosecuting the war. He did, however, subject himself to the charge of inconsistency, by exempting from the operation of his proclamation West Virginia and such parts of the other Southern States as were in the possession of the Federal forces; by proclaiming freedom to the slave where his authority could not be exercised, and leaving, where it was felt and acknowledged, many thousands in bondage. Nothing was or could be gained by not including all slaves in his proclamation of freedom, and his failure to do it greatly prejudiced the Union cause in Great Britain and other European states. The right to confiscate the property that could be reached in the South was unquestionable; his right to liberate the slaves, which was one form of confiscation, where the Confederate authority was dominant, was at least doubtful. Fortunately for the country, this was not left an open question. The doom of slavery in the United States was sealed by the amendments of the Constitution soon after the war was ended.

Whether Mr. Lincoln would have been competent to deal with the questions which were presented after the war, in the reconstruction of the Southern States—whether he would have exhibited the qualities of a statesman—is, I know, regarded by many as somewhat doubtful ; but it is, I think, only fair to infer, from the ability which he displayed as President, that he would have been equal to the new duties which he would have been called to perform, if he had completed the term for which he had been elected. He was well versed in constitutional law, his mind was well balanced, he was free from vindictiveness, and he was eminently patriotic. He would not have quarreled with his party, as his successor, Mr. Johnson, did. He had the confidence of the people, and could, therefore, have given direction to reconstructive legislation. His aim would have been to bring about by honorable conciliation harmonious relations between the sections, to secure the supremacy of the government without interference with the reserved rights of the States. There is nothing on his record to indicate that he would have favored the immediate and full enfranchisement of those who, having been always in servitude, were unfitted for an intelligent and independent use of the ballot. In the plan for the rehabilitation of the South which he and his Cabinet had partially agreed upon, and which Mr. Johnson and the same Cabinet endeavored to perfect and carry out, no provision was made for negro suffrage. This question was purposely left open for further consideration and for Congressional action, under such amendments of the Constitution as the changed condition of the country might render necessary. From some of his incidental expressions, and from his well-known opinions upon the subject of suffrage and the States to regulate it, my conclusion is that he would have been disposed to let that question remain as it stood before the war; with, however, such amendments of the Constitution as would have prevented any but those who were permitted to vote in Federal elections from being included in the enumeration for representatives in Congress, thus inducing the recent slave States, for the purpose of increasing their Congressional influence and power, to give the ballot to black men as well as white.

Nor would Mr. Lincoln have been vindictive against the masses who had been in arms against the government. Educated, as the people of the South had been, in the doctrine that the Union was a confederation of States, from which any State or number of States might withdraw when, in the opinion of a majority of their citizens, it had failed to accomplish the object for which it was formed, he would not have regarded the attempted secession as being treason, in the ordinary acceptation of the term ; nor would he have regarded as traitors any of the Southern people except those who, while continuing to hold Federal offices and to draw their pay from the Federal Treasury, used the influence of their positions to overthrow the government whose servants they were. For *them* he would have favored no forgiveness, to *them* he would have granted no pardons. *They* were guilty of treason, for which there could be no palliation. These, however, were comparatively few. The war on the part of the South was revolutionary. It was not only so considered by other nations, but by those who administered the government after the war was ended. Officers of high standing in the Confederate army were appointed to Federal offices by General Grant. The Vice-President of the Confederacy, when subsequently in Congress, was treated with great respect by both parties. Two of the members of the present Cabinet, and nearly every one of the Southern Senators in the last and present Congress, held distinguished civil or military positions under the Confederate Government. This would not, could not, have been the case had they been guilty of treason. They were revolutionists, not traitors, and as such they would have been treated by Mr. Lincoln.

Nor would Mr. Lincoln have appointed to Southern offices such men as, unfortunately, were appointed, whose chief mission seemed to have been to enrich themselves, overload the States with debt, and perpetuate the sectional discord which had always, to some extent, existed, and which had been aggravated and intensified by the war. His sympathy was as broad as his patriotism. Devoted to the Union—not merely a geographical union, but a true national Union—his aim would have been to build up the waste places, give new life to Southern industry, and bind together North and South, the people of the country and the whole country, by ties of mutual respect, brotherhood and interest.

In what, then, consisted Mr. Lincoln's greatness? Not in his legal acquirements; not in his skill as a writer or effectiveness as a speaker; not in his executive ability—although in these respects he commanded great respect; but in the strength of his convictions; his unwavering adherence to the principles which he avowed; his personal uprightness; his sound judgment; his knowledge of the people, gained rather by a study of himself than of them; his love of country; his humanity; his sublime faith in Republican institutions.

It was these qualities, rarely found in combination, which made him great and fitted him for the high position which he filled with so much credit to himself and with lasting honor and benefit to the nation.

HUGH McCULLOCH.

LINCOLN'S FIRST
NOMINATION AND HIS VISIT TO RICHMOND

I.

THE one political convention surpassing all others in enthusiasm, earnestness of purpose, and fidelity to principle, was that of the Republican Party held in Chicago, May, 1860. The spirit animating it was prefigured in the erection of the "wigwam," an edifice in which it was held. The convention was the sudden bursting into flower of the growing spirit of the free States against the aggressions of slavery.

The enthusiasm was stimulated by the conviction that through the dissensions of the Democratic Party the nominee of the convention would in all probability receive a majority of the electoral votes.

It was the opinion of most men east of Ohio that Mr. Seward of New York would receive the nomination. There were three other prominent candidates—Salmon P. Chase of Ohio, Edward Bates of Missouri, and Abraham Lincoln of Illinois.

Several weeks prior to the assembling of the convention, I started from Boston on a tour of observation through New York, New Jersey, Pennsylvania, to Baltimore, attending the Whig Convention in that city, which nominated John Bell of Tennessee, and Edward Everett of Massachusetts. It was the last assembling of that party which had numbered among its leaders Daniel Webster and Henry Clay—the raking together the embers of a dying political organization, appropriately held in an old church from which worshipers had forever departed. Southern men controlled the convention. They were enthusiastic over the nomination of Bell, but moderate in their demonstration over Everett's name, although public opinion in the Northern States regarded Everett as by far the greater statesman of the two. One editor called it the "kangaroo" ticket, and said that its hind legs were longest. It was noticeable that the antagonism of the Southern Whigs was manifestly greater toward the "black Republicans" than toward either wing of the divided Democratic Party.

From Baltimore I passed on to Washington, finding the name of Mr. Seward upon the lips of most Republicans as the probable nominee of the approaching convention. Mr. Seward expected to be nominated. I recall a day in the Senate Chamber, and a conversation with Henry Wilson, Senator from Massachusetts. We were seated on a sofa, when Mr. Seward entered from the cloak-room.

" There is our future President," said Mr. Wilson. " He will be nominated at Chicago, and elected. He feels it. You can see it in his bearing."

Of the public men of the period, there was no keener observer than Senator Wilson—Thaddeus Stevens of Pennsylvania being a possible exception —no one whose fingers detected more closely the beating of the heart of the people of the Northern States. Mr. Wilson knew every phase of public sentiment in Massachusetts, comprehended New England far beyond any other man, but he did not fully comprehend the trend of thought and feeling in the great West—the rapid growth and change which was going on during those spring days in the Republican States beyond the Alleghanies. Had he seen what I saw a week later he would not have so readily concluded that Mr. Seward was to be the next President.

My journey from Philadelphia to Pittsburg sufficed to convince me that Mr. Seward would not receive the votes of Pennsylvania in the convention. A quarter of a century ago there was a rivalry between the two States for political prestige and power which has disappeared with the changed condition of affairs. New York gloried in being the "Empire" State, while Pennsylvania plumed herself upon being the "keystone" which sustained the Republic. It was plain to me that Pennsylvanian

Republicans had no intention of giving their votes to the favorite son of New York, but would withhold them from any candidate till they could be given with decisive result.

In Ohio I found a moderate enthusiasm for Mr. Chase, but I could discover no particular organization to promote his candidacy. Of public sentiment in Indiana I could form no definite opinion. There had been no crystallizing of sentiment other than that the nominee must be a Western man.

II.

Arriving in Chicago several days in advance of the assembling of the convention, I found a number of delegates from Missouri actively advocating the nomination of Mr. Bates. In no city of the Union had there been so rapid a development of Republican sentiment as in St. Louis. The Republicans of that city believed, or affected to believe, that with Mr. Bates they could secure the electoral vote of the State.

There was but one name on the lips of the Republicans of Illinois—that of Abraham Lincoln. They knew him personally; had looked into his face at the mass meetings in the memorable contest with Douglas; had listened to his plain, incisive arguments, as clear and demonstrable as a proposition from Euclid. Outside of Illinois he was the "rail-splitter"—a plain, ungainly man, a *homespun* candidate, once member of Congress, but unacquainted with public affairs as the ruler of a nation.

Thurlow Weed had charge of Mr. Seward's affairs, and employed all the means and appliances known to New York political managers—even to enrolling delegates who reported themselves from Texas. I discovered a band of *claquers* in the interest of Mr. Seward, who hurrahed upon the streets and in the convention at every mention of his name. They overdid their part.

Mr. Norman B. Judd had charge of Mr. Lincoln's canvass, but there had been no such systematic pulling of distant wires or organization on his part. Nor was there need. It was manifest from the outset that there was a ground-swell of public opinion, if I may use the term, which promised to sweep all before it, and which rose, like the tides of the sea, during the second day of the convention, brought into quick action by the determination to devour Weed's organized band.

Arnold, in his *Life of Lincoln*, has narrated how it was done, by the employment of a Dr. Ames, who had a voice sufficiently powerful to be heard above the uproar of the lake in the wildest storm. He was a Democrat, but readily consented to shout for Lincoln. With an organized band he was placed at one end of the wigwam; another body was stationed at the opposite end. Mr. Cook, of Ottawa, delegate, was upon the platform. Whenever he waved his handkerchief they were to cheer. It was that handkerchief which set the ten thousand Illinoisians in the wigwam wild with enthusiasm, and which nominated Abraham Lincoln on the second ballot.

During the convention I chanced to sit at a small table with Thurlow Weed, and had an excellent opportunity to study his face. I doubt if during his long and eventful life he ever experienced a greater disappointment or a keener sorrow than at that moment. I saw him press his fingers *hard* upon his eyelids to keep back the tears. His plans had all miscarried. It was the sinking of a great hope. The rail-splitter, story teller—the ungainly, uneducated practitioner of the Sangamon bar—was the nominee instead of the able, learned, classical, polished senator. The mob had nominated him ! Mr. Weed did not comprehend that the *mob* in the wigwam was the best possible representative of the rising public opinion. All this is preliminary, but needful to adequately set forth subsequent scenes.

III.

On the morning after the adjournment of the convention a single passenger car, drawn by one of the fastest locomotives of the Illinois Central road, glided out from the Grand Central depot, bearing

the committee appointed by the convention to no-
tify Mr. Lincoln of his nomination. These were
George Ashman, president of the convention, who
had won great respect by his ability, manifested as a
presiding officer ; Julius A. Andrews of Massachusetts, in the vigor of manhood, who had electrified
the convention by his eloquence and plain common
sense ; George G. Fogg of New Hampshire, editor
of the Independent *Democrat*, printed at Concord,
who, next to John P. Hale, had been instrumental in
making New Hampshire a Republican State, afterwards Minister to Switzerland ; Wm. B. Kelly of
Pennsylvania, the veteran member of Congress, still
representing his steadfast constituents ; Caleb Smith
of Indiana, appointed to Mr. Lincoln's Cabinet ;
Amos Tuck of New Hampshire, member of Congress with Mr. Lincoln ; Norman B. Judd of Chicago, who had managed Mr. Lincoln's affairs, afterward Minister to Berlin ; Judge Carter of Ohio (appointed to a Washington judgeship), humorist, wit
and off-hand speaker, who addressed the crowds at
the railway stations, his speeches ending with the
words, " In the race for the Presidency, the Little
Giant (Douglas) will find that his coat-tails are too
near the ground to beat Old Abe." It was an allu-
sion to the difference in stature between the two
candidates, responded to by a yell of delight on the
part of Republicans, with groans from Democrats.

There were in all, including correspondents, about thirty persons.

The sun was setting when we reached Springfield. A crowd was gathering in the public square, not to welcome the committee but to listen to a speech from John A. McClelland (afterwards general), member of Congress from that district, in support of Mr. Douglas.

It was past eight o'clock Saturday evening when the committee called upon Mr. Lincoln at his home —a plain, comfortable, two-storied house, a hallway in the center, a plain white paling in front. The arrival of the committee had awakened no enthusiasm on the part of the townspeople. A dozen citizens gathered in the street. One of Mr. Lincoln's sons was perched on the gate-post. The committee entered the room at the left hand of the hall. Mr. Lincoln was standing in front of the fireplace, wearing a black frock-coat. He bowed, but it was not gracefully done. There was an evident constraint and embarrassment. He stood erect, in a stiff and unnatural position, with downcast eyes. There was a diffidence like that of an ungainly school-boy standing alone before a critical audience. Mr. Ashman stated briefly the action of the convention and the errand of the committee. Then came the reply, found in every "life" of Mr. Lincoln. It was a sympathetic voice, with an indescribable charm in the tones. There was no study of inflection or cadence for effect, but a sincerity which won instant confidence. The lines upon his face, the large ears, sunken cheeks, enormous nose, shaggy hair, the deep-set eyes, sparkling with humor, and which seemed to be looking far away, were distinguishing facial marks. I do not know that any member of the company, other than Mr. Tuck of New Hampshire and some of the Western men, had ever seen him before, but there was that about him which commanded instant admiration. A stranger meeting him on a country road, ignorant of his history, would have said, "He is no ordinary man."

Mr. Lincoln's reply was equally brief. With the utterance of the last syllable his manner instantly changed. A smile, like the sun shining through the rift of a passing cloud sweeping over the landscape, illuminated his face, lighting up every homely feature, as he grasped the hand of Mr. Kelly.

"You are a tall man, Judge. What is your height?"

"Six feet three."

"I beat you. I am six feet four without my high-heeled boots."

"Pennsylvania bows to Illinois. I am glad that we have found a candidate for the Presidency whom we can look up to, for we have been informed that there were only *little giants* in Illinois," was Mr. Kelly's graceful reply.

All embarrassment was gone. Mr. Lincoln was no longer the ungainly school-boy. The unnatural dignity which he had assumed for the moment, as a barrister of the English bar assumes gown and horse-hair wig in court, was laid aside. Conversation flowed as freely and laughingly as a meadow brook. There was a bubbling up of quaint humor, fragrant with Western idiom, making the hour exceedingly enjoyable.

"Mrs. Lincoln will be pleased to see you, gentlemen," said Mr. Lincoln. "You will find her in the other room. You must be thirsty after your long ride. You will find a pitcher of water in the library."

I crossed the hall and entered the library. There were miscellaneous books on the shelves, two globes, celestial and terrestrial, in the corners of the room, a plain table with writing materials upon it, a pitcher of cold water, and glasses, but no wines or liquors. There was humor in the invitation to take a glass of water, which was explained to me by a citizen, who said that when it was known that the committee was coming, several citizens called upon Mr. Lincoln and informed him that some entertainment must be provided.

"Yes, that is so. What ought to be done? Just let me know and I will attend to it," he said.

"O, we will supply the needful liquors," said his friends.

"Gentlemen," said Mr. Lincoln, "I thank you for your kind intentions, but must respectfully decline your offer. I have no liquors in my house, and have never been in the habit of entertaining my friends in that way. I cannot permit my friends to do for me what I will not myself do. I shall provide cold water—nothing else."

What Mr. Lincoln's feelings may have been over his nomination will never be known; doubtless he was gratified, but there was no visible elation. After the momentarily assumed dignity he was himself again—plain Abraham Lincoln—man of the people.

IV.

I pass over a year and a half to October 21, 1861. I was in Washington. The Army of the Potomac was in camp on Arlington Heights, and at Alexandria McClellan was having his weekly reviews. There was much parade but no action. "All quiet on the Potomac," sent nightly by the correspondents to their papers, had become a by-word. The afternoon was lovely—a rare October day. I learned early in the day that something was going on up the Potomac near Edwards' Ferry, by the troops under General Banks. What was going on no one knew, even at McClellan's head-quarters. It was near sunset when, accompanied by a fellow-correspondent, I went once more to ascertain what was taking place. We entered the anteroom and sent our cards to General McClellan. While waiting, President Lincoln came in, recognized us, reached out his hand, spoke of the beauty of the afternoon, while waiting for the return of the young lieutenant who had gone to announce his arrival. The lines were deeper in the President's face than when I saw him in his own home, the cheeks more sunken. They were lines of care and anxiety. For eighteen months he had borne a burden such as has fallen upon few men—a burden as weighty as that which rested upon the great law-giver of Israel.

" Please to walk this way," said the lieutenant.

We could hear the click of the telegraph in the adjoining room, and low conversation between the President and General McClellan, succeeded by silence, excepting the click-click of the instrument, which went on with its tale of disaster.

Five minutes passed, and then Mr. Lincoln, unattended, with bowed head, and tears rolling down his furrowed cheeks, his face pale and wan, his heart heaving with emotion, passed through the room. He almost fell as he stepped into the street, and we sprang involuntarily from our seats to render assistance, but he did not fall. With both hands pressed upon his heart he walked down the street, not returning the salute of the sentinel pacing his beat before the door.

General McClellan came a moment later. " I have not much news to give you," he said. " There has been a movement of troops across the Potomac at Edwards' Ferry, under General Stone, and Colonel Baker is reported killed. That is about all I can give you."

At that moment the finale of the terrible disaster at Ball's Bluff was going on—the retreat to the river, the plunge into the swirling water to escape the murderous fire flaming upon them from the rifles of the victorious Confederates. It was the news of the death of Colonel E. D. Baker which stunned President Lincoln. They were old-time friends, members of the Sangamon bar, had ridden the circuits together, been opponents in debate, but friends ever. So strong was the friendship, that Mr. Lincoln had named his second son Edward Baker. Colonel Baker had succeeded him in Congress, had emigrated to California, to return a Senator, to become President Lincoln's strong right arm, to advance at a bound to the front as one of the most eloquent orators of that body. Well do I recall his tireless activity, commanding presence and height, and sparkling eye. His presence was an inspiration. Ah ! what a scene was that a few weeks later when President Lincoln, supported by Senators Trumbull and Browning of Illinois, en-

tered the draped chamber to attend the funeral ob-
sequies of his old friend! Again the tears rolled
down his cheeks, as he heard the words of Senator
McDougall, recalling the by-gone scenes. Turning
toward Lincoln, he said, " He loved freedom, Anglo-
Saxon freedom. Many years ago I heard him, on a
star-lit night on the plains of the far West, recite the
Battle of Ivry. At Ball's Bluff he was Henry of
Navarre—

> " 'And if my standard-bearer fall, as fall full well he may,
> For never saw I promise yet of such a bloody fray—
> Press where ye see my white plume shine amid the rank of war,
> And be your oriflamme to-day the helmet of Navarre.' "

I doubt if any other of the many tragic events of
President Lincoln's life ever stunned him so much
as that unheralded message which came over the
wires while he was beside the instrument on that
mournful day, October 21, 1861.

V.

I come to the spring of 1865. I had been in Savannah, witnessed the departure of Sherman's army
on its triumphant northern holiday march, had seen
the old flag wave once more over Sumter, had
heard the colored troops march through the streets
of Charleston, singing "John Brown's body lies
moldering in the grave," and was back once more at

City Point to witness the last drawing of the scene to Five Forks, which was designed by Grant to put an end to the struggle. President Lincoln was on the *Ocean Queen*, a river steamer, at City Point. Sherman had reached Goldsboro. His army was in need of supplies. He had opened the railroad to Newberne, but could not move on to Bucksville without provisions. He wished to confer with Grant before making the last move, and arrived at City Point on the afternoon of March 27. Grant had not expected him, and I doubt not his coming was an agreeable surprise, as it would enable the two commanders to act in concert.

I was early at General Grant's head-quarters on the morning of the 28th. Adjutant-General Bowers, whose acquaintance I made in 1862 on the *Tennessee*, was ever courteous. I was examining a map of the military situation which he laid before me, when, looking down the line of log huts which constituted the head-quarters' camp, I saw General Grant step upon the plank-walk, smoking as usual, and then the tall form of President Lincoln, wearing his stove-pipe hat. It was a mild spring morning, but he wore an overcoat. Next to emerge from the hut was Sherman, wearing an old slouch hat, his pantaloons tucked into his boots, his uniform faded and worn. He was talking rapidly and emphasizing his points with gesticulation. The three, Lincoln in the center, formed the front rank, and walked slowly toward the Adjutant-General's office, Sherman talking, the others respectful listeners. In the second rank came Generals Meade, Ord, and Crook. It was a historical group—names which will live long in history. There were several other officers who had called to pay their respects to the President.

They came into the Adjutant-General's office, the President taking the precedence. He saw and recognized me, extended his hand, and said smilingly :

" What news have you ?" I never have been able to settle in my own mind the significance of the question, but I think humor prompted it, for in those days correspondents often sent news which was not altogether reliable.

" I have just arrived from Charleston and Savannah," I replied.

" Indeed ! " It was a tone indicative of a pleasant surprise. " Well, I am right glad to see you. How do the people like being back in the Union again?" he said, as he sat down in the chair placed for him by General Bowers.

" I think some of them are reconciled to it," I replied, " if we may draw conclusions from the action of one planter, who, while I was there, came down the Savannah River with his whole family— wife, children, negro woman and her children, of whom he was father—and with his crop of cotton, which he was anxious to sell at the highest price.."

The President's eyes sparkled, as they always did when his humor was aroused.

"Oh, yes, I see," he said with a laugh which was peculiarly his own—"I see; patriarchal times once more; Abraham, Sarah, Isaac, Hagar and Ishmael, all in one boat!" He chuckled a moment, and added:

"I reckon they'll accept the situation now that they can sell their cotton."

The maps were being placed for his inspection, that he might see the situation of the two armies—Grant's stretching beyond Thatcher's Run, ready to make its final move; Sherman's at Goldsboro, in position to move upon Bucksville.

"We shall be in position to catch Lee between our two thumbs," said Sherman, who did pretty much all the talking, Grant taking but little part. The stay was brief, the President going on board the *Ocean Queen*, and Sherman a little later going on board the *Bat*, a fleet craft which steamed rapidly down the James, carrying him to Moorehead City. During the afternoon Sheridan's cavalry was moving south past Petersburg and on to Five Forks.

VI.

I come to the morning of April 3d.   It was not far from three o'clock when there was an explosion which aroused the whole army from its slumbers. The Confederates had blown up their ironclads in the James.   Five Forks had been fought.   Lee's lines were broken and his army in retreat.   I was early in Petersburg.   The Union troops, flushed with victory, conscious that the last hours of the Confederacy had arrived, were sweeping through the streets with wild hurrahs.   I heard the whistle of the locomotive on the military railroad leading to City Point, and saw the train, a single car, which brought President Lincoln to the scene.   The soldiers saw him, swung their hats, and gave a yell of delight. He lifted his hat and bowed.   Perhaps I was mistaken, but the lines upon his face seemed far deeper than I had ever seen them before.   There was no sign of exultation in his demeanor.   He mounted a horse, and under a small cavalry escort rode through the town.   I did not follow him, but put spurs to my horse and rode alone to Richmond, over ground which twenty-four hours before had been swept by shot and shell, entering the city while the flames were still rolling heavenward from the buildings fired by the departing Confederates.   The fire was raging on two sides of the Spotswood Hotel when I entered it. The clerk was the only person visible. He bowed from habit.

"Can I have a room?" I asked.

"Take any room you please. I dare say you won't occupy it long. You see we are liable to be burnt out any moment."

I took up the pen and wrote my name and residence large—the first Yankee after the long list of majors, colonels and generals of the "C. S. A."

The clerk looked at it and smiled. I wandered at will through the streets, beholding a woe-begone crowd gazing mournfully upon the scene of desolation, guarding the piles of furniture heaped upon the grass springing fresh and green in the Capitol square—bedding, tables, chairs, looking-glasses, crockery, children, weeping women, groups of old men, weak and irresolute, trying to guard the wreck of their property from the crowd of pilferers ready to seize the plunder. The troops of General Deven's division were doing provost guard duty, and the soldiers shared their rations with the women and children.

VII.

During the following forenoon I was in the Representatives' Chamber in the Capitol, when a plain, quick-stepping gentleman entered—Admiral Farragut, who had hastened in from Norfolk to take a look at the situation. Having the latest account of what the army had done, I gave him the details of the last movement to Five Forks. He listened with intense interest, and said, " Thank God, it is about over."

In the afternoon of the same day I was standing on the bank of the James, when I saw a boat pulled by twelve sailors coming up the river, and a moment later recognized the tall form of the President, with Admiral Porter by his side, Captain Adams of the Navy, Lieutenant Clemens of the Signal Corps, and the President's son Tad.

Near at hand was a lieutenant directing the construction of a bridge across the canal. The men under his charge were negroes who had been impressed into service, and who were eager to work for their rations.

" Would you like to see the man who made you free ? " I said to one of the negroes.

" What, massa ? "

" Would you like to see Abraham Lincoln, who made you free ? "

" Yes, massa."

" There he is, that man with the tall hat."

" Be dat Massa Linkinn ? "

" That is President Lincoln."

" Hallelujah ! Hurrah, boys, Massa Linkinn's come ! "

He swung his old straw hat, slapped his hands and

jumped into the air. In an instant the fifty negroes under the lieutenant were shouting it. They ran towards the landing, yelling and shouting like lunatics. I could hear the cry running up the streets and lanes, " Massa Linkinn—Massa Linkinn," and the next moment there was a crowd of sable-hued men and women and children with wondering white eyeballs rushing pell-mell towards the landing.

President Lincoln recognized me. "Can you direct us to General Wirtzel's head-quarters?" he asked.

I informed him that I could do so. The boat came alongside the landing. Six marines in blue caps and jackets, armed with carbines, stepped on shore, then the President and little Tad, Admiral Porter and the rest, followed by six more marines. I indicated to Captain Adams the direction, and the procession under his lead began its march up the street toward Capitol Hill, the crowd increasing every moment, the cry of the delighted colored people rising like the voice of many waters.

I recall a negro woman who was jumping in ecstasy, clapping her hands, and shouting, "Glory! glory! glory!" She could find no other words.

Another had for her refrain, "Bress de Lord! bress de Lord! bress de Lord!"

The tropical exuberance of sentiment characteristic of the African race burst into full flower upon the

instant, and no wonder.   Abraham Lincoln was their
Saviour, their Moses, who had brought them through
the Red Sea and the desert to the promised land;
their Christ, their Redeemer.   We who have always
had our liberty, we cool-blooded Anglo-Americans,
can have no adequate realization of the ecstasy of
that moment on the part of those colored people of
Richmond.   They were drunk with ecstasy.   They
leaped into the air, hugged and kissed one another,
surged around the little group in a wild delirium of
joy.   They would gladly have prostrated themselves
before him—allowed him to walk on their bodies—if
by so doing they could have expressed their joy.

We reached the base of Capitol Hill.   The afternoon was warm, and the President desired to rest.
The procession halted.   The crowd had become so
dense that it was difficult to advance, and a cavalry-
man rode to General Shepley, who was placed in
command of the city, for an escort.   While thus
resting, an old negro, wearing a few rags, whose
white, crisp hair appeared through his crownless
straw hat, lifted the hat from his head, kneeled
upon the ground, clasped his hands, and said, "May
de good Lord bress and keep you safe, Massa
President Linkum."

Mr. Lincoln lifted his own hat and bowed to the
old man.   The moisture gathered in his eyes.   He
brushed the tears away, and the procession moved

on up the hill, a half dozen cavalrymen, with General Shepley, opening the way.

The procession reached Wirtzel's head-quarters— the mansion from which Jefferson Davis had taken his quick departure the previous Sunday.

President Lincoln wearily ascended the steps, and by chance dropped into the very chair usually occupied by Mr. Davis when at his writing-table.

Such was the entrance of the Chief of the Republic into the capital of the late Confederacy. There was no sign of exultation, no elation of spirit, but, on the contrary, a look of unutterable weariness, as if his spirit, energy and animating force were wholly exhausted.

The gentlemen who had been deputed to meet General Wirtzel in the early morning came in and were introduced. They were courteously and kindly received.

Later in the afternoon I saw President Lincoln riding through the streets, taking a hasty glance at the scene of desolation and woe. There was no smile upon his face. Paler than ever his countenance, deeper than ever before the lines upon his forehead. The driver turned his horses towards the landing. The visit to the capital of the Confederacy was ended.

I never saw him again. A few weeks later the bullet of the assassin accomplished its fatal work,

ending the earthly labors of this man of the people
—whose influence was far wider than the Republic—
held in such reverence that three years later I found
,myself drawn along the railway crossing the Apen-
nines by the locomotive Abraham Lincoln.

CHARLES CARLTON COFFIN.

VII

LINCOLN AND THE CABINET

FEW men have had the opportunity to render services so important and beneficial to the country and humanity as Abraham Lincoln. But we may question whether his career as President and Emancipator through the trying scenes of the great Civil War, or even the tragic and touching incidents of his untimely death, would have excited and kept alive the affectionate and ever-increasing interest in his character, if that character had not been marked by traits, some of them quaint, original and homely, that appealed to the common heart of mankind and revealed that touch of nature that makes the whole world kin. It has been often and truthfully said of him that he was a man whose heart lay close to the great popular heart and felt its beatings. Even after he had reached the perilous elevation of the White House, where the truth is apt to be seen through very refracted mediums, he never for a moment lost the faculty of reading the mind of those whom he called " the plain people." In truth he was, by birth, education, experience and sympathy, one of " the plain people " himself, and the traits that make him so uniquely interesting were simply the outgrowth of a mind original and vigorous, and a kindly heart developed by and taking shape from the modes of thought and expression, the habits and manner of life of the people amid whom he had been brought up and lived. Born in England or Massachusetts, and educated in conventional fashion at Oxford or Harvard, he would doubtless have been a man of mark and power, but he would not have been the Abraham Lincoln whom the people knew and loved. The training of the schools would probably have polished away, not indeed the native humor and shrewd faculty of observation, but that quaint and original habit of thought and speech which found constant expression in racy and effective phrase and in stories of Western life, often homely but never obscene, and always singularly apt in illustration.

But I am not writing an essay on Mr. Lincoln's character or genius. My less ambitious work is to record a few examples of his " preaching by parables," and of his habit of condensing an idea into a single telling phrase.

When these incidents happened I may premise that I was in the public service, and, by virtue of a custom established by Mr. Lincoln, I had occasional access to the Cabinet meetings during the absence of my departmental chief, the Attorney-General.

The skill and success with which Mr. Lincoln would dispose of an embarrassing question or avoid premature committal to a policy advocated by others is well known. He knew how to send applicants away in good humor even when they failed to extract the desired response.

A story told of him after General Cameron's retirement from the War Department illustrates this habit. Every one knows that Mr. Lincoln's Cabinet was chosen chiefly from his rivals for the Presidential nomination, and from considerations largely political. But the exigencies of the war demanded, in the opinion of many good Republicans, a reorganization of the Cabinet based on the special fitness of each member for the great work in hand. Of this opinion were some of the leading Republican Senators. After the retirement of General Cameron they held a caucus and appointed a committee to wait on the President. The committee represented that, inasmuch as the Cabinet had not been chosen with reference to the war, and had more or less lost the confidence of the country, and since the President had decided to select a new War Minister, they thought the occasion was opportune to change the whole seven Cabinet Ministers. They therefore earnestly advised him to make a clean sweep and select seven new men, and so restore the waning confidence of the country.

The President listened with patient courtesy, and when the Senators had concluded he said, with a characteristic gleam of humor in his eye:

"Gentlemen, your request for a change of the whole Cabinet because I have made one change reminds me of a story I once heard in Illinois of a farmer who was much troubled by skunks. They annoyed his household at night, and his wife insisted that he should take measures to get rid of them. One moonlight night he loaded his old shot-gun and stationed himself in the yard to watch for the intruders, his wife remaining in the house anxiously awaiting the result. After some time she heard the shot-gun go off, and in a few minutes the farmer entered the house. 'What luck had you?' said she. 'I hid myself behind the wood-pile,' said the old man, 'with the shot-gun pointed toward the hen-roost, and before long there appeared not one skunk but *seven*. I took aim, blazed away, killed one, and he raised such a fearful smell that I concluded it was best to let the other six go.'"

With a hearty laugh the Senators retired, and nothing more was heard of Cabinet reconstruction.

One of Mr. Lincoln's most amiable qualities was the patience and gentleness with which he would listen to people who thought they had wrongs to redress or claims to enforce. But sometimes, when his patience had been abused for selfish or unworthy purposes, he was quite capable of administering a caustic rebuke in his own way.

One day, when he was alone and busily engaged on an important subject, involving vexation and anxiety, he was, by some mischance, disturbed by the unwarranted intrusion of three men, who, without apology, proceeded to lay their claim before him. The spokesman of the three reminded the President that they were the owners of some torpedo or other warlike invention which, if the government would only adopt it, would soon crush the rebellion. "Now," said the spokesman, "we have been here to see you time and again; you have referred us to the Secretary of War, to the Chief of Ordnance, and the General of the Army, and they give us no satisfaction. We have been kept here waiting, till money and patience are exhausted, and we now come to demand of you a final reply to our application."

Mr. Lincoln listened quietly to this insolent tirade, and at its close the old twinkle came into his eye.

"You three gentlemen remind me of a story I once heard," said he, "of a poor little boy out West who had lost his mother. His father wanted to give him a religious education, and so placed him in the family of a clergyman, whom he directed to instruct the little fellow carefully in the Scriptures. Every day the boy was required to commit to memory and recite one chapter of the Bible. Things proceeded

smoothly until they reached that chapter which details the story of the trials of Shadrach, Meshach, and
Abednego in the fiery furnace.   The boy got on well
until he was asked to repeat these three names, but
he had forgotten them.   His teacher told him he
must learn them, and gave him another day to do so.
Next day the boy again forgot them.   'Now,' said
the teacher, 'you have again failed to remember
those names, and you can go no further till you have
learned them.   I will give you another day on this
lesson, and if you don't repeat the names I will punish you.'   A third time the boy came to recite, and
got down to the stumbling-block, when the clergyman said: 'Now tell me the names of the men in the
fiery furnace.'   'Oh,' said the boy, 'here come those
three infernal bores!   I wish the devil had them!'"

Having received their "final answer" the three
patriots retired, and at the Cabinet meeting which
followed directly after, the President, in high good
humor, related how he had dismissed his untimely
visitors.

The humorous aspect of a subject never failed to
strike him, and the illustrative story was as ready
for a grave matter of business as in its lighter
hours.   Often during the war United States marshals made arrests and seizures, the legality of which
would be tested by judicial proceedings against
them.   For their protection Congress appropriated

$100,000, to be expended under the direction of the President in defending United States officers in such suits. Some of the marshals thus sued had been clamorous for orders from the Attorney-General to the United States district-attorneys to defend these suits. But when it became known that the President had $100,000 for this purpose the marshals ceased to importune the Attorney-General for counsel, and "went" for the money.

In submitting to the President some rules for his approval under which the fund should be paid to the marshals, I spoke of the fact that they no longer sought the aid of the district-attorneys but were all anxious to get control of the money. "Yes," said he, "they will now all be after the money and be content with nothing else. They are like a man in Illinois, whose cabin was burned down, and according to the kindly custom of early days in the West, his neighbors all contributed something to start him again. In his case they had been so liberal that he soon found himself better off than before the fire, and he got proud. One day, a neighbor brought him a bag of oats, but the fellow refused it with scorn. 'No,' said he, 'I'm not taking oats now. I take nothing but money.'"

A friend of mine was one of a delegation who called on Mr. Lincoln to ask the appointment of a gentleman as Commissioner to the Sandwich Islands. They presented their case as earnestly as possible, and, besides his fitness for the place, they urged that he was in bad health, and a residence in that balmy climate would be of great benefit to him. The President closed the interview with this discouraging remark:

"Gentlemen, I am sorry to say that there are eight other applicants for that place, and they are all sicker than your man."

Many examples might be given of felicitous phrases, often of rustic origin, that gave point to his speech. Once, presenting to him an eminent lawyer, the President courteously said he was familiar with the Judge's professional reputation. The Judge responded:

"And we do not forget that you, too, Mr. President, are a distinguished member of the bar."

"Oh," said Mr. Lincoln modestly, "I'm only a *mast-fed* lawyer."

If there be any who do not see the point of this quaint suggestion of a self-educated lawyer, let them look at the illustration from Dr. South under the word "mast" in Webster's Dictionary.

When Attorney-General Bates resigned, late in 1864 (following the resignation of Postmaster-General Blair earlier in that year), the Cabinet was left without a Southern member. A few days before the meeting of the Supreme Court, which then met in December, Mr. Lincoln sent for me and said :

"My Cabinet has *shrunk up* North, and I must find a Southern man. I suppose if the twelve Apostles were to be chosen nowadays the shrieks of locality would have to be heeded. I have invited Judge Holt to become Attorney-General, but he seems unwilling to undertake the Supreme Court work. I want you to see him, remove his objection if you can, and bring me his answer."

I then had charge of the government cases in the Supreme Court, and they were all ready for argument. I saw Judge Holt, explained the situation, and assured him that he need not appear in court unless he chose to do so. He had, however, decided to decline the invitation, and I returned to the President and so informed him.

"Then," said he, "I will offer it to James Speed, of Louisville, a man I know well, though not so well as I know his brother Joshua. That, however, is not strange, for I slept with Joshua for four years, and I suppose I ought to know him well. But James is an honest man and a gentleman, and if he comes here you will find he is one of those well-poised men, not too common here, who are not spoiled by a big office."

Mr. Lincoln was himself a perfect illustration of that remark. His modest, manly nature was quite

unaffected by the accidents of place and power. It
was a common saying that he was far more acces-
sible than many a chief of bureau or clerk. Many
authentic anecdotes are told to show the kindness
with which he received and heard the stories of
those whom the sorrows of the war brought to him
for relief, and no bruised heart ever came to him to
invoke Executive clemency or assistance that did
not go away, if not healed, at least consoled and
grateful for patient hearing and kindly sympathy.

In the spring of 1863, a very handsome and attractive young lady from Philadelphia came to my
office with a note from a friend, asking me to assist
her in obtaining an interview with the President.
Some time before she had been married to a young
man who was a lieutenant in a Pennsylvania regiment. He had been compelled to leave her the day
after the wedding to rejoin his command in the
Army of the Potomac. After some time he obtained
leave of absence, returned to Philadelphia, and
started on a brief honeymoon journey with his bride.
A movement of the army being imminent, the War
Department issued a peremptory order requiring all
absent officers to rejoin their regiments by a certain
day on penalty of dismissal in case of disobedience.
The bride and groom, away on their hurried wedding
tour, failed to see the order, and on their return he
was met by a notice of his dismissal from the service.

The young fellow was completely prostrated by the disgrace, and his wife hurried to Washington to get him restored. I obtained for her an interview with the President. She told her story with simple and pathetic eloquence, and wound up by saying:

"Mr. Lincoln, won't you help us? I promise you, if you will restore him, he will be faithful to his duty."

The President had listened to her with evident sympathy, and a half-amused smile at her earnestness, and as she closed her appeal he said with parental kindness:

"And you say, my child, that Fred was compelled to leave you the day after the wedding? Poor fellow, I don't wonder at his anxiety to get back, and if he stayed a little longer than he ought to have done we'll have to overlook his fault this time. Take this card to the Secretary of War and he will restore your husband."

She went to the War Department, saw the Secretary, who rebuked her for troubling the President, and dismissed her somewhat curtly. As it happened, on her way down the War Department stairs, her hopes chilled by the Secretary's abrupt manner, she met the President ascending. He recognized her, and with a pleasant smile said:

"Well, my dear, have you seen the Secretary?"

"Yes, Mr. Lincoln," she replied, "and he seemed

very angry with me for going to you. Won't you speak to him for me?"

"Give yourself no trouble," said he. "I will see that the order is issued."

And in a few days her husband was remanded to his regiment. I am sorry to add that, not long after, he was killed at the battle of Gettysburg, thus sealing with his blood her pledge that he should be faithful to his duty.

Attorney-General Bates, who was a Virginian by birth and had many relatives in that State, one day heard that a young Virginian, the son of one of his old friends, had been captured across the Potomac, was a prisoner of war, and was not in good health. Knowing the boy's father to be in his heart a Union man, Mr. Bates conceived the idea of having the son paroled and sent home, of course under promise not to return to the army. He went to see the President and said:

"I have a personal favor to ask. I want you to give me a prisoner."

And he told him of the case. The President said:

"Bates, I have an almost parallel case. The son of an old friend of mine in Illinois ran off and entered the rebel army. The young fool has been captured, is a prisoner of war, and his old broken-hearted father has asked me to send him home, promising of course to keep him there. I have not seen my way clear to do it, but if you and I unite our influence with this administration I believe we can manage it together and make two loyal fathers happy. Let us make them our prisoners."

And he did so.

I often heard the Attorney-General say on his return from important Cabinet meetings that the more he saw of Mr. Lincoln the more was he impressed with the clearness and vigor of his intellect and the breadth and sagacity of his views, and he would add:

"He is beyond question the master-mind of the Cabinet."

No man could talk with him on public questions without being struck with the singular lucidity of his mind and the rapidity with which he fastened on the essential point.

A day or two after the news came of the stopping of the English steamer *Trent* by Admiral Wilkes, and the forcible capture of Mason and Slidell, the President walked into the Attorney-General's room, and as he seated himself said to that officer:

"I am not getting much sleep out of that exploit of Wilkes', and I suppose we must look up the law of the case. I am not much of a prize lawyer, but it seems to me pretty clear that if Wilkes saw fit to make that capture on the high seas he had no right to turn his quarter-deck into a prize court."

His mind quickly saw the point which, first of all, gave the act its gravest and most indefensible aspect.

The memory of Abraham Lincoln is and always will be precious to the American people, and the better his character and conduct are understood the brighter will he shine among those names that the world will not willingly let die.

TITIAN J. COFFEY.

VIII

LINCOLN AND SLAVERY

"Without doubt the greatest man of rebellion times, the one matchless among forty millions for the peculiar difficulties of the period, was Abraham Lincoln."

JAMES LONGSTREET.

MR. LINCOLN'S greatness was founded upon his devotion to truth, his humanity and his innate sense of justice to all.

In his career as a lawyer, he traversed a wide range of territory in Illinois ; he attended many courts and had many professional engagements, some remunerative and others not. In all his conflicts at the bar, wherein it may be said he was successful in every case that he ought to have been, he never inflicted an unnecessary wound upon an adversary, and no one ever thought of uttering a rude word to him. He affected no superior wisdom over his fellows, yet he was often appealed to by the judge to say what rule of law ought to be applied in a given case, and what disposition the parties ought to make of it, and his opinion, when expressed, always seemed to be so reasonable, fair and just, that the parties accepted it. He was never known to rebuke any one for intemperance, profanity, or other violation of social duty. While he professed nothing in these respects, people did not drink immoderately in his presence, neither were they vulgar nor profane. When he appeared, every one seemed to be happy ; they wanted to hear him talk ; he always had something to say that would amuse or instruct them— something that they had not heard before. He argued great causes, in which principle and property were involved, logically, and with wonderful ability. Trifling causes he met with ridicule, and often by an anecdote, in the use of which he was unsurpassed : the cause would be abandoned in a gale of merriment, the losing party being neither provoked nor angry.

A man endowed with such qualities was bound to be a successful politician ; and, if he turned his attention in that direction, none who knew him could doubt upon which side he would be, or with which party he would unite. He was a Whig, because he believed the principles of that party best conduced to the welfare of his fellow-man. He believed that the true principles of government were those which Mr. Clay advocated. He believed in the protection of American industries. He believed that the slavery of men was wrong in principle, and impossible of justification, and he held in profound veneration and respect the founders of the State of

Illinois, who had, by constitutional provision, forever prevented the existence of that institution in the State.

His opinions upon this subject would have remained a sentiment only, for he manifested no disposition by word or act to interfere with slavery where it existed, but for the violent attempt to introduce slavery in Kansas and Nebraska upon the repeal of the Missouri Compromise. Mr. Douglas, the author of the repeal, sought to justify his act by the claim that the Kansas-Nebraska act submitted the question of slavery to the people of those territories, when they should come to adopt a constitution and apply for admission into the Union as States. Upon the questions involved the debates between him and Mr. Lincoln occurred.

There were comparatively few Abolitionists, in the strict sense of the term, in the State of Illinois. Their doctrines and pretensions were very unpopular. But a few years had gone by since Lovejoy was mobbed and killed at Alton, his press thrown into the river, and his murder passed unavenged; and yet Lovejoy neither said nor published anything more hostile to slavery than Lincoln uttered in those debates. But Lovejoy was an avowed Abolitionist; Lincoln was not. Mr. Douglas said at Freeport, in the northern part of the State, that Mr. Lincoln would not dare to speak at Carlisle, in the southern

14

part of the State, where they were soon to appear, in the same terms he did at Freeport. When they reached Carlisle, Mr. Lincoln referred to Mr. Douglas's remark, and spoke in the same strain as before, and no one remonstrated. He could do this because the people believed he was entirely sincere. His earnest and gentle manners compelled them to respect and tolerate the freedom of speech. At Charleston he said : " Because I do not want and would not have a negro woman for a slave it does not follow that I want her for a wife." This expression illustrates his aptness in enforcing an argument. A committee from the convention sitting in Richmond, which finally passed the Virginia ordinance of secession, went to Washington with the request that the President should order the evacuation by Major Anderson of Fort Sumter. During the colloquy which occurred between Mr. Lincoln and this committee, Mr. Lincoln said :

" I understand you claim and believe yourselves to be Union men, that the Richmond Convention is opposed to a dissolution of the Union, and that you believe a majority of the people of the State want to remain in the Union."

They said : " Yes."

Then Mr. Lincoln replied :

" I can't understand it at all ; Virginia wants to remain in the Union, and yet wants me to let South

Carolina go out and the Union be dissolved, in order that Virginia may stay in."

The masterly debates between Douglas and Lincoln made Lincoln the nominee of the Republican Party for President at the Chicago Convention in 1860, to the great disappointment of Mr. Seward and his supporters. The election came on, and resulted in the election of a majority of Republican electors; but these electors did not receive a majority of the public vote by nearly a million of votes, which fact Mr. Lincoln often referred to during his administration. The Republican Party, as such, stood pledged to the maintenance, inviolate, of the rights of the States, and especially the right of each State to order and control its own domestic institutions according to its own judgment exclusively. To that pledge Mr. Lincoln determined rigorously to adhere, and if, during his administration, there was any seeming digression from that resolve, it was brought about and compelled by the exigencies of the war. In his first inaugural address he expressed himself as follows:

"I have no purpose, directly or indirectly, to interfere with the institution of slavery in the States where it exists. I believe I have no lawful right to do so, and I have no inclination to do so."

This, he said, was quoted from one of his former speeches, and, further, that the same sentiment would be found in nearly all his public speeches. In the course of his address he said :

" No State upon its own mere motion can lawfully get out of the Union ; resolves and ordinances to that effect are legally void, and acts of violence within any State or States, against the authority of the United States, are insurrectionary or revolutionary, according to circumstances."

Then followed a declaration that, in his view of the Constitution and the laws, the Union was unbroken, and that to the extent of his ability he would take care that the laws of the Union be faithfully executed in all the States ; that there need be no bloodshed or violence in doing this, and that there would be none unless it was forced upon the national authority. It is needless to say that these pledges were kept.

The frankness of this inaugural address, and the pledges contained in it, inspired the devotees of the Union in the North with the hope that peace would finally prevail. It is plain that Mr. Lincoln entertained such hope, and he had ample reason for it if he considered the popular vote. It was but fair to assume that the votes cast for Messrs. Douglas and Bell, with the fusion vote of Pennsylvania for Breckinridge, were, with but few exceptions, the votes of Union men. They, with the votes cast for him, amounted to nearly 4,000,000 votes, leaving only

600,000 or 700,000 who voted for Breckinridge, who were for the most part disunionists. It was incredible that these Union voters would join in a rebellion for the dissolution of the Union over the express pledge in the inaugural address that "the government will not assail you. You can have no conflict without being yourselves the aggressors."

Mr. Bell was nominated as a Union man ; his supporters were Unionists of the strictest order ; at any rate they professed to be, and undoubtedly they were. But the mass of them were in the South, and more or less interested in the institution of slavery, and were inconsiderate enough to say during the canvass that if Mr. Lincoln should be elected, and should attempt to maintain the Union by force, they would, with the Breckinridge men, resist. When the war came, they felt the force of their pledge. They joined the rebellion, and, as was said at the time, they were generally placed in the front, and made to bear the brunt of the battle.

During the canvass which terminated in the election of Mr. Lincoln, Mr. Douglas omitted no occasion to express his devotion to the preservation of the Union. He traversed the whole country, and in all his speeches left no room to doubt his determination to stand by the government, no matter who was elected. The pledges then made he kept, and they were of immense value to the Union cause, and for them Mr. Lincoln never omitted to express his gratification and his obligation to Mr. Douglas.

In a retrospect of the scenes of those times, until the firing upon Fort Sumter, it must be apparent to all that good fortune attended Mr. Lincoln. The Secessionists dominated both Houses, and they had it in their power to prevent the counting of the electoral vote. They could have prevented his peaceful inauguration. It can hardly be supposed that Mr. Jefferson Davis would ever have permitted the canvassing of the electoral vote, and the subsequent inauguration of Mr. Lincoln, by which, in the form prescribed by the Constitution, he was invested with the executive authority of the nation, if he had supposed Mr. Lincoln would have forcibly resisted the dissolution of the Union. In contemplating the awful crime of the rebellion, and the great destruction of life which Mr. Davis, if he possessed the abilities which his friends ascribe to him, ought to have realized, how is his conduct to be accounted for in permitting the vote to be canvassed and Mr. Lincoln inaugurated? It is in vain to say that he failed to inaugurate anarchy because it was criminal, when he was preparing to enter upon a line of conduct which he ought to have known, if persisted in, would within a very brief time lead to a destructive war. It adds nothing to his fame if, in charity, it be said that he expected a peaceful separation; that the nation would voluntarily consent to a dissolution of the Union and to its own death.

Mr. Seward was in the Senate with Mr. Davis in the last session of Congress of 1860–1861. He was satisfied that Mr. Davis believed there would be a peaceful dissolution of the Union; that Davis expected to be President of the Southern Confederacy then already taking shape, and that Mr. Seward would be Secretary of State under Mr. Lincoln. Mr. Seward was apprehensive that Mr. Davis might inaugurate the rebellion before Mr. Lincoln was to be inaugurated—that he would resist the canvassing of the electoral vote, and this apprehension led to his famous Astor House speech. Mr. Seward afterward, at a dinner at Willard's Hotel, gave the following version of that affair. Referring to a speech that Mr. Oakey Hall had then lately made in the City of New York, he said :

" Oakey Hall says I am the most august liar in the United States ; that I said in the winter before the war, in a speech at the Astor House, that the trouble would all be over and everything settled in sixty days. I would have Mr. Oakey Hall to know that when I made that speech the electoral vote was not counted, and I knew it never would be if Jeff Davis believed there would be war. We both knew that he was to be President of the Southern Confederacy, and that I was to be Secretary of State under Mr.

requested Mr. Greeley to come to Washington and make known in person his complaints, to the end that they might be obviated if possible. The managing editor of the *Tribune* came. Mr. Lincoln said:

"You complain of me. What have I done or omitted to do which has provoked the hostility of the *Tribune?*"

The reply was: "You should issue a proclamation abolishing slavery."

Mr. Lincoln answered: "Suppose I do that. There are now 20,000 of our muskets on the shoulders of Kentuckians, who are bravely fighting our battles. Every one of them will be thrown down or carried over to the rebels."

The reply was: "Let them do it. The cause of the Union will be stronger if Kentucky should secede with the rest than it is now."

Mr. Lincoln answered: "Oh, I can't think that!"

No matter to what political party any man had been attached, if he was in good faith for the maintenance of the Union he had the confidence of Mr. Lincoln. During his administration he recognized but two parties, one for the Union and the other against it. He repelled no one; he strove to make friends, not for himself so much as for the preservation of the government, and seeing clearly from the beginning that property in slaves was in the way of many, he urged them to accept compensation. His wisdom and foresight is now apparent to all. If the Border States would have accepted compensation for slaves, or if Virginia had adhered to the Union, there would have been no war, and slavery would have been abolished by agreement and compensation.

Mr. Lincoln in his inaugural said to the malcontents:

"Suppose you go to war, you cannot fight always; and when after much loss on both sides, and no gain on either, you cease fighting, the identical old questions as to terms of intercourse are again upon you."

Failing to bring about the emancipation of the slaves in the Border States by agreement and compensation, Mr. Lincoln set about the restoration of government in the States in rebellion. On the 8th of December, 1863, he issued his Proclamation of Amnesty. By that proclamation it was declared that whenever in any of the seceding States a number of persons, not less than one-tenth in number of the votes cast in such State at the Presidential election of 1860, shall have taken the oath required, and not violated it, and being qualified voters by the election law of the State existing immediately before the so-called Act of Secession, and excluding all others, shall re-establish a State government which shall be Republican, such shall be recognized as the true government of the State, and be protected by the United States, as a State, against invasion and domestic violence. It will be observed that the persons who were authorized to re-establish a State government were to be qualified voters of the State before secession. Mr. Chase insisted that this paragraph of the proclamation should be changed, and the word citizens inserted in the place of qualified voters. The Attorney-General had given an opinion to Mr. Chase, November 29, 1862, that colored men born in the United States were citizens of the United States. That was the law of Mr. Lincoln's administration, so that if he had adopted the views of Mr. Chase the tenth in number necessary to organize a State might have been legally composed of colored men. There was no argument upon this proposition. Mr. Chase insisted. Mr. Seward quietly observed: " I think it is very well as it is." Mr. Lincoln made no reply.

There is abundant evidence, however, proving that Mr. Lincoln had no thought of restoring State governments in seceded States through any other instrumentality than by the qualified voters of those States before secession was inaugurated.

It was the purpose of the President to issue a proclamation looking to the emancipation of slaves during the summer of 1862, but in consequence of the unexpected misadventure of General McClellan in the Peninsula before Richmond, it was considered prudent to delay the proclamation until some decisive advantage should be gained by the armies in the field. Accordingly, soon after the battle of Antietam, the first Proclamation of Emancipation was made. By that, one hundred days were given the States in rebellion to resume their normal condition in the government. In the preparation of the final Proclamation of Emancipation, of January 1, 1863, Mr. Lincoln manifested great solicitude. He had his original draft printed, and furnished each member of his Cabinet with a copy, with the request that each should examine, criticise, and suggest any amendments that occurred to them. At the next meeting of the Cabinet, Mr. Chase said:

"This paper is of the utmost importance, greater than any state paper ever made by this government. A paper of so much importance, and involving the liberties of so many people, ought, I think, to make some reference to Deity. I do not observe anything of the kind in it."

Mr. Lincoln said:

"No; I overlooked it. Some reference to Deity must be inserted. Mr. Chase, won't you make a draft of what you think ought to be inserted?"

Mr. Chase promised to do so, and at the next meeting presented the following:

"And upon this Act, sincerely believed to be an

act of justice, warranted by the Constitution, upon military necessity, I invoke the considerate judgment of mankind, and the gracious favor of Almighty God."

When Mr. Lincoln read the paragraph, Mr. Chase said: "You may not approve it, but I thought this or something like it would be appropriate."

Lincoln replied: "I do approve it; it cannot be bettered, and I will adopt it in the very words you have written."

When the parts of the proclamation containing the exception from its operation of States and parts of States were considered, Mr. Montgomery Blair spoke of the importance of the proclamation as a state paper, and said that persons in after times, in seeking correct information of the occurrences of those times, would read and wonder why the thirteen parishes and the City of New Orleans in Louisiana, and the counties in Virginia about Norfolk, were excepted from the proclamation; they were in the "very heart and back of slavery," and unless there was some good reason which was then unknown to him, he hoped they would not be excepted.

Mr. Seward said: "I think so, too; I think they should not be excepted."

Mr. Lincoln replied: "Well, upon first view your objections are clearly good; but after I issued the proclamation of September 22, Mr. Bouligny, of Louisiana, then here, came to see me. He was a great invalid, and had scarcely the strength to walk up stairs. He wanted to know of me if these parishes in Louisiana and New Orleans should hold an election, and elect Members of Congress, whether I would not except them from this proclamation. I told him I would."

Continuing, he said : " No, I did not do that in so many words ; if he was here now he could not repeat any words I said which would amount to an absolute promise. But I know he understood me that way, and that is just the same to me. They have elected members, and they are here now, Union men, ready to take their seats, and they have elected a Union man from the Norfolk district."

Mr. Blair said : " If you have a promise out, I will not ask you to break it."

Seward said : " No, no. We would not have you do that."

Mr. Chase then said : " Very true, they have elected Hahn and Flanders, but they have not yet got their seats, and it is not certain that they will."

Mr. Lincoln rose from his seat, apparently irritated, and walked rapidly back and forth, across the room. Looking over his shoulder at Mr. Chase, he said : " There it is, sir. I am to be bullied by Congress, am I ? If I do I'll be durned."

Nothing more was said. A month or more thereafter Hahn and Flanders were admitted to their seats.

The only differences in the Cabinet were upon this very question. Mr. Lincoln adhered strictly to the opinions expressed in his inaugural: that the resolves and ordinances of secession were void; that the insurgent States were never out of the Union; that all that was necessary for them or the people of those States to do was to lay down their arms and cease fighting, acknowledge the Constitution and laws of the United States, and conform to their requirements. Mr. Chase, with a great many other Union men, had a different view of that subject, the discussion of which is not now important, further than to state that they held that Congress had the right and power to enact such laws for the government of the people of those States as they might deem expedient for the public safety, including the bestowal of suffrage upon negroes. Mr. Lincoln thought that suffrage, if it ever came to the negroes, should come in other ways. In his Amnesty Proclamation of December 8, 1863, will be found a fair indication of his mind concerning the freed people. He said that any provision by such State " which shall recognize and declare their permanent freedom, provide for their education, and which may yet be consistent, as a temporary arrangement, with their present condition as a laboring, landless, and home-less class, will not be objected to by the national executive."

In all his state papers and writings to that date there can be found no assertion that he intended to force negro suffrage upon the people of the slave-holding States. Doubtless he contemplated that some time in the future suffrage would be volun-tarily yielded to the blacks by the people of those States. From all that could be gathered by those who observed his conduct in those times, it seemed that his hope was that the people in the insurgent States, upon exercising authority under the Consti-tution and laws of the United States, necessarily recognizing the extinction of slavery, would find it necessary to make suitable provision, not only for the education of the freedmen, as specified in his Amnesty Proclamation, but also for the acquisition of property, and its security in their possession; and, to insure that, would find it necessary and expedient to bestow suffrage upon them in some degree at least. We have some evidence that such was his expecta-tion and hope. In a letter to Governor Hahn, con-gratulating him upon having his name fixed in his-tory as the first Free State Governor of Louisiana, he said :

"Now, you are about to have a convention, which, among other things, will probably define the

15

elective franchise. I barely suggest for your private consideration whether some of the colored people may not be let in—as, for instance, the very intelligent, and especially those who have fought gallantly in our ranks. They would probably help, in some trying time to come, to keep the jewel of liberty within the family of freedom. But this is only a suggestion—not to the public, but to you alone."

It was apparent to all who bore intimate relations with Mr. Lincoln, that, foreseeing the termination of the war by the submission of the insurgents, his mind was seriously affected in contemplation of the new responsibilities which would devolve upon him. His speech grew more grave, and his aspect more serious. His second inaugural address was a faithful mirror of his mind. He seemed to be oppressed with a great care, conscious that changes were about to occur which would impose upon him new duties in which he might possibly find himself in conflict with many of the public men who had supported the government in the war. There seemed to be as many minds as there were men, and in a majority of cases inclined to adhere to their own opinions, without regard to the opinions of Mr. Lincoln or any one else ; yet he felt that the responsibility all rested upon him.

A short time before the capitulation of General Lee, General Grant had told him that the war must necessarily soon come to an end, and wanted to know of him whether he should try to capture Jeff Davis, or let him escape from the country if he would. He said:

"About that, I told him the story of an Irishman who had taken the pledge of Father Mathew. He became terribly thirsty, and applied to a bartender for a lemonade, and while it was being prepared he whispered to him, 'And couldn't ye put a little brandy in it all unbeknown to meself?' I told Grant if he could let Jeff Davis escape all unbeknown to himself, to let him go. I didn't want him."

When he returned from the James, where he met Messrs. Stephens, Campbell, and Hunter, he related some of his conversations with them. He said that at the conclusion of one of his discourses, detailing what he considered to be the position in which the insurgents were placed by the law, they replied:

"Well, according to your view of the case we are all guilty of treason, and liable to be hanged."

Lincoln replied:

"Yes, that is so."

They, continuing, said:

"Well, we suppose that would necessarily be your view of our case, but we never had much fear of being hanged while you were President."

From his manner in repeating this scene he seemed to appreciate the compliment highly. There is no evidence in his record that he ever contemplated executing any of the insurgents for their treason. There is no evidence that he desired any of them to leave the country, with the exception of Mr. Davis. His great, and apparently his only object, was to have a restored Union. Soon after his return from the James, the Cabinet was convened, and he read to it for approval a message which he had prepared to be submitted to Congress, in which he recommended that Congress appropriate $300,000,000, to be apportioned among the several slave States, in proportion to slave population, to be distributed to the holders of slaves in those States upon condition that they would consent to the abolition of slavery, the disbanding of the insurgent army, and would acknowledge and submit to the laws of the United States.

The members of the Cabinet were all opposed. He seemed somewhat surprised at that, and asked : " How long will the war last?" No one answered, but he soon said : " A hundred days. We are spending now in carrying on the war $3,000,000 a day, which will amount to all this money, besides all the lives."

With a deep sigh he added : " But you are all opposed to me, and I will not send the message."

From time to time persons, probably desiring to extol and magnify Mr. Lincoln, have represented that he was, during the war, frequently discouraged and quite in despair. About nothing in his career has he been more misrepresented than by these persons in this matter. There was never an hour during all the war in which he had any doubt of the ultimate success of the Union arms. He was often disappointed, and grieved at the disappointment. He expected that McClellan would be successful on the Peninsula, and afterward that he would follow up his victory at Antietam, and that Meade would follow up his at Gettysburg; and in speaking of that battle and the omission of Meade to pursue and fight, he said :

"He did so well at Gettysburg that I cannot complain of him."

As to Grant, after the Vicksburg campaign he never expressed a doubt of his success nor seemed to have the slightest apprehension that disaster would overtake him.

Persons may have fallen into the error of supposing that he was dejected and discouraged from his appearance in repose. When not engaged in conversation his countenance wore a sad expression, but that was no index of the operation of his mind. Chief among his great characteristics were his gentleness and humanity, and yet he did not hesitate promptly to approve the sentences of Kennedy and Beall.

During the entire war there are but few other evidences to be found of a willingness on his part that any one should suffer the penalty of death. His great effort seemed to be to find some excuse, some palliation for offences charged. He strove at all times to relieve the citizens on both sides of the inconveniences and hardships resulting from the war. It has often been reported that Secretary of War Stanton arbitrarily refused to carry out his orders. In all such cases reported it will be found that the President had given directions to him to issue permits to persons who had applied to go through the lines into the insurgent districts. The President said at one time, referring to Stanton's refusal to issue the permits and the severe remarks made by the persons who were disobliged :

" I cannot always know whether a permit ought to be granted, and I want to oblige everybody when I can, and Stanton and I have an understanding that if I send an order to him that cannot be consistently granted, he is to refuse it, which he sometimes does; and that led to a remark which I made the other day to a man who complained of Stanton, that I hadn't much influence with this administration, but expected to have more with the next."

J. P. USHER.

IX

LINCOLN
AND THE PROCLAMATION OF EMANCIPATION

MY first meeting with Mr. Lincoln was in January, 1861, when I visited him at his home in Springfield.

I had a curiosity to see the famous "rail-splitter," as he was then familiarly called, and as a member-elect of the Thirty-seventh Congress I desired to form some acquaintance with the man who was destined to play a conspicuous part in the impending national crisis. Although I had zealously supported him in the canvass, and was strongly impressed by the grasp of thought and aptness of expression which marked his great debate with Douglas, yet, as a thorough-going Free Soiler and a member of the Radical wing of Republicanism, my prepossessions were against him. He was a Kentuckian, and a conservative Whig, who had supported General Taylor in 1848, and General Scott four years later, when the Whig party finally sacrificed both its character and its life on the altar of slavery. His nomination, moreover, had been secured through the diplomacy of conservative Republicans, whose mor-

bid dread of "abolitionism" unfitted them, as I believed, for leadership in the battle with slavery which
had now become inevitable, while the defeat of Mr.
Seward had been to me a severe disappointment and
a real personal grief.   Still, I did not wish to do Mr.
Lincoln the slightest injustice, while I hoped and believed his courage and firmness would prove equal to
the emergency.

On meeting him, I found him far better-looking
than the campaign pictures had represented.   These,
as a general rule, were wretched caricatures.   His
face, when lighted up in conversation, was not un-
handsome, and the kindly and winning tones of his
voice pleaded for him, as did the smile which played
about his rugged features.   He was full of anecdote
and humor, and readily found his way to the hearts
of those who enjoyed a welcome to his fireside.   His
face, however, was sometimes marked by that touching expression of sadness which became so generally
noticeable in the following years.   I was much pleased
with our first Republican Executive, and returned
home more fully inspired than ever with the purpose
to sustain him to the utmost in facing the duties of
his great office.

The chief purpose of this visit, however, related
to another matter.   The rumor was then current and
generally credited, that Simon Cameron and Caleb
B. Smith were to be made Cabinet ministers, and I

desired to enter my protest against such a movement. Mr. Lincoln heard me patiently, but made no committal; and the subsequent selection of these representatives of Pennsylvania and Indiana Republicanism, along with Seward and Chase, illustrated the natural tendency of his mind to mediate between opposing forces. This was further illustrated a little later when some of his old Whig friends pressed the appointment of an incompetent and unfit man for an important position. When I remonstrated against it, Mr. Lincoln replied: "There is much force in what you say, but, in the balancing of matters, I guess I shall have to appoint him." This "balancing of matters" was a source of infinite vexation during his administration, as it has been to his successors; but it was then easier to criticise this policy than to point the way to any practicable method of avoiding it.

I did not see Mr. Lincoln again till the day of his inauguration, when he entered the Senate-chamber arm-in-arm with Mr. Buchanan. The latter was so withered and bowed with age that in contrast with the towering form of his successor he seemed little more than half a man. The public curiosity to see the President-elect reached its climax as he made his appearance on the east portico of the Capitol. All sorts of stories had been told and believed about his personal appearance. His character had been grossly misrepresented and maligned in both sections of the Union ; and the critical condition of the country naturally whetted the appetite of men of all parties to see and hear the man who was now the central figure of the Republic.   The tone of moderation, tenderness, and good-will which breathed through his inaugural speech made a profound impression in his favor ; while his voice, though not very strong or full-toned, rang out over the acres of people before him with surprising distinctness, and, I think, was heard in the remotest parts of his audience.

The pressure for office during the first few months of the new administration was utterly unprecedented and beggared all description.   It was a sort of epidemic, and Mr. Lincoln, at times, was perfectly appalled by it.   It gave him no pause, but pursued him remorselessly night and day ; and there were moments when his face was the picture of an indescribable weariness and despair.   It jarred upon his sentiment of patriotism, when the country was just entering upon the awful struggle for its life, and seemed to make him sick at heart.   Sometimes he lost his temper.   An instance of this occurred soon after his inauguration, which also illustrates his fidelity to his friends.   A delegation of California Republicans called on him with a proposed political slate covering the chief offices on the Pacific coast. Their programme was opposed, in part, by Senator

Baker, of Oregon, who quite naturally claimed the right to be consulted respecting the patronage of his section of the Union. Some of the Californians very unwisely sought the accomplishment of their purpose by assailing both the public and private character of the Oregon Senator, who was an old-time friend of the President. The anger of Mr. Lincoln was kindled instantly, and blazed forth with such vehemence and intensity that everybody present quailed before it. His wrath was simply terrible, as he put his foot down and told the delegation that Senator Baker was his friend ; that he would permit no man to assail him in his presence ; and that it was not possible for them to accomplish their pur pose by any such methods. The result was that the charges against Senator Baker were summarily with-drawn and apologized for, and such a disposition of the offices on the Pacific slope finally made as proved satisfactory to all parties. These facts I learned at the time from an intimate personal friend who formed a part of the delegation, and who was afterward honored by an important appointment in his State.

This is not the only case in which Mr. Lincoln lost his habitual good temper. After my nomination for re-election in the year 1864, Mr. Holloway, who was holding the position of Commissioner of Patents, and was one of the editors of a Republican newspaper in my district, refused to recognize me as the party candidate, and kept the name of my defeated competitor standing in his paper. It threatened discord and mischief, and I went to the President with these facts, and on the strength of them asked for Mr. Holloway's removal from office.

"Your nomination," said Mr. Lincoln, "is as binding on Republicans as mine, and you can rest assured that Mr. Holloway shall support you, openly and unconditionally, or lose his head."

This was entirely satisfactory, but after waiting a week or two for the announcement of my name, I returned to the President with the information that Mr. Holloway was still keeping up his fight, and that I had come to ask of him decisive measures. I saw in an instant that his ire was roused. He rang the bell for his messenger, and said to him in a very excited and emphatic way,

"Tell Mr. Holloway to come to me!"

The messenger hesitated, looking somewhat surprised and bewildered, when Mr. Lincoln said in a tone still more emphatic,

" *Tell Mr. Holloway to come to me!* "

It was perfectly evident that the business would now be attended to, and in a few days my name was duly announced, and the work of party insubordination ceased.

But the temper of the President was far more seriously tried early in the year 1862, touching the conduct of the war. General McClellan had disregarded the general order of the President, dated the 19th of January, for a movement of all our forces. He had protested against the order of January 31st, directing an expedition for the purpose of seizing upon the railroad south-west of Manassas Junction. He had opposed all forward movements of the Army of the Potomac, and again and again refused to co-operate with the Navy in breaking up the blockade of that river. And his movement early in March in the direction of the enemy at Centreville and Manassas was undertaken with very great reluctance, and after the enemy had evacuated these positions. Mr. Lincoln had clung to General McClellan with great pertinacity and in the face of much popular clamor, but his patience was now completely exhausted, and his passions carried him by storm. According to Senator Chandler, from whom I obtained my information, the scene strikingly suggested that described by Colonel Lear, when General Washington received the news of St. Clair's defeat by the Indians in 1791. I well remember the delight and exultation of the Michigan Senator as he related the circumstances to me, and predicted the victory for our arms which he believed it foreshadowed. "Old Abe," said he, " is mad, and the war will now go on."

During the month of January, 1863, I called with the Indiana delegation to see the President respecting the appointment of Judge Otto, of Indiana, as Assistant Secretary of the Interior. He was soon after appointed, but Mr. Lincoln then only responded to our application by treating us to four anecdotes.

Senator Lane told me that when he heard a story that pleased him he took a memorandum of it, and filed it away among his papers. This was probably true. At any rate, by some method or other, his supply seemed inexhaustible, and always aptly available. He entered into the enjoyment of his stories with all his heart, and completely lived over again the delight he had experienced in telling them on previous occasions. When he told a particularly good story, and the time came to laugh, he would sometimes throw his left foot across his right knee, and clenching his foot with both hands and bending forward, his whole frame seemed to be convulsed with the effort to give expression to his sensations. His laugh was like that of the hero of *Sartor Resartus*, "a laugh of the whole man, from head to heel." I believe his anecdotes were his great solace and safeguard in seasons of severe mental depression. I remember that when I called on him on the 2d of July, 1862, at the time our forces were engaged in a terrific conflict with the enemy near Richmond, and everybody was anxious as to the result, he seemed quite as placid as usual, and at once yielded to his ruling passion for story-telling. If I had not known his peculiarities, I should have pronounced him incapable of any deep earnestness of feeling; but his manner was so kindly, and so free from the ordinary crookedness of the politician and the vanity and self-importance of official position, that nothing but good will was inspired by his presence.

In March following I called on the President respecting the appointments I had recommended under the conscription law, and took occasion to refer to the failure of General Fremont to obtain a command. He said he did not know where to place him, and that it reminded him of the old man who advised his son to take a wife, to which the young man responded, "Whose wife shall I take?" He proceeded to point out the practical difficulties in the way by referring to a number of important commands which might suit Fremont, but which could only be reached by removals he did not wish to make. I remarked that I was very sorry if this was true, and that it was unfortunate for our cause, as I believed his restoration to duty would stir the country as no other appointment could. He said:

" It would stir the country favorably on one side, and stir it the other way on the other. It would please Fremont's friends, and displease the conservatives; and that is all I can see in the *stirring* argument. My proclamation," he added, "was to stir the country; but it has done about as much harm as good."

These observations were characteristic, and showed how reluctant he still was to turn away from the conservative counsels he had so long heeded.

It has often been asserted that Secretary Stanton ruled Mr. Lincoln. This is a mistake. The Secretary would frequently overawe and sometimes browbeat others, but he was never imperious in dealing with the President. This I have from Mr. Watson, for some time Assistant Secretary of War, and Mr. Whiting, while Solicitor of the War Department. Lincoln, however, had the highest opinion of Stanton, and their relations were always most kindly. The following anecdote illustrates the character of the two men, and Mr. Lincoln's method of dealing with a dilemma. It is related that a committee of Western men, headed by Mr. Lovejoy, procured from the President an important order looking to the exchange of Eastern and Western soldiers, with a view to more effective work. Repairing to the office of the Secretary, Mr. Lovejoy explained the scheme, as he had done before to the President, but was met by a flat refusal.

"But we have the President's order, sir," said Lovejoy.

"Did Lincoln give you an order of that kind?" said Stanton.

" He did, sir."

" Then he is a d——d fool," said the irate Secretary.

" Do you mean to say the President is a d——d fool ? " asked Lovejoy, in amazement.

" Yes, sir, if he gave you such an order as that."

The bewildered Congressman from Illinois betook himself at once to the President, and related the result of his conference.

" Did Stanton say I was a d——d fool ? " asked Lincoln, at the close of the recital.

" He did, sir; and repeated it."

After a moment's pause, and looking up, the President said :

" If Stanton said I was a d——d fool, then I must be one, for he is nearly always right, and generally says what he means.   I will step over and see him."

Notwithstanding Mr. Lincoln's proverbial caution and diplomacy in dealing with difficult problems, he was completely armed with the courage of his convictions, after his conclusions had been carefully matured.   No man was more ready to take the responsibility when his sense of duty commanded him. This was strikingly illustrated in the summer of 1862, when he refused to sign the confiscation act of the 17th of July, without a modification first made exempting the fee of rebel land-owners from its operation.   Congress was obliged to make the modifi-

16

cation required as the only means of securing the important advantages of other features of the measure; but the action of the President was inexpressibly provoking to a large majority of Congress. It was bitterly denounced as an anti-Republican discrimination between real and personal property, when the nation was struggling for its life against a rebellious aristocracy founded on the monopoly of land and the ownership of negroes. The President was charged with thus prolonging the war and aggravating its cost by paralyzing one of the most potent means of putting down the rebellion, and purposely leaving the owners of large estates in full possession of their lands at the end of the struggle. He was arraigned as the deliberate betrayer of the freedmen and poor whites, who had been friendly to the Union, while the confiscation of life-estates as a war measure could prove of no practical advantage to the government or disadvantage to the enemy.

The popular hostility to the President at this time cannot be described, and was wholly without precedent, and the opposition to him in Congress was still more intense. But Mr. Lincoln accepted the situation, and patiently abode his time.

Two years later, when the fortunes of the war and his own reflections had wrought a change in his opinion, his frankness and courage in avowing it were as creditable to him as had been his firmness in facing a hostile public. Having heard of this change, I called to see him on the 2d of July, 1864, and asked him if I might say to the people that what I had learned on this subject was true, assuring him that I would make a far better fight for our cause if he would permit me to do so. He replied that when he prepared his veto of our law on the subject two years before he had not examined the matter thoroughly, but that on further reflection, and on reading Solicitor Whiting's law argument, he had changed his view, and would now sign a bill striking at the fee of rebel land-holders, if we would send it to him. I was much gratified by this statement, which was of great service to the cause in the canvass ; but, unfortunately, constitutional scruples respecting such legislation had gained ground, and although both houses of Congress at different times endorsed the measure, it never became a law, owing to unavoidable differences between the President and Congress on the question of reconstruction.

Perhaps the most charming trait in the character of Mr. Lincoln was his geniality. With the exception of occasional seasons of deep depression, his nature was all sunshine. His presence seemed a message of peace and good-will. Early in the war, after the Hutchinson family had been ordered out of the Army of the Potomac by General McClellan for the offense of singing Whittier's songs, he repeated-

ly welcomed them to the White House and listened
to the music which had been considered detrimental
to the service. He was delighted with it, selecting
his favorite songs, and testifying his satisfaction by
alternate laughter and tears. He said that if these
were the songs they had been singing, he wished
them to continue in the business, and that they
should have a pass wherever they desired to go.

Mr. Lincoln used to attend the rousing anti-
slavery meetings that were held in the Smithsonian
Institute, in the fall and winter of 1861–2, which
were addressed by several of the leading orators of
Abolitionism. At one of these meetings, Horace
Greeley delivered a written address, which Mr. Lincoln listened to and very greatly admired. I sat by
his side, and at the conclusion of the discourse he
said to me:

"That address is full of good thoughts, and I
would like to take the manuscript home with me
and carefully read it over some Sunday."

During the progress of the war, he and Mr. Greeley had some radical difference of opinion about its
prosecution and the duty of the government in dealing with the question of slavery ; but he had, I know,
the most profound personal respect for Mr. Greeley,
and placed the highest estimate upon his services as
an independent writer and thinker.

Mr. Lincoln had no resentments. He had kind

words for men who bitterly assailed him. He joined in no outcry against men in civil or military life who went astray. When the Republicans were denouncing Andrew Johnson after his maudlin speech on the 4th of March, 1865, he only said, " Poor Andy," and expressed the charitable hope that he would profit by his dreadful mistake.

Few subjects have been more debated and less understood than the Proclamation of Emancipation. Mr. Lincoln was himself opposed to the measure, and when he very reluctantly issued the preliminary proclamation in September, 1862, he wished it distinctly understood that the deportation of the slaves was, in his mind, inseparably connected with the policy. Like Mr. Clay and other prominent leaders of the old Whig party, he believed in colonization, and that the separation of the two races was necessary to the welfare of both. He was at that time pressing upon the attention of Congress a scheme of colonization in Chiriqui, in Central America, which Senator Pomeroy espoused with great zeal, and in which he had the favor of a majority of the Cabinet, including Secretary Smith, who warmly indorsed the project. Subsequent developments, however, proved that it was simply an organization for land-stealing and plunder, and it was abandoned ; but it is by no means certain that if the President had foreseen this fact his preliminary notice to the rebels would have been given. There are strong reasons for saying that he doubted his right to emancipate under the war power, and he doubtless meant what he said when he compared an Executive order to that effect to "the Pope's Bull against the comet." In discussing the question, he used to liken the case to that of the boy who, when asked how many legs his calf would have if he called its tail a leg, replied, "Five," to which the prompt response was made that *calling* the tail a leg would not *make* it a leg.

But the right to emancipate by such an edict and the legal effect of it when issued were not the only questions with which the President was obliged to deal. The demand for it was wide-spread and rapidly extending in the Republican party. The popular current had become irresistible. The power to issue it was taken for granted. All doubts on the subject were consumed in the burning desire of the people, or forgotten in the travail of war. The anti-slavery element was becoming more and more impatient and impetuous. Opposition to that element now involved more serious consequences than offending the Border States. Mr. Lincoln feared that enlistments would cease, and that Congress would even refuse the necessary supplies to carry on the war, if he declined any longer to place it on a clearly defined antislavery basis. He finally yielded to this pressure, and in doing so he became the liberator of the slaves through the triumph of our arms which it insured.

The authority to emancipate under the war power was therefore a side issue. It undoubtedly existed, but it could only be asserted over territory occupied by our armies. Each commanding general, as fast as our flag advanced, could have offered freedom to the slaves, as could the President himself. This was the view of Secretary Chase. A paper proclamation of freedom, as to States in the power of the enemy, could have no more validity than a paper blockade of their coast. Mr. Lincoln's proclamation did not apply to the Border States, which were loyal, and in which slavery was of course untouched. It did not pretend to operate upon the slaves in other large districts, in which it would have been effective at once, but studiously excluded them, while it applied mainly to States and parts of States within the military occupation of the enemy, where it was necessarily void.

But even if the proclamation could have given freedom to the slaves according to its scope, their permanent enfranchisement would not have been secured, because the *status* of slavery, as it existed under the local laws of the States prior to the war, would have remained the same after the re-establishment of peace. All emancipated slaves found in those States, or returning to them, would have been subject to slavery as before, for the simple reason that no military proclamation could operate to abolish their municipal laws. Nothing short of a constitutional amendment could at once give freedom to our black millions and make their re-enslavement impossible; and "this," as Mr. Lincoln declared in earnestly urging its adoption, "is a king's-cure for all evils. It winds the whole thing up." All this is now attested by very high authorities on international and constitutional law; and while it takes nothing from the glory of Mr. Lincoln as the great Emancipator, it shows how wisely he employed a splendid popular delusion in the salvation of his country. His proclamation had no present legal effect within territory not under the control of our arms; but as an expression of the spirit of the people and the policy of the administration, it had become both a moral and a military necessity. The simple truth should now be told, and the honor, due to Mr. Lincoln, be placed upon its just foundation.

But no picture of Abraham Lincoln which leaves out his private life can do him justice. Every lineament of his grand public career should have the setting of his rare personal worth. In all the qualities that go to make up character, he was a thoroughly genuine man. His sense of justice was perfect and ever present. His integrity was second only to that of Washington, and his ambition as stainless. His sympathy for the unfortunate and the down-trodden earned for him the fitting title of "Father Abraham," and made him the idol of the common people. His devotion to wife and children was as abiding and unbounded as his love of country, and his happiest hours in the White House were spent in the companionship of his little boy "Tad," who used to gambol about his knees. When death entered his household his sorrow was so consuming that it could only be measured by the singular depth and intensity of his love. He was human in the best and highest sense of the word. The record of too many of our famous men has been marred by personal vices; but in him, were happily blended the qualities which adorn public station and dignify private life.

GEORGE W. JULIAN.

X

SOME OF LINCOLN'S PROBLEMS

I.

I AM asked to give some reminiscences of Abraham Lincoln. I have so many and pleasant ones that I do not know where to begin unless at the beginning.

I first saw Lincoln in 1840, making a speech in that memorable campaign, in the City Hall at Lowell; and not again till I was more than twenty-one years older, when I called on him at the White House to make acknowledgments for my appointment as major-general. When he handed me the commission, with some kindly words of compliment, I replied: " I do not know whether I ought to accept this. I received my orders to prepare my brigade to march to Washington while trying a cause to a jury. I stated the fact to the court and asked that the case might be continued, which was at once consented to, and I left to come here the second morning after, my business in utter confusion." He said: " I guess we both wish we were back trying cases," with a quizzical look upon his countenance. I said: "Besides, Mr.

President, you may not be aware that I was the Breckinridge candidate for Governor in my State in the last campaign, and did all I could to prevent your election." " All the better," said he ; " I hope your example will bring many of the same sort with you." " But," I answered, "I do not know that I can support the measures of your administration, Mr. President." " I do not care whether you do or not," was his reply, " if you will fight for the country." " I will take the commission and loyally serve while I may, and bring it back to you when I can go with you no further." "That is frank ; but tell me wherein you think my administration wrong before you resign," said he. " Report to General Scott."

I was assigned to the command of the Department of Virginia and North Carolina, and didn't see Mr. Lincoln again until after the capture of Hatteras, about the first of September, the news of which I was able to bring him in person, and he gave me leave to come home and look after my private business, as I had been relieved from command at Fortress Monroe by Brevet Lieutenant-General Wool.

When I returned to Washington, Lincoln sent for me, and after greetings said : " General, you are out of a job ; now, if we only had the troops, I would like to have an expedition either against Mobile, New Orleans, or Galveston. Filling up regiments is going on very slowly." I said : " Mr. President, you gave me permission to tell you when I differed from the action of the administration." He said hastily : " You think we are wrong, do you ? " I said : " Yes, in this: You are making this too much a party war. That perhaps is not the fault of the administration but the result of political conditions. All the northern Governors are Republicans, and they of course appoint only their Republican friends as officers of regiments, and then the officers only recruit Republicans. Now this war cannot go on as a party war. You must get the Democrats in it, and there are thousands of patriotic Democrats who would go into it if they could see any opportunity on equal terms with Republicans. Besides, it is not good politics. An election is coming on for Congressmen next year, and if you get all the Republicans sent out as soldiers and the Democrats not interested, I do not see but you will be beaten." He said : " There is meat in that, General," a favorite expression of his ; " what is your suggestion ? " I said: " Empower me to raise volunteers for the United States and select the officers, and I will go to New England and raise a division of 6,000 men in sixty days. If you will give me power to select the officers I shall choose all Democrats. And if you put epaulets on their soldiers they will be as true to the country as I hope I am." He said: " Draw such an order as you want, but don't get me into any scrape with the Governors about the appointments of the officers if you can help it." The order was signed, the necessary funds were furnished the next day, and I started for New England; in ninety days I had 6,000 men enlisted, and was ordered to make preparations for an expedition to Ship Island, and the last portion of that expedition sailed on the 25th of February, 1862.

All the New England Governors appointed Democratic officers of my selection save one. And this plan was followed by Governors of the Northern and Western States, which had not been done before in cases of civilians who had not been educated at West Point. Before I left Washington I called upon the President to take leave of him. He received me very cordially, and said : " Good-by, Genral ; get into New Orleans if you can, and the backbone of the rebellion will be broken. It is of more importance than anything else that can now be done; but don't interfere with the slavery question, as Fremont has done at St. Louis, and as your man Phelps has been doing on Ship Island." I said : " May I not arm the negroes ?" He said : " Not yet ; not yet." I said : " Jackson did." He answered : " But not to fight against their masters, but with them." I replied : " I will wait for the word or the necessity, Mr. President." " That's right ; God be with you."

On my return from New Orleans the first of January, 1863, I received from an officer of a revenue cutter in New York harbor a kindly note from Lincoln asking me to come to Washington at once, with which I complied. After greetings, I said: "Why was I relieved, Mr. President, from command at New Orleans?" "I do not know, General," was the answer; "something about foreign affairs; ask Seward. Do you want to go back again to the Mississippi River, General?" "No, Mr. President, not unless I can go back to New Orleans." He then produced a map which had been colored according to the proportion of white and slave population in the United States bordering on the Mississippi, and said: "See that black cloud, General. If it is not under some control soon, shall we not have trouble there? Hadn't you better go down to Vicksburg?" "No," I said, "the black cloud you can control by coming up river as well as going down. I prefer to go home rather than to go anywhere else in the south-west than to New Orleans." He said: "I am sorry, General, that you won't go. I can't send you to New Orleans without doing injustice to General Banks, who has not yet been tried there." "And I can't consistently with self-respect go anywhere else in the south-west from which I have just been relieved."

Some months after this interview, being at Washington on some business matter, I called to pay my respects to the President, and he said to me jocosely, "Well, General, you have had some time with nothing to do but to look on ; any more criticisms ? " I said : " Yes, Mr. President, the bounties which are now being paid to new recruits cause very large desertions. Men desert and go home, and get the bounties and enlist in other regiments." " That is too true," he replied, " but how can we prevent it ! " " By vigorously shooting every man who is caught as a deserter until it is found to be a dangerous business." A saddened, weary look came over his face which I had never seen before, and he slowly replied, " You may be right—probably are so ; but God help me, how can I have a butcher's day every Friday in the Army of the Potomac ? " The subject seemed to me to be too painful to him to be further pursued. In the later summer I was invited by the President to ride with him in the evening out to the Soldiers' Home, some two miles, a portion of the way being quite lonely. He had no guard—not even an orderly on the box. I said to him : " Is it known that you ride thus alone at night out to the Soldiers' Home ? " " Oh, yes," he answered, " when business detains me until night. I do go out earlier as a rule." I said : " I think you peril too much. We have passed a half dozen places where a well-directed bullet might have taken you off." " Oh," he replied, " assassination of public officers is not an American crime. But perhaps it would relieve the anxiety of anxious friends which you express if I had a guard." The next morning I spoke to Stanton about it, and he afterward insisted upon the President having a guard.

In November, 1863, I received an order to proceed to Fort Monroe and resume command of the Department of Virginia and North Carolina, relieving General Foster. *En route* through Washington I called upon the President and thanked him for this mark of confidence, and he said : "Yes, General, I believe in you, but not in shooting deserters. As a commander of a department, you can now shoot them for yourself. But let me advise you not to amuse yourself by playing billiards with a rebel officer who is a prisoner of war." And it was thus that I learned one of the causes for General Foster's being relieved, which was for playing billiards with General Fitz Hugh Lee, then a prisoner of war. He then said : "I wish you would give all the attention you can to raising negro troops ; large numbers of negroes will probably come in to you. I believe you raised the first ones in New Orleans." I said : "Yes, Mr. President, except General Hunter at South Carolina, whose negro troops were disbanded by your order." "Yes," he said, laughing, "Hunter is a very good fellow, but he was a little too previous in that." He then said good-naturedly : "Don't let Davis catch you, General ; he has put a price on your head ; he will hang you sure." I answered : "That's a game two can play at, Mr. Presi-

17

dent. If I ever catch him I will remember your scruples about capital punishment, and relieve you from any trouble with them in his case. He has outlawed me, and if I get hold of him I shall give him the law of the outlaw after a reasonable time to say his prayers."

Lincoln visited my department twice while I was in command. He was personally a very brave man, and gave me the worst fright of my life. He came to my head-quarters and said: "General, I should like to ride along your lines and see them, and see the boys and how they are situated in camp." I said, "Very well, we will go after breakfast." I happened to have a very tall, easy-riding, pacing horse, and as the President was rather long legged, I tendered him the use of him while I rode beside him on a pony. He was dressed, as was his custom, in a black suit, a swallow-tail coat, and tall silk hat. As there rode on the other side of him at first Mr. Fox, the Secretary of the Navy, who was not more than five feet six inches in height, he stood out as a central figure of the group. Of course the staff officers and orderly were behind. When we got to the line of intrenchment, from which the line of rebel pickets was not more than 300 yards, he towered high above the works, and as we came to the several encampments the boys all turned out and cheered him lustily. Of course the enemy's attention was

wholly directed to this performance, and with the
glass it could be plainly seen that the eyes of their
officers were fastened upon Lincoln; and a personage riding down the lines cheered by the soldiers
was a very unusual thing, so that the enemy must
have known that he was there. Both Mr. Fox and
myself said to him, " Let us ride on the side next to
the enemy, Mr. President. You are in fair rifle-shot
of them, and they may open fire; and they must
know you, being the only person not in uniform,
and the cheering of the troops directs their attention
to you." "Oh, no," he said laughing, "the commander-in-chief of the army must not show any
cowardice in the presence of his soldiers, whatever
he may feel." And he insisted upon riding the
whole six miles, which was about the length of my
intrenchments, in that position, amusing himself at
intervals, where there was nothing more attractive,
in a sort of competitive examination of the com-
manding-general in the science of engineering,
much to the amusement of my engineer-in-chief,
General Weitzel, who rode on my left, and who was
kindly disposed to prompt me while the examination
was going on, which attracted the attention of Mr.
Lincoln, who said, " Hold on, Weitzel, I can't beat
you, but I think I can beat Butler."

I give this incident to show his utter unconcern
under circumstances of very great peril, which kept

the rest of us in a continued and quite painful anxiety. When we reached the left of the line we turned off toward the hospitals, which were quite extensive and kept in most admirable order by my medical director, Surgeon McCormack. The President passed through all the wards, stopping and speaking very kindly to some of the poor fellows as they lay on their cots, and occasionally administering a few words of commendation to the ward master. Sometimes when reaching a patient who showed much suffering the President's eyes would glisten with tears. The effect of his presence upon these sick men was wonderful, and his visit did great good, for there was no medicine which was equal to the cheerfulness which his visit so largely inspired.

I accompanied him to Fort Monroe, and afterward to Fort Wool, which is on the middle ground between the channels at Hampton Roads. As we sat at dinner, before we took the boat for Washington, his mind seemed to be preoccupied, and he hardly did justice to the best dinner our resources could provide for him. I said, " I hope you are not unwell; you do not eat, Mr. President?" " I am well enough," was the reply; " but would to God this dinner or provisions like it were with our poor prisoners in Andersonville.

Not long afterward I had occasion to visit Washington, and I took with me the record of a court-martial wherein I had approved a sentence of death, and, upon reflection and re-examination of the record, had some doubt as to the entire sufficiency of the evidence. The order for execution at a future day had been promulgated, and although I might have commuted the sentence even then, yet I thought a pardon had better come from the President, perhaps induced by the thought that a pardon from him would be no reflection upon the court, or intimation that the commading general ever had any occasion to change his mind upon such matter. I called upon the President, laid the record down before him, and in a few words explained it. He looked up and said, "You asking me to pardon some poor fellow! Give me that pen." And in less time than I can tell it the pardon was ordered without further investigation.

Indeed the President didn't keep his promise to allow me to execute whom I pleased as Commander of the Department, for he was not unfrequently sending down telegraphic orders to have some convicted person sent to the Dry Tortugas.

I have given only such incidents, free from all observation of my own, as will tend to illustrate his character, and will content myself with one which develops another phase.

It will be remembered that, like all Southern men, Mr. Lincoln did not understand the negro character.

He doubted very much whether the negro and the white man could possibly live together in any other condition than that of slavery ; and early after the emancipation proclamation he proposed to Congress to try the experiment of negro colonization in order to dispose of those negroes who should come within our lines. And, as I remember, speaking from memory only, attempted to make some provision at Demerara, through the agency of Senator Pomeroy, for colonizing the negroes. The experiment was not fully carried out, the reasons for which are of no moment here.

Lincoln was very much disturbed after the surrender of Lee, and he had been to Richmond, upon the question of what would be the results of peace in the Southern States as affected by the contiguity of the white and black races. Shortly before the time, as I remember it, when Mr. Seward was thrown from his carriage and severely injured, being then in Washington, the President sent for the writer, and said, " General Butler, I am troubled about the negroes. We are soon to have peace. We have got some one hundred and odd thousand negroes who have been trained to arms. When peace shall come I fear lest these colored men shall organize themselves in the South, especially in the States where the negroes are in preponderance in numbers, into guerrilla parties, and we shall have down there a warfare between the whites and the negroes. In the course of the reconstruction of the Government it will become a question of how the negro is to be disposed of. Would it not be possible to export them to some place, say Liberia, or South America, and organize them into communities to support themselves? Now, General, I wish you would examine the practicability of such exportation. Your organization of the flotilla which carried your army from Yorktown and Fort Monroe to City Point, and its success show that you understand such matters. Will you give this your attention, and, at as early a day as possible, report to me your views upon the subject." I replied, "Willingly," and bowed and retired. After some few days of examination, with the aid of statistics and calculations, of this topic, I repaired to the President's office in the morning, and said to him, " I have come to report to you on the question you have submitted to me, Mr. President, about the exportation of the negroes." He exhibited great interest, and said, "Well, what do you think of it?" I said: "Mr. President, I assume that if the negro is to be sent away on shipboard you do not propose to enact the horrors of the middle passage, but would give the negroes the air-space that the law provides for emigrants." He said, "Certainly." "Well, then, here are some calculations which will show you that if you undertake to export all of the negroes—and I do not see how you can take one portion differently from another—negro children will be born faster than your whole naval and merchant vessels, if substantially all of them were devoted to that use, can carry them from the country; especially as I believe that their increase will be much greater in a state of freedom than of slavery, because the commingling of the two races does not tend to productiveness." He examined my tables carefully for some considerable time, and then he looked up sadly and said: "Your deductions seem to be correct, General. But what can we do?" I replied: "If I understand you, Mr. President, your theory is this: That the negro soldiers we have enlisted will not return to the peaceful pursuits of laboring men, but will become a class of guerrillas and criminals. Now, while I do not see, under the Constitution, even with all the aid of Congress, how you can export a class of people who are citizens against their will, yet the Commander-in-Chief can dispose of soldiers quite arbitrarily. Now, then, we have large quantities of clothing to clothe them, large quantities of provision with which to supply them, and arms and everything necessary for them, even to spades and shovels, mules and wagons. Our war has shown that an army organization is the very best for digging up the soil and making intrenchments. Witness the very many miles of in-

trenchments that our soldiers have dug out. I know
of a concession of the United States of Colombia
for a tract of thirty miles wide across the Isthmus
of Panama for opening a ship canal. The enlistments of the negroes have all of them from two to
three years to run. Why not send them all down
there to dig the canal? They will withstand the
climate, and the work can be done with less cost
to the United States in that way than in any
other. If you choose, I will take command of the
expedition. We will take our arms with us, and I
need not suggest to you that we will need nobody
sent down to guard us from the interference of any
nation. We will proceed to cultivate the land and
supply ourselves with all the fresh food that can be
raised in the tropics, which will be all that will be
needed, and your stores of provisions and supplies
of clothing will furnish all the rest. Shall I work
out the details of such an expedition for you, Mr.
President?" He reflected for some time, and then
said: "There is meat in that suggestion, General
Butler; there is meat in that suggestion. Go and
talk to Seward, and see what foreign complication
there will be about it. Then think it over, get your
figures made, and come to me again as soon as you
can. If the plan has no other merit, it will rid the
country of the colored soldiers." "Oh," said I, "it
will do more than that. After we get down there

we shall make a humble petition for you to send our wives and children to us, which you can't well refuse, and then you will have a United States colony in that region which will hold its own against all comers, and be contented and happy." "Yes, yes," said he, "that's it; go and see Seward."

I left the office, called upon the Secretary of State, who received me kindly, and explained in a few words what the President wanted. He said: "Yes, General, I know that the President is greatly worried upon this subject. He has spoken to me of it frequently, and yours may be a solution of it; but to-day is my mail day. I am very much driven with what must be done to-day; but I dine, as you know, at six o'clock. Come and take a family dinner with me, and afterward, over an indifferent cigar, we will talk this matter over fully."

But that evening Secretary Seward, in his drive before dinner, was thrown from his carriage and severely injured, his jaw being broken, and he was confined to his bed until the assassination of Lincoln, and the attempted murder of himself by one of the confederates of Booth, so that the subject could never be again mentioned to Mr. Lincoln.

II.

There are two incidents in regard to the nomination of Vice-President in 1864 which for obvious
reasons did not get into the newspapers of that day,
but which bit of history may be of interest.

It will be remembered that Mr. Chase was using
his position as Secretary of the Treasury to aid in
his candidature for the Presidency as early as the winter and spring of 1864.   That was supposed to have
created some coolness between him and Mr. Lincoln.

Early in the spring of that year, a prominent
Treasury official, who held his office directly from
Mr. Chase, without the intervention of either the
President or the Senate, but yet who controlled the
disposition of more property and the avenues of
making more fortunes than any other subordinate
Treasury official, and who afterward held as large
a controlling influence with Mr. Seward, but in quite
a different direction, came to the head-quarters of
the Department of Virginia and North Carolina,
ostensibly upon official business.

After that was finished, the actual object of his
visit was disclosed by a question, in substance as
follows :

" There has been some criticism, General, based
on the assertion that Mr. Chase is using the powers

of his office to aid his Presidential aspirations. What do you think of Mr. Chase's action, assuming the reports true?"

"I see no objection to his using his office to advance his Presidential aspirations, by every honorable means, providing Lincoln will let him do it. It is none of my business, but I have for some time thought that Mr. Lincoln was more patient than I should have been, and if he does not object, nobody else has either the power or right to do so."

"Then, General, you approve of Mr. Chase's course in this regard?"

"Yes, certainly; he has a right to use in a proper manner every means he has to further a laudable ambition."

"As Chase is a Western man," said my visitor, "the Vice-Presidency had better come from the East. Who, General, do you think will make a good candidate with Mr. Chase?"

"There are plenty of good men," I answered; "but as Chase is very pronounced as an antislavery man and free-soiler, I think that General John A. Dix, of New York, ought to be selected to go on his ticket, and thus bring to his banner, both in convention and at the polls, the war Democrats, of whom Mr. Dix claims to be a fair representative."

"You are a war Democrat, General; would you take that position with Mr. Chase yourself?"

"Are you specifically authorized by Mr. Chase to put to me that question, and report my answer to him for his consideration?"

"You may rest assured," was the reply, "that I am fully empowered by Mr. Chase to put the question, and he hopes the answer will be favorable."

"Say, then, to Mr. Chase that I have no desire to be Vice-President. I am but forty-five years old; I am in command of a fine army; the closing campaign of the war is about beginning, and I hope to be able to do some further service for the country, and I should not, at my time of life, wish to be Vice-President if I had no other position. Assure him that my determination in this regard has no connection with himself personally. I will not be a candidate for any elective office whatever until this war is over."

"I will report your determination to Mr. Chase, and I can assure you that from what I know of his feelings he will hear it with regret."

Within three weeks afterward a gentleman who stood very high in Mr. Lincoln's confidence came to me at Fort Monroe. This was after I had learned that Grant had allotted to me a not unimportant part in the coming campaign around Richmond, of the results of which I had the highest hope, and for which I had been laboring, and the story of which has not yet been told, but may be hereafter.

The gentleman informed me that he came from

Mr. Lincoln; this was said with directness, because the messenger and myself had been for a very considerable time in quite warm, friendly relations, and I owed much to him, which I can never repay save with gratitude.

He said: "The President, as you know, intends to be a candidate for re-election, and as his friends indicate that Mr. Hamlin is no longer to be a candidate for Vice-President, and as he is from New England, the President thinks that his place should be filled by some one from that section; and aside from reasons of personal friendship which would make it pleasant to have you with him, he believes that, being the first prominent Democrat who volunteered for the war, your candidature would add strength to the ticket, especially with the war Democrats, and he hopes that you will allow your friends to co-operate with his to place you in that position."

I answered: "Please say to Mr. Lincoln, that while I appreciate with the fullest sensibility this act of friendship and the compliment he pays me, yet I must decline. Tell him," I said laughingly, "with the prospects of the campaign, I would not quit the field to be Vice-President, even with himself as President, unless he will give me bond with sureties, in the full sum of his four years' salary, that he will die or resign within three months after his inauguration. Ask him what he thinks I have done to deserve the

punishment, at forty-six years of age, of being made
to sit as presiding officer over the Senate, to listen
for four years to debates, more or less stupid, in
which I can take no part nor say a word, nor even be
allowed a vote upon any subject which concerns the
welfare of the country, except when my enemies
might think my vote would injure me in the estimation of the people, and therefore, by some parliamentary trick, make a tie on such question, so I
should be compelled to vote ; and then at the end of
four years (as nowadays no Vice-President is ever
elected President), and because of the dignity of the
position I had held, not to be permitted to go on
with my profession, and therefore with nothing left
for me to do save to ornament my lot in the cemetery tastefully, and get into it gracefully and respect-
ably, as a Vice-President should do. No, no, my
friend ; tell the President I will do everything I can
to aid in his election if nominated, and that I hope
he will be, as until this war is finished there should
be no change of administration."

"I am sorry you won't go with us," replied my
friend, "but I think you are sound in your judgment."

I asked : "Is Chase making any headway in his
candidature ? "

"Yes, some ; but he is using the whole power of
the Treasury to help himself."

"Well, that's the right thing for him to do."

"Do you really think so?"

"Yes; why ought not he to do it, if Lincoln lets him?"

"How can Lincoln help letting him?"

"By tipping him out. If I were Lincoln I should say to Mr. Chase, 'My Secretary of the Treasury, you know that I am a candidate for re-election, as I suppose it is proper for me to be. Now every one of my equals has a right to be a candidate against me, and every citizen of the United States is my equal who is not my subordinate. Now, if you desire to be a candidate, I will give you the fullest opportunity to be one, by making you my equal and not my subordinate, and I will do that in any way that will be the most pleasant to you, but things cannot stay as they now are.' You see, I think it is Mr. Lincoln's and not Mr. Chase's fault that he is using the Treasury against Mr. Lincoln."

"Right again!" said my friend, "I will tell Mr. Lincoln every word you have said."

What happened after is a matter of history.

BENJAMIN F. BUTLER.

XI

LINCOLN AND THE WAR DEPARTMENT

THE first time I saw Mr. Lincoln was shortly after his inauguration. He had appointed Mr. Seward to be his Secretary of State, and some of the Republican leaders of New York, who had been instrumental in preventing Mr. Seward's nomination to the Presidency and in securing that of Mr. Lincoln, had begun to fear that they would be left out in the cold in the distribution of the offices. General James S. Wadsworth, George Opdyke, Lucius Robinson, T. B. Carroll, and Henry B. Stanton were among the number of these gentlemen. Their apprehensions were somewhat mitigated by the fact that Mr. Chase, to whom we were all friendly, was Secretary of the Treasury. But, notwithstanding, they were afraid that the superior tact and pertinacity of Mr. Seward and Mr. Weed would get the upper hand, and that the power of the Federal Administration would be put into the control of the rival faction. Accordingly, several of them determined to go to Washington, and I was asked to go with them.

I believe the appointment for our interview with

during this period, I was not myself either a principal actor or a personal witness, but I knew all about it.

My friend and colleague, the Hon. Peter H. Watson, who was the earliest Assistant Secretary of War appointed by Mr. Stanton, had caught some quartermasters in extensive frauds in forage furnished to the Army of the Potomac. The mode of the fraud consisted in a dishonest mixture of oats and Indian corn for the horses and mules of the army. By changing the proportions of the two sorts of grain, they were able to make a great difference in the cost of the bushel, and it was quite difficult to detect the cheat. However, Watson found it out and at once arrested the two officers who were most directly involved. They soon surrendered a large sum of money. If my memory serves me correctly, they returned $175,000 from the product of the swindle. They were men of some political importance about Lycoming, and eminent politicians took a hand in getting them out of the scrape. Among these the Hon. David Wilmot, then Senator of the United States and author of the famous Wilmot Proviso, was very active. He went to Mr. Lincoln and made such representations and appeals that finally the President consented to go with him over to the War Department and see Watson in his office. Wilmot remained outside, and Mr. Lincoln went in to labor with the Assistant Secretary. Watson eloquently described to him the nature of the fraud and the extent to which it had already been developed by his partial investigation. The fact that $175,000 had been refunded by the guilty men was dwelt upon, and when the President urged the safety of the cause and the necessity of preserving united the powerful support which Pennsylvania was giving to the Administration in suppressing the rebellion, Watson answered :

"Very well, Mr. President, if you wish to have these men released, all that is necessary is to give the order; but I shall ask to have it in writing. In such a case as this it would not be safe for me to obey a verbal order; and let me add that, if you do release them, the fact and the reason will necessarily become known to the public."

Finally Mr. Lincoln took up his hat and went out, and when Wilmot, who was waiting in the corridor, met him, he said :

"I can't do anything with Watson; he won't release them."

The reply which the Senator made to this remark cannot be printed here, but it did not affect the judgment of the President. The men were retained for a long time afterward. The fraud was fully investigated, and future swindles of the kind were rendered impossible. If Watson could have had his

way, the guilty parties—and there were some whose
names never got to the public—would have been
tried by court-martial and sternly dealt with. But
all my reflections upon the subject since lead me to
the conclusion that the moderation of the President
was wiser than the unrelenting justice of the Assistant Secretary would have been.

Another incident connected with Pennsylvania re-
curs to my memory which interested me greatly at
that time as showing the habitual breadth of Mr.
Lincoln's judgment and action.

In the spring of 1864 some question arose about
affairs in that State, and, Mr. Stanton being absent,
Mr. Lincoln sent for me. I found Mr. Seward with
him in the President's room. Mr. Lincoln entered
at once upon the subject, and Mr. Seward said, "My
advice is to send for Aleck McClure." After a few
words between them on the subject, and the reiterated expression of Mr. Seward's opinion, Mr. Lincoln said, "We will do it," and asked Mr. Seward
to forward the necessary telegram. Then he turned
to me, "What do you say, Dana?" "Well, sir," I
replied, "McClure is very good, but I would suggest that it would be well to send for Wayne Mac-
Veagh also." Mr. Seward thought this would not
be necessary, and I took my leave with the impression that my advice was not to be heeded. Next
morning, however, MacVeagh came into my office.

"Did Mr. Lincoln send for you?" I asked. "Yes, he did," was the answer, "and I think it will be all right;" and so it was. The cause of anxiety proved to be more than half imaginary.

The relations between Mr. Lincoln and the members of his Cabinet were always friendly and sincere on his part. He treated every one of them with unvarying kindness; but though several of them were men of extraordinary force and self-assertion—this is true especially of Mr. Seward, Mr. Chase, and Mr. Stanton—and though there was nothing of selfhood or domination in his manner toward them, it was always plain that he was the master and they the subordinates. They constantly had to yield to his will, and if he ever yielded to theirs it was because they convinced him that the course they advised was judicious and appropriate. I fancied during the whole time of my intimate intercourse with him and with them that he was always prepared to receive the resignation of any one of them; and at the same time I do not recollect a single occasion when either of the members of the Cabinet had got his mind ready to quit his post from any feeling of dissatisfaction with the orders or the conduct of the President.

In the beginning of May, Grant moved the Army of the Potomac across the Rappahannock and fought the battle of the Wilderness. For two days we had no authentic news in Washington, and both Mr.

Lincoln and the Secretary of War were very much troubled about it. One night at about ten o'clock I was sent for to the War Department, and on reaching the office I found the President and the Secretary together.

"We are greatly disturbed in mind," said Mr. Lincoln, "because Grant has been fighting two days and we are not getting any authentic account of what has happened since he moved. We have concluded to send you down there. How soon will you be ready to start?"

"I will be ready," I said, "in half an hour, and will get off just as soon as a train and an escort can be got ready at Alexandria."

"Very good," said the President; "go then, and God bless you."

I at once made the necessary preparations and gave orders for a train from Alexandria to the Rappahannock. At the appointed time, just before midnight, I was on board the cars in Maryland Avenue, which were to take me and my horse to Alexandria, when an orderly rode up in haste to say that the President wanted to see me at the War Department. Riding there as fast as I could I found the President still there.

"Since you went away," said he, "I have been feeling very unhappy about it. I don't like to send you down there. We hear that Jeb Stewart's cavalry is riding all over the region between the Rappahannock and the Rapidan, and I don't want to expose you to the danger you will have to meet before you can reach Grant."

"Mr. Lincoln," I said, "I have got a first-rate horse, and twenty cavalrymen are in readiness at Alexandria. If we meet a small force of Stewart's people, we can fight, and if they are too many, they will have to have mighty good horses to catch us."

"But are you not concerned about it at all?" said he.

"No, sir," said I, "don't feel any hesitation on my account. Besides it is getting late, and I want to get down to the Rappahannock by daylight."

"All right," said he; "if you feel that way, I won't keep you any longer. Good-night, and good-by."

Another side of this remarkable character was illustrated on the evening of election day in November. The political struggle had been most intense, and the interest taken in it, both in the White House and in the War Department, had been almost painful. All the power and influence of the War Department, then something enormous from the vast expenditure and extensive relations of the war, had been employed to secure the re-election of Mr. Lincoln; and after the arduous toil of the canvass there was necessarily a great suspense of feeling until the result of the voting should be ascertained.

I went over to the War Department about half-past eight in the evening and found the President and Mr. Stanton together in the Secretary's office. General Eckert, who then had charge of the telegraph department of the War Office, was coming in continually with telegrams containing election returns. Mr. Stanton would read them and the President would look at them and comment upon them. Presently there came a lull in the returns, and Mr. Lincoln called me up to a place by his side.

"Dana," said he, "have you ever read any of the writings of Petroleum V. Nasby?" "No, sir," I said, "I have only looked at some of them, and they seemed to me quite funny."

"Well," said he, "let me read you a specimen," and, pulling out a thin yellow-covered pamphlet from his breast-pocket, he began to read aloud. Mr. Stanton viewed this proceeding with great impatience, as I could see, but Mr. Lincoln paid no attention to that. He would read a page or a story, pause to con a new election telegram, and then open the book again and go ahead with a new passage. Finally Mr. Chase came in and presently Mr. Whitelaw Reid, and then the reading was interrupted. Mr. Stanton went to the door and beckoned me into the next room. I shall never forget the fire of his indignation at what seemed to him to be mere nonsense. The idea that when the safety of the

Republic was thus at issue, when the control of an empire was to be determined by a few figures brought in by the telegraph, the leader, the man most deeply concerned, not merely for himself but for his country, could turn aside to read such balderdash and to laugh at such frivolous jests, was to his mind something most repugnant and damnable. He could not understand, apparently, that it was by the relief which these jests afforded to the strain of mind under which Lincoln had so long been living and to the natural gloom of a melancholy and desponding temperament—this was Mr. Lincoln's prevailing characteristic—that the safety and sanity of his intelligence was maintained and preserved.

Another interesting incident occurs to me. A spy whom we employed to report to us the proceedings of the Confederate Government and its agents, and who passed continually between Richmond and St. Catherines, reporting at the War Department upon the way, had come in from Canada and had put into my hands an important dispatch from Mr. Clement C. Clay, Jr., addressed to Mr. Benjamin. Of course the seal was broken and the paper read immediately. It showed unequivocally that the Confederate agents in Canada were making use of that country as a starting point for warlike raids which were to be directed against frontier towns like St. Albans in Vermont. Mr. Stanton thought it important that

this dispatch should be retained as a ground of re-
clamation to be addressed to the British Government.   It was on a Sunday that it arrived, and he
was confined to his house by a cold.   At his directions I went over to the President and made an
appointment with him to be at the Secretary's office
after church.   At the appointed time he was there,
and I read the dispatch to them.   Mr. Stanton
stated the reasons why it should be retained, and
before deciding the question Mr. Lincoln turned to
me, saying :

"Well, Dana?"

I observed to them that this was a very important
channel of communication, and that if we stopped
such a dispatch as this it was at the risk of never obtaining any more information through that means.

"Oh," said the President, "I think you can manage that.   Capture the messenger, take the dispatch
from him by force, put him in prison, and then let
him escape.   If he has made Benjamin and Clay believe his lies so far, he won't have any difficulty in
telling them new ones that will answer for this case."

This direction was obeyed.   The paper was sealed
up again and was delivered to its bearer.   General
Augur, who commanded the District, was directed to
look for a Confederate messenger at such a place on
the road south that evening.   The man was arrested,
brought to the War Department, searched, the paper

found upon him and identified, and he was committed to the Old Capitol Prison. He made his escape about a week later, being fired upon by the guard. A large reward for his capture was advertised in various papers East and West, and when he reached St. Catherines with his arm in a sling, wounded by a bullet which had passed through it, his story was believed by Messrs. Clay and Jacob Thompson, or, at any rate, if they had any doubts upon the subject, they were not strong enough to prevent his carrying their messages afterward.

The last time I saw Mr. Lincoln to speak with him was in the afternoon of the day of his murder. The same Jacob Thompson was the subject of our conversation. I had received a report from the Provost Marshal of Portland, Maine, saying that Mr. Thompson was to be in that town that night for the purpose of taking the steamer for Liverpool; and what orders had the Department to give? I carried the telegram to Mr. Stanton. He said promptly, "Arrest him;" but as I was leaving his room, he called me back, adding, "You had better take it over to the President." It was now between four and five o'clock in the afternoon, and business at the White House was completed for the day. I found Mr. Lincoln with his coat off in a closet attached to his office washing his hands. "Halloo, Dana," said he, as I opened the door, "what is it now?" "Well, sir," I said, "here is the Provost Marshal of Portland, who reports that Jacob Thompson is to be in that town tonight, and inquires what orders we have to give." "What does Stanton say?" he asked. "Arrest him," I replied. "Well," he continued, drawling his words, "I rather guess not. When you have an elephant on hand, and he wants to run away, better let him run."

This answer I carried back to the War Department, and, accordingly, no reply was sent to the Provost Marshal. That night Mr. Lincoln was shot, and in the room adjoining the small chamber in which he lay unconscious and breathing heavily, Mr. Stanton, the only member of the Administration who seemed to retain his self-possession and undiminished energy, gave all the orders for hours that seemed necessary to carry on the government. I left him at about two o'clock in the morning and went home to sleep. But at five o'clock Colonel Pelouse knocked at my front door. Opening the window, I asked, "What is it?" "Mr. Dana," said he, "Mr. Lincoln is dead, and Mr. Stanton directs you to arrest Jacob Thompson."

The order was sent to Portland, but Thompson did not come there. Some years afterward he told me that he had thought it safer to go to England by way of Halifax.

CHARLES A. DANA.

XII

TWO STORIES OF LINCOLN

NEW YORK, *Oct.* 26, 1885.

DEAR SIR:

In the first draft of his book, Gen. Grant had fixed upon quite a large number of anecdotes which were afterward omitted. Among the number I find the following, for which, as will be seen, he was indebted to President Lincoln.

Respectfully,

F. D. GRANT.

ALLEN THORNDIKE RICE, ESQ.

I.

JUST after receiving my commission as lieutenant-general, the President called me aside to speak to me privately. After a brief reference to the military situation, he said he thought he could illustrate what he wanted to say by a story, which he related as follows: "At one time there was a great war among the animals, and one side had great difficulty in getting a commander who had sufficient confidence in himself. Finally, they found a monkey, by the name of Jocko, who said that he thought he could command their army if his tail could be made a little longer. So they got more tail and spliced it on to his caudal appendage. He looked at it admiringly, and then thought he ought to have a little more still. This was added, and again he called for more. The splicing process was repeated many times, until they had coiled Jocko's tail around the room, filling all the space. Still he called for more tail, and, there being no other place to coil it, they began wrapping it around his shoulders. He continued his call for more, and they kept on winding the additional tail about him until its weight broke him down."

I saw the point, and, rising from my chair, replied: " Mr. President, I will not call for more assistance unless I find it impossible to do with what I already have."

II.

Upon one occasion, when the President was at my head-quarters at City Point, I took him to see the work that had been done on the Dutch Gap Canal. After taking him around and showing him all the points of interest, explaining how, in blowing up one portion of the work that was being excavated, the explosion had thrown the material back into, and

filled up, a part already completed, he turned to me
and said : " Grant, do you know what this reminds
me of ? Out in Springfield, Illinois, there was a
blacksmith named ——. One day, when he did not
have much to do, he took a piece of soft iron that
had been in his shop for some time, and for which he
had no special use, and, starting up his fire, began to
heat it. When he got it hot he carried it to the anvil
and began to hammer it, rather thinking he would
weld it into an agricultural implement. He pounded
away for some time until he got it fashioned into
some shape, when he discovered that the iron would
not hold out to complete the implement he had in
mind. He then put it back into the forge, heated it
up again, and recommenced hammering, with an ill-
defined notion that he would make a claw hammer,
but after a time he came to the conclusion that there
was more iron there than was needed to form a
hammer. Again he heated it, and thought he would
make an axe. After hammering and welding it into
shape, knocking the oxydized iron off in flakes, he
concluded there was not enough of the iron left to
make an axe that would be of any use. He was now
getting tired and a little disgusted at the result of
his various essays. So he filled his forge full of coal,
and, after placing the iron in the center of the heap,
took the bellows and worked up a tremendous blast,
bringing the iron to a white heat. Then with his

19

tongs he lifted it from the bed of coals, and thrust-
ing it into a tub of water near by, exclaimed with an
oath, 'Well, if I can't make anything else of you, I
will make a fizzle, anyhow.'"

I replied that I was afraid that was about what
we had done with the Dutch Gap Canal.

ULYSSES S. GRANT.

XIII

LINCOLN'S KINDNESS OF HEART

ONE morning, early in the spring of 1863, a middle-aged lady appeared at the garrison gate of Fort McHenry, and applied for permission to visit head-quarters.

This was some time after the battle fought at Nashville, Tennessee, where our troops were victorious under the command of General Franklin.

The lady's request was sent up to head-quarters by the officer of the guard. At that time, I was chief of staff to General W. W. Morris, of the regular army, then commanding the defenses of Baltimore. Representing my chief, who was absent, I granted the lady's request.

Her appearance, as she entered head-quarters, inspired every one with the deepest interest, for, with the calm self-possession and distinguished bearing of an accomplished lady, there was an expression of profound sadness in her face which appealed touchingly to every heart.

She told me her story with modest dignity. She was a widow, she said, and resided near Nashville,

Tennessee, but, although a native of that State, she had no sympathy with the rebellion. She had an only son. At the outbreak of the war he was a student in a Southern college. Without her knowledge or consent he enlisted in a rebel regiment, and was severely wounded at the battle of Nashville, taken prisoner, and carried North.

The day after the battle, to her great astonishment and grief, she first heard of these facts. She at once applied to the commanding general for leave to go through the lines and follow her son. Leave was granted. She first found her son at Louisville, then followed him to Wheeling, West Virginia, and thence to Fort McHenry, Baltimore. Here he was placed in the garrison hospital.

The mother desired the privilege of seeing her son in order to learn his present condition, and to furnish him any little comforts he might need which were not supplied under army regulations.

Only a short time before, an order had been received from the War Department prohibiting all intercourse between citizens and prisoners of war.

I expressed my regret that, under this order, I must deny her request, but assured her that she should be fully informed as to her son's condition, and have permission to send him anything for his comfort that the post surgeon should approve of.

The post surgeon was sent for, but said that he

had not personally examined the case of this special prisoner, but added that she might go with him to his office in the hospital, and he would make inquiries. She went, and learned that her son's wound had been aggravated by his journey from Wheeling, but that with rest and careful treatment he was certain to recover.

To remove all doubts from her mind as to the comforts furnished patients who were our prisoners of war, the surgeon said to her, as she arose to go:

"Let me show you, madam, one or two of our prisoners' wards, so that you may see for yourself how our government provides for the sick and wounded of the enemy who are captured."

Gladly the mother accepted the invitation. Hardly had they entered, when the lady, descrying her boy through a half-open door in an adjoining room, rushed from the surgeon's side. Rapidly following her, he saw "a scene," which, he said, "was too sacred to interrupt." The mother was on her knees by the cot of her pale and emaciated boy, exclaiming, as she clasped him to her bosom:

"Oh! my blessed child! I *must* see you if I die for it!"

The kind-hearted surgeon turned away and left the mother and son undisturbed.

Soon the lady returned to the waiting officer, her

face suffused with tears, but beaming with hope and joy, as she said :

" Oh, sir! my blessed boy is sorry he entered the army, and wishes to give his parole and leave the Confederate service forever. Will the authorities permit him to do this? Can I go again to head-quarters ? "

They came together to head-quarters. She approached me with a look of mingled fear and exultation that greatly puzzled me ; but she recounted all that had occurred at the hospital with perfect frankness, and said :

" If I have done wrong, punish me ; but I could not help it."

Of course I did not utter a word of censure, but in answer to her request to have her son paroled, I told her that this power was vested in the President or Secretary of War alone, and advised her to go to Washington and appeal to Secretary Stanton.

The next day she went, taking with her a letter of introduction to the Commissary-General of Prisoners.

In two days she returned to Fort Henry, disappointed and crushed in heart at the treatment she had received from Secretary Stanton. She told me her story.

" I took your note of introduction to General Hoffman," she said, " and he kindly spoke to the

Secretary of my purpose in visiting Washington, and afterward he went with me and introduced me at the War Department.

"As we entered the Secretary's office, Mr. Stanton was writing at his desk. General Hoffman said :

"'Mr. Secretary, this is the lady I spoke to you about. She wishes to consult you about releasing her son, who is a prisoner of war, wounded, in the hospital at Fort Henry.' The General then turned and left the room. I was standing near the door of the office. Mr. Stanton never looked at me nor spoke. After a minute or two the Secretary turned round in his chair, and abruptly, in a severe tone, said :

"'So, *you* are the woman who has a son prisoner of war in Fort McHenry.'"

"'I am so unfortunate,' I said.

"The Secretary then answered in a still louder and sterner tone of voice, leaving me standing all the time :

"'I have nothing to say to you, and no time to waste on you. If you have raised up sons to rebel against the best government under the sun, you and they must take the consequences.'

"I attempted to say to him," continued the lady, "that my son was a mere boy, scarcely seventeen years old, and had entered the Confederate service without my knowledge or approval, but before I had uttered five words he fairly yelled at me, as if in an insane rage :

"'I don't want to hear a word from you. I've no time to waste on you. I want you to go at once. I'll do nothing for you.'

"I left," she said, "and am thankful I got out of Washington alive. Oh! why are *such* men intrusted with power?"

And she sobbed as if her heart would break.

After a brief silence, I asked her if she could go to Washington again?

"What! to see *that* man? No, sir! Not for all Washington," she exclaimed, before she had given a moment for explanation.

After ascertaining that the necessary action would not be hampered by poverty—that she had means enough to pay traveling expenses—I drew up, next day, a paper addressed to the President, concisely stating the case, and asking a parole for the boy. She signed it; the surgeon certified it. She was advised to call on the President, and given directions how and when to get an interview.

After an absence of three days, she returned to Fort McHenry. As she approached the desk of the officer commanding, tears glistened in her eyes, but they were tears of gratitude. Her whole countenance was luminous with joy. Handing to me the same official envelope which had inclosed the document prepared for her to present to the President, she pointed to an order written *in pencil* upon it, and exclaimed with deep emotion :

"My boy is free ! Thank God for such a President ! He is the soul of goodness and honor !"

The order was as follows :

"EXECUTIVE MANSION,
March 13, 1863.

" *To the Commandant at Fort McHenry :*

" GENERAL :—You will deliver to the bearer, Mrs. Winston, her son, now held a prisoner of war in Fort McHenry, and permit her to take him where she will, upon his taking the proper parole never again to take up arms against the United States.

"ABRAHAM LINCOLN."

I asked her how the President received her when she met him ?

"With the kindness of a brother," she replied. "When I was ushered into his presence he was alone. He immediately arose, and, pointing to a chair by his side, said :

" 'Take this seat, madam, and then tell me what I can do for you.'

"I took the envelope, and asked him if he would read the inclosures."

" 'Certainly,' he said, and he proceeded to read the statements I had signed very deliberately. When he had finished reading it he turned to me, and, with emotion, he said :

"'Are you, madam, the unhappy mother of this wounded and imprisoned son ?'

"'I am,' I said.

"'And do you believe he will honor his parole if I permit him to take it and go with you ?'

"'I am ready, Mr. President, to peril my personal liberty upon it,' I replied.

"'You shall have your boy, my dear madam,' he said. 'To take him from the ranks of rebellion and give him to a loyal mother is a better investment for this government than to give him up to its deadly enemies.'

"Then, taking the envelope, he wrote with his own pencil the order which you see upon it. As he handed it to me he said :

"'There! Give that to the commanding officer of Fort McHenry, and you will be permitted to take your son with you where you will; and God grant he may prove a great blessing to you and an honor to his country.'"

It need hardly be added, that the young prisoner was soon removed from the garrison ; and, under the tender nursing of this heroic and devoted mother, was able, after a few months, to resume his studies in one of our Northern colleges. A beautiful and most touching letter, subsequently received at Fort

McHenry from Mrs. Winston, expressed, in touching terms, her gratitude and that of her son to all who had rendered her aid in that hour of her great trial.

The National Cemetery at Gettysburg was dedicated on the 17th of November, 1863. Shortly before the dedication was to take place the President sent an invitation to my chief, General W. W. Morris, and his staff, to join him at Baltimore and accompany him on his special train to Gettysburg. General Morris was sick at the time, and requested me, as his chief of staff, to represent him on that occasion. The General was suffering from one of the troubles which tried the patience of Job.

On the day appointed, therefore, I presented myself, with two other members of the staff, to President Lincoln, on his arrival at Baltimore, and offered the apology of my chief for his absence.

After cordially greeting us and directing us to make ourselves comfortable, the President, with quizzical expression, turned to Montgomery Blair (then Postmaster-General), and said:

"Blair, did you ever know that fright has sometimes proved a sure cure for boils?"

"No, Mr. President. How is that?"

"I'll tell you. Not long ago, when Colonel ——, with his cavalry, was at the front, and the Rebs were making things rather lively for us, the colonel was ordered out on a *reconnaissance*. He was troubled at the time with a big boil where it made horseback riding decidedly uncomfortable. He hadn't gone more than two or three miles when he declared he couldn't stand it any longer, and dismounted and ordered the troops forward without him. He had just settled down to enjoy his relief from change of position when he was startled by the rapid reports of pistols and the helter-skelter approach of his troops in full retreat before a yelling rebel force. He forgot everything but the yells, sprang into his saddle, and made capital time over fences and ditches till safe within the lines. The pain from his boil was gone, and the boil too, and the colonel swore that there was no cure for boils so sure as fright from rebel yells, and that the secession had rendered to loyalty *one* valuable service at any rate."

During the ride to Gettysburg the President placed every one who approached him at his ease, relating numerous stories, some of them laughable, and others of a character that deeply touched the hearts of his listeners.

I remember well his reply to a gentleman who stated that his "only son fell on 'Little Round Top' at Gettysburg, and I am going to look at the spot."

President Lincoln replied:

"You have been called upon to make a terrible sacrifice for the Union, and a visit to that spot, I fear, will open your wounds afresh. But oh! my dear sir, if we had reached the end of such sacrifices, and had nothing left for us to do but to place garlands on the graves of those who have already fallen, we could give thanks even amidst our tears ; but when I think of the sacrifices of life yet to be offered and the hearts and homes yet to be made desolate before this dreadful war, so wickedly forced upon us, is over, my heart is like lead within me, and I feel, at times, like hiding in deep darkness."

At one of the stopping-places of the train, a very beautiful little child, having a bouquet of rose-buds in her hand, was lifted up to an open window of the President's car. With a childish lisp she said : "Flowrth for the President!"

The President stepped to the window, took the rose-buds, bent down and kissed the child, saying :

"You're a sweet little rose-bud yourself. I hope your life will open into perpetual beauty and goodness."

We had taken with us from Fort McHenry the Second United States Artillery band, one of the oldest and finest of the army.

After our arrival at Gettysburg, two gentlemen, who represented themselves as members of the Committee of Arrangements, applied to me for this band to serenade the President and the several Governors of States who had arrived.

The band was placed at their disposal and the serenades given. But, presently, information was given me that, for some reason, Governor Seymour, of New York, had been omitted in the serenades. After ascertaining that the information was correct, I resolved that this omission should be corrected, whether it had resulted from a mistake or a deliberate intention, and that the New York troops at least, who were a majority of those present, and were from "the defenses of Baltimore," should have an opportunity to join in a serenade of their beloved Governor, the soldiers' friend.

Accordingly, arrangements having been made for the presence of the band, and liberty having been given to the members of the several commands from "the defenses of Baltimore" to be present, at about ten o'clock in the evening a crowd of thousands of citizens and soldiers had assembled in front of and around the Governor's quarters.

The night was clear and delightful, and the moonlight rested in beauty on the town and the surrounding scenery. The band seemed inspired by the scene and the occasion, and played exquisitely a number of their sweetest and most appropriate airs.

At length, at a pause in the music, the Governor stepped out on the balcony. Instantly cheers burst from the vast multitude, as hearty, long-continued, and soul-stirring as ever found utterance from enthusiastic hearts.

When silence was restored, the Governor, evidently laboring under deep emotion, commenced an address which held enchained his great audience from beginning to end. I had listened to the eloquence of Governor Seymour on other occasions, but now he seemed to rise into the empyrean of the inspired orator. Never were sentiments of loftier patriotism uttered.

And when, with touching pathos, the Governor addressed the citizens and soldiers before him, and told them of the deep and tender anxiety felt for them by loved ones they had left behind, and how their prayers and the prayers of millions of loyal hearts were constantly ascending to Heaven for their success and safe return; and then spoke of the thousands of cheeks still wet with falling tears for husbands, fathers, brothers, sons, now sleeping in the graves on yonder hill-side, I doubt if a dry eye could have been found in that vast throng of enthralled listeners. And when he closed, for a moment there was profound silence, and not till he turned to leave the balcony did the pent-up feelings of the deeply affected crowd break forth; when in the wildest cheers, and cries of "God bless Governor Seymour," and "Long live the Union," the thousands of hearts, "both by tumultuous rapture and tender sympathy swayed," found such utterance as has rarely been awarded to the eloquence of man.

President Lincoln, on learning the next morning of the occasion of the demonstration late the night before, said to me :

"I am glad Governor Seymour was specially honored. He deserves it. No man has shown greater interest and promptness in his co-operation with us. The New York soldiers may well admire and honor him."

The ceremonies of the dedication were imposing and most interesting. The great procession, civic and military, the splendid music, the impressive religious exercises, the great oration by Edward Everett (the last public effort of his life), the dedication, of the ground chosen, in an address by President Lincoln, of beauty and pathos never surpassed —all amidst the scenes where thousands but recently had freely offered up their lives for the life of the Republic—made the day one to be remembered as long as our Union shall last.

Around the platform, on which the addresses were delivered, the military were formed in hollow square several ranks deep. Inside of this square, and but a few feet from the platform, I had my position, and thus enjoyed the best opportunities to see and hear.

The oration of Mr. Everett, although, perhaps,

not equal in rhetorical beauty and lofty eloquence to some of his previous efforts, was rich in historical instruction and glowing with patriotic sentiment, and was received with great applause.

At length, and in the name of the American Republic, the President came forward formally to dedicate the place, which had drank so freely of the life-blood of her sons, as their peaceful resting-place till time should be no more, pledging the fidelity and honor and power of the government to its preservation for this sacred purpose while that government should last.

A description of the President's famous address is needless ; it has already become a classic ; it is impossible to conceive of anything more beautiful and appropriate for the occasion.

But I may say a word of the appearance of the orator.

President Lincoln was so put together physically that, to him, gracefulness of movement was an impossibility. But his awkwardness was lost sight of in the interest which the expression of his face and what he said awakened.

On this occasion he came out before the vast assembly, and stepped slowly to the front of the platform, with his hands clasped before him, his natural sadness of expression deepened, his head bent forward, and his eyes cast to the ground.

20

In this attitude he stood for a few seconds, silent, as if communing with his own thoughts; and when he began to speak, and throughout his entire address, his manner indicated no consciousness of the presence of tens of thousands hanging on his lips, but rather of one who, like the prophet of old, was overmastered by some unseen spirit of the scene, and passively gave utterance to the memories, the feelings, the counsels and the prophecies with which he was inspired.

In his whole appearance, as well as in his wonderful utterances, there was such evidence of a wisdom and purity and benevolence and moral grandeur, higher and beyond the reach of ordinary men, that the great assembly listened almost awe-struck as to a voice from the divine oracle.

I was still on duty in "the defenses of Baltimore" when the Presidential campaign of 1864 occurred. I had been a life-long Democrat, and I favored the election of General McClellan, the candidate of my party.

One evening in September, 1864, I was invited by a few friends to go with them to a Democratic meeting, and listen to a distinguished orator who was to advocate the claims of McClellan. As I could not well refuse, I agreed to go for a few minutes only. To my surprise and annoyance, I was called on by the audience for a speech, and the calls were so persistent that I was placed in a most embarrassing position. Forced to say something, I contented myself with a brief expression of my high regard for McClellan as a soldier, and a statement of my intention to vote for him. I made no reference of Mr. Lincoln, and soon left the hall.

Next day an order came from Secretary Stanton directing me to be mustered out of the service. No reason was assigned, nor opportunity given for defense. As I was and had always been an unwavering Union man, as I had a brother and three sons in the military service of the Union, and as I had learned that my action at the meeting when reported to Secretary Stanton had made him very angry and caused him to utter severe threats against me, I determined to go, and did go, to Washington to know the reason of this attempt to disgrace me. As no other pretext could be given for such action, I resolved to appeal to the President.

I gave my papers setting forth these facts into the hands of a personal friend, a Republican member of Congress, with the request that he would ask Mr. Lincoln whether the revocation of my commission was by his order, knowledge or consent. He did so.

The President immediately replied : " I know nothing about it. Of course Stanton does a thousand things in his official character which I can know nothing about, and which it is not necessary that I should know anything about."

Having heard the case, he then added: "Well, that's no reason. Andrews has as good a right to hold on to his Democracy, if he chooses, as Stanton had to throw *his* overboard. If I should muster out all my generals who avow themselves Democrats there would be a sad thinning out of commanding officers in the army. No!" he continued, "when the *military* duties of a soldier are fully and faithfully performed, he can manage his politics in his own way; we've no more to do with *them* than with his religion. Tell this officer he can return to his post, and if there is no other or better reason for the order of Stanton than the one he suspects, it shall do him no harm; the commission he holds will remain as good as new. Supporting General McClellan for the Presidency is no violation of army regulations, and as a question of taste of choosing between him and me, well, I'm the longest, but he's better looking."

And so I resumed my service, and was never afterward molested by the Secretary of War.

E. W. ANDREWS.

XIV

LINCOLN AND NEW YORK

MY relations with President Lincoln were cordial. I was a member of the House of Representatives when he entered upon the duties of President, and remained in the House until December, 1864, when I resigned my seat for the office of Governor of New York.

In the summer and fall of 1864—during the Presidential canvass—there was great anxiety in respect to the decision of the people at the ballot-box, as well as to our varying success on the field of arms. The war for the Union had prospered slowly. Determining results had not been realized. Its frightful proportions were more apparent as the days increased. Patriotic people became restless. Many of our Republican friends thought the war was not prosecuted with sufficient vigor and wisdom. Party spirit was embittered by conflicting sympathies, and severe criticisms were ventured touching the conduct of the war. The Democratic party had in terms even declared it to be "a failure." To add intensity to the anxiety on the Republican side at this condition of affairs, the government of New York State was in Democratic hands. Our principal commercial port, our great city and center of money and exchange, was within the boundary of the State, and State and local authorities, or the practices under them, might at any time seriously embarrass the General Government in the farther prosecution of the war. Hence, New York was a stake of mighty import. Each party was certain to exert itself to the utmost. And, even beyond the electoral vote of the State as a possible factor in merely deciding who should be President, the case was surrounded with the gravest concern, especially for those in charge of the government, and whose war purposes and policy were clearly defined.

On the 22d day of August, I received a telegram from Mr. John G. Nicolay, Private Secretary, saying that the President desired to see me. I arrived in Washington next day. The President, speaking to me said, in language as nearly as I can remember: "You are to be nominated by our folks for Governor of your State. Seymour of course will be the Democratic nominee. You will have a hard fight. I am very desirous that you should win the battle. New York should be on our side by honest possession. There is some trouble among our folks over there, which we must try and manage. Or, rather, there is one man who may give us trouble, because of his indifference, if in no other way. He has great influence, and his feelings may be reflected in many of his friends. We must have his counsel and co-operation if possible. This, in one sense, is more important to you than to me, I think, for I should rather expect to get on without New York, but you can't. But in a larger sense than what is merely personal to myself, I am anxious for New York, and we must put our heads together and see if the matter can't be fixed."

In a word, Mr. Thurlow Weed was dissatisfied with the disposition of the federal patronage in the city of New York. Especially he felt that Mr. Simeon Draper, Collector of the Port, and Mr. Rufus F. Andrews, Surveyor, were unfriendly to him, and that he had no voice in those places of influence and power. Patronage had a welcome in the public service then. Removals and appointments were made upon the judgment or caprice of those at the head. The Republican convention in New York to place a candidate for Governor before the people was to come off early in September.

As a result of this consultation with Mr. Lincoln, in the evening of the day after my arrival in Washington, Mr. Nicolay and I left for New York, and in Room No. 11, Astor House, next forenoon, I had a talk with Mr. Weed. I need not speak of the particulars of that conference. It is enough to say that Mr. Nicolay returned to Washington with the resignation of Mr. Rufus F. Andrews, and that Mr. Abram Wakeman—zealous friend of Mr. Weed—at once became his successor as Surveyor. From that time forward Mr. Weed was earnest and helpful in the canvass. The small majority in New York in November—less than 7,000 for the Republican electoral ticket—justified the anxiety of Mr. Lincoln, and serves to illustrate his political sagacity and tact. He was always politician as well as statesman.

Mr. Lincoln was not a successful impromptu speaker. He required a little time for thought and arrangement of the thing to be said. I give an instance in point. After the election to which I have referred, just before I resigned my seat in Congress to enter upon my official duties as Governor at Albany, New Yorkers and others in Washington thought to honor me with a serenade. I was the guest of ex-Mayor Bowen. After the music and speaking usual upon such occasions, it was proposed to call on the President. I accompanied the committee in charge of the proceedings, followed by bands and a thousand people. It was full nine o'clock when we reached the Mansion. The President was taken by surprise, and said he "didn't know just what he could say to satisfy the crowd and himself." Going from the library room down the stairs to the portico front, he asked me to say a few words first, and give him if I could "a peg to hang on." It was just when General Sherman was *en route* from Atlanta to the sea, and we had no definite news as to his safety or whereabouts. After one or two sentences, rather commonplace, the President farther said he had no war news other than was known to all, and he supposed his ignorance in regard to General Sherman was the ignorance of all ; that "we all knew where Sherman went in, but none of us knew where he would come out." This last remark was in the peculiarly quaint, happy manner of Mr. Lincoln, and created great applause. He immediately withdrew, saying he "had raised a good laugh and it was a good time for him to quit." In all he did not speak more than two minutes, and, as he afterward told me, because he had no time to think of much to say.

A few days after I succeeded to the office of Governor I was led to an investigation in regard to the quota of men for New York for the field, under the President's call for 300,000 of December 19th just previous. My search led me to doubt the correctness of the assignment of quotas to several localities, and, as between several localities or districts, it was, to my mind, unequal and unjust. I do not mean that it was so intended. It was a difficult and perplexing matter ; differences in respect to methods were liable to arise and errors were likely to creep in. And, more-over, the total number, 61,000, for the State seemed to me clearly excessive. Thus impressed, accom-panied by General George W. Palmer of my military staff, I went to Washington on the 21st of January.

My interviews with the Secretary of War and the Provost-marshal General did not end favorably to my views. The Secretary of War was more than firm. He was indeed rigid in adhering to the assign-ment for New York as then made. Not doubting the right and justice of my claim for reduction and re-assignment as to the districts, I called on Mr. Lincoln. He gave me time and listened attentively and patiently to all I had to say. At the close he remarked, "I guess you have the best of it, and I must advise Stanton and Fry to ease up a little." He wrote upon a card to Mr. Stanton, and gave it to me to carry to him, as follows:

> The Governor has a pretty good case. I feel sure he is more than half right. We don't want him to feel cross and we in the wrong. Try and fix it with him.
>   A. LINCOLN.

I write from the card, which the gruff and great Stan-ton allowed me to retain.

Neither he nor General Fry could go over the matter with a view to the further precise adjustment during my sojourn. The Legislature of my State was in session and I could not tarry. I will only add that the quota as finally arranged was fully 9,000 less, and the equality between the several districts was in a great measure restored. It was mainly satisfactory to the people. And the State had the proud honor, as theretofore, of unhesitatingly and heroically meeting this further demand upon her patriotism.

Turning back out of the order of events to the fall and early winter of 1861, General McClellan, with an army which some authorities place at full 150,000 men, was then in camp and quarters around about Washington. It was said to be intended to move "on to Richmond," or at least toward the Confederate forces, some time before the rains of the winter months should set in. Congress convened the first week in December. The army seemed to be in good condition but impatient. The roads were exceptionally dry and good for the season of the year. The loyal people, through the press and otherwise, were calling for a forward movement, and the representatives of the people in Congress were ready to open upon General McClellan with wrathful eloquence because of the delay. One, two, and more weeks passed and the army did not move. It was felt that something must be done to avert the threatened heated discussion at Washington ; something to prevent further dissatisfaction and distrust among the soldiers and the people. Galusha A. Grow was Speaker of the House of Representatives.

About the 18th, the Speaker, the Hon. Schuyler Colfax, and myself called on Mr. Lincoln to plan with him if need be, or better to say, to have his judgment as to a way of escape from the danger of an aroused hostile public sentiment which then seemed imminent.

Mr. Lincoln was keenly alive to the situation. The character and opinions of this rugged-featured and intellectually great man always enforced respect and confidence whatever the pleasantry of his manner. He said Providence, with favoring sky and earth, seemed to beckon the army on, but General McClellan, he supposed, knew his business and had his reasons for disregarding these hints of Providence. " And," said Mr. Lincoln, " as we have got to stand by the General, I think a good way to do it may be for Congress to take a recess for several weeks, and by the time you get together again, if McClellan is not off with the army, Providence is very likely to step in with hard roads and force us to say, ' the army can't move.' " He continued : " You know Dickens said of a certain man that if he would always follow his nose he would never stick fast in the mud. Well, when the rains set in it will be impossible for even our eager and gallant soldiers to keep their noses so high that their feet will not stick in the clay mud of Old Virginia." I have given very nearly the words of Mr. Lincoln. His felicity in stating a case and his good sense always impressed me, and my memory loses nothing in vividness with the lapse of years.

The Congress was adjourned for the holiday period quite as early and quite as long as usual, notwithstanding pressing public affairs were requiring the attention of the law-making power. When it reassembled—January 5th, as I remember—the rain had come, the Virginia roads were well-nigh impassable, and the army was still in and around Washington. Verily, to move then was to stick fast in the mud, and the Congress and the country reluctantly became reconciled, in a measure, to the situation.

R. E. FENTON.

XV

LINCOLN AND THE COLORED TROOPS

I DO not know more about Mr. Lincoln than is known by countless thousands of Americans who have met the man. But I am quite willing to give my recollections of him and the impressions made by him upon my mind as to his character.

My first interview with him was in the summer of 1863, soon after the Confederate States had declared their purpose to treat colored soldiers as insurgents, and their purpose not to treat any such soldiers as prisoners of war subject to exchange like other soldiers. My visit to Mr. Lincoln was in reference to this threat of the Confederate States. I was at the time engaged in raising colored troops, and I desired some assurances from President Lincoln that such troops should be treated as soldiers of the United States, and when taken prisoners exchanged like other soldiers; that when any of them were hanged or enslaved the President should retaliate. I was introduced to Mr. Lincoln on this occasion by Senator Pomeroy, of Kansas; I met him at the Executive Mansion.

I was somewhat troubled with the thought of meeting one so august and high in authority, especially as I had never been in the White House before, and had never spoken to a President of the United States before. But my embarrassment soon vanished when I met the face of Mr. Lincoln. When I entered he was seated in a low chair, surrounded by a multitude of books and papers, his feet and legs were extended in front of his chair. On my approach he slowly drew his feet in from the different parts of the room into which they had strayed, and he began to rise, and continued to rise until he looked down upon me, and extended his hand and gave me a welcome. I began, with some hesitation, to tell him who I was and what I had been doing, but he soon stopped me, saying in a sharp, cordial voice :

"You need not tell me who you are, Mr. Douglass, I know who you are. Mr. Sewell has told me all about you."

He then invited me to take a seat beside him. Not wishing to occupy his time and attention, seeing that he was busy, I stated to him the object of my call at once. I said :

"Mr. Lincoln, I am recruiting colored troops. I have assisted in fitting up two regiments in Massachusetts, and am now at work in the same way in Pennsylvania, and have come to say this to you, sir, if you wish to make this branch of the service successful you must do four things :

"First—You must give colored soldiers the same pay that you give white soldiers.

"Second—You must compel the Confederate States to treat colored soldiers, when taken prisoners, as prisoners of war.

"Third—When any colored man or soldier performs brave, meritorious exploits in the field, you must enable me to say to those that I recruit that they will be promoted for such service, precisely as white men are promoted for similar service.

"Fourth—In case any colored soldiers are murdered in cold blood and taken prisoners, you should retaliate in kind."

To this little speech Mr. Lincoln listened with earnest attention and with very apparent sympathy, and replied to each point in his own peculiar, forcible way. First he spoke of the opposition generally to employing negroes as soldiers at all, of the prejudice against the race, and of the advantage to colored people that would result from their being employed as soldiers in defense of their country. He regarded such an employment as an experiment, and spoke of the advantage it would be to the colored race if the experiment should succeed. He said that he had difficulty in getting colored men into the United States uniform ; that when the pur-

21

pose was fixed to employ them as soldiers, several different uniforms were proposed for them, and that it was something gained when it was finally determined to clothe them like other soldiers.

Now, as to the pay, we had to make some concession to prejudice. There were threats that if we made soldiers of them at all white men would not enlist, would not fight beside them. Besides, it was not believed that a negro could make a good soldier, as good a soldier as a white man, and hence it was thought that he should not have the same pay as a white man. But said he,

"I assure you, Mr. Douglass, that in the end they shall have the same pay as white soldiers."

As to the exchange and general treatment of colored soldiers when taken prisoners of war, he should insist to their being entitled to all privileges of such prisoners. Mr. Lincoln admitted the justice of my demand for the promotion of colored soldiers for good conduct in the field, but on the matter of retaliation he differed from me entirely. I shall never forget the benignant expression of his face, the tearful look of his eye and the quiver in his voice, when he deprecated a resort to retaliatory measures.

"Once begun," said he, "I do not know where such a measure would stop."

He said he could not take men out and kill them in cold blood for what was done by others. If he could get hold of the persons who were guilty of killing the colored prisoners in cold blood, the case would be different, but he could not kill the innocent for the guilty.

Before leaving Mr. Lincoln, Senator Pomeroy said :

" Mr. President, Mr. Stanton is going to make Douglass Adjutant-General to General Thomas, and is going to send him down the Mississippi to recruit."

Mr. Lincoln said in answer to this :

" I will sign any commission that Mr. Stanton will give Mr. Douglass."

At this point we parted.

I met Mr. Lincoln several times after this interview.

I was once invited by him to take tea with him at the Soldiers' Home. On one occasion, while visiting him at the White House, he showed me a letter he was writing to Horace Greeley in reply to some of Greeley's criticisms against protracting the war. He seemed to feel very keenly the reproaches heaped upon him for not bringing the war to a speedy conclusion ; said he was charged with making it an Abolition war instead of a war for the Union, and expressed his desire to end the war as soon as possible. While I was talking with him Governor Buckingham sent in his card, and I was amused by his telling the

messenger, as well as by the way he expressed it, to
"tell Governor Buckingham to wait, I want to have
a long talk with my friend Douglass."

He used those words.   I said : "Mr. Lincoln, I
will retire."   "Oh, no, no, you shall not, I want
Governor Buckingham to wait," and he did wait for
at least a half hour.   When he came in I was introduced by Mr. Lincoln to Governor Buckingham, and
the Governor did not seem to take it amiss at all
that he had been required to wait.

I was present at the inauguration of Mr. Lincoln,
the 4th of March, 1865.   I felt then that there was
murder in the air, and I kept close to his carriage on
the way to the Capitol, for I felt that I might see
him fall that day.   It was a vague presentiment.

At that time the Confederate cause was on its last
legs, as it were, and there was deep feeling.   I could
feel it in the atmosphere here.   I did not know exactly what it was, but I just felt as if he might be
shot on his way to the Capitol.   I cannot refer to
any incident, in fact, to any expression that I heard,
it was simply a presentiment that Lincoln might fall
that day.   I got right in front of the east portico of
the Capitol, listened to his inaugural address, and
witnessed his being sworn in by Chief Justice Chase.
When he came on the steps he was accompanied
by Vice-President Johnson.   In looking out in the
crowd he saw me standing near by, and I could see

he was pointing me out to Andrew Johnson. Mr. Johnson, without knowing perhaps that I saw the movement, looked quite annoyed that his attention should be called in that direction. So I got a peep into his soul. As soon as he saw me looking at him, suddenly he assumed rather an amicable expression of countenance. I felt that, whatever else the man might be, he was no friend to my people.

I heard Mr. Lincoln deliver this wonderful address. It was very short; but he answered all the objections raised to his prolonging the war in one sentence—it was a remarkable sentence.

"Fondly do we hope, profoundly do we pray, that this mighty scourge of war shall soon pass away, yet if God wills it continue until all the wealth piled up by two hundred years of bondage shall have been wasted, and each drop of blood drawn by the lash shall have been paid for by one drawn by the sword, we must still say, as was said three thousand years ago, the judgments of the Lord are true and righteous altogether."

For the first time in my life, and I suppose the first time in any colored man's life, I attended the reception of President Lincoln on the evening of the inauguration. As I approached the door I was seized by two policemen and forbidden to enter. I said to them that they were mistaken entirely in what they were doing, that if Mr. Lincoln knew that

I was at the door he would order my admission, and I bolted in by them. On the inside I was taken charge of by two other policemen, to be conducted as I supposed to the President, but instead of that they were conducting me out the window on a plank.

"Oh," said I, "this will not do, gentlemen," and as a gentleman was passing in I said to him, "Just say to Mr. Lincoln that Fred. Douglass is at the door."

He rushed in to President Lincoln, and almost in less than a half a minute I was invited into the East Room of the White House. A perfect sea of beauty and elegance, too, it was. The ladies were in very fine attire, and Mrs. Lincoln was standing there. I could not have been more than ten feet from him when Mr. Lincoln saw me; his countenance lighted up, and he said in a voice which was heard all around: "Here comes my friend Douglass." As I approached him he reached out his hand, gave me a cordial shake, and said: "Douglass, I saw you in the crowd to-day listening to my inaugural address. There is no man's opinion that I value more than yours: what do you think of it?" I said: "Mr. Lincoln, I cannot stop here to talk with you, as there are thousands waiting to shake you by the hand;" but he said again: "What did you think of it?" I said: "Mr. Lincoln, it was a sacred effort," and then I walked off. " I am glad you liked it," he said. That was the last time I saw him to speak with him.

In all my interviews with Mr. Lincoln I was impressed with his entire freedom from popular prejudice against the colored race. He was the first great man that I talked with in the United States freely, who in no single instance reminded me of the difference between himself and myself, of the difference of color, and I thought that all the more remarkable because he came from a State where there were black laws. I account partially for his kindness to me because of the similarity with which I had fought my way up, we both starting at the lowest round of the ladder. I must say this for Mr. Lincoln, that whenever I met him he was in a very serious mood. I heard of those stories he used to tell, but he never told me a story. I remember of one of Mr. Lincoln's stories being told me by General Grant. I had called on him, and he said : " Douglass, stay here, I want to tell you about a little incident. When I came to Washington first, one of the first things that Lincoln said to me was, ' Grant, have you ever read the book by Orpheus C. Kerr ?' 'Well, no, I never did,' said I. Mr. Lincoln said : 'You ought to read it, it is a very interesting book. I have had a good deal of satisfaction reading that book. There is one poem there that describes a meeting of the animals. The substance of it being that the animals and a dragon, or some dreadful thing, was near by and had to be conquered, and it was a question as to who would undertake the job. By and by a monkey stepped forward and proposed to do the work up. The monkey said he thought he could do it if he could get an inch or two more put on his tail. The assemblage voted him a few inches more to his tail, and he went out and tried his hand. He was unsuccessful and returned, stating that he wanted a few more inches put on his tail. The request was granted, and he went again. His second effort was a failure. He asked that more inches be put on his tail and he would try a third time.' At last," said General Grant, "it got through my head what Lincoln was aiming at, as applying to my wanting more men, and finally I said: 'Mr. Lincoln, I don't want any more inches put on my tail.'" It was a hit at McClellan, and General Grant told me the story with a good deal of gusto. I got the book afterward and read the lines of Orpheus C. Kerr.

There was one thing concerning Lincoln that I was impressed with, and that was that a statement of his was an argument more convincing than any amount of logic. He had a happy faculty of stating a proposition, of stating it so that it needed no argument. It was a rough kind of reasoning, but it went right to the point. Then, too, there was another feeling that I had with reference to him, and that was that while I felt in his presence I was in the presence of a very great man, as great as the greatest, I felt as though I could go and put my hand on him if I wanted to, to put my hand on his shoulder. Of course I did not do it, but I felt that I could. I felt as though I was in the presence of a big brother, and that there was safety in his atmosphere.

It was often said during the war that Mrs. Lincoln did not sympathize fully with her husband in his anti-slavery feeling, but I never believed this concerning her, and have good reason for being confirmed in my impression of her by the fact that, when Mr. Lincoln died and she was about leaving the White House, she selected his favorite walking cane and said: "I know of no one that would appreciate this more than Fred. Douglass." She sent it to me at Rochester, and I have it in my house to-day, and expect to keep it there as long as I live.

FREDERICK DOUGLASS.

XVI

LINCOLN AND THE NEWSPAPER CORRESPONDENTS

THE election of Abraham Lincoln as President was very acceptable to the older Washington correspondents. They remembered him well in the XXXth Congress, when, as the Representative from the Sangamon district, he was the only Whig in the Illinois delegation, then but seven in number. In the drawing for seats his name had been one of the last called, and he had been obliged to content himself with a desk in the very outer row, about midway on the Speaker's left hand, where he had on one side of him Harmon S. Conger, of New York, and on the other John Gayle, of Alabama. There he used to sit patiently listening to the eloquence of John Quincy Adams, Robert Toombs, David M. Barringer, Andrew Johnson, and others whose genius and learning adorned the old Hall, and to the verbose platitudes of those less gifted. His own voice was never heard unless when he voted "aye" or "nay."

During the Christmas holidays Mr. Lincoln found his way into the small room used as the post-office of the House, where a few jovial *raconteurs* used to meet almost every morning, after the mail had been distributed into the members' boxes, to exchange such new stories as any of them might have acquired since they had last met. After modestly standing at the door for several days, Mr. Lincoln was "reminded" of a story, and by New Year's he was recognized as the champion story-teller of the Capitol. His favorite seat was at the left of the open fire-place, tilted back in his chair, with his long legs reaching over to the chimney jamb. He never told a story twice, but appeared to have an endless repertoire of them, always ready, like the successive charges in a magazine gun, and always pertinently adapted to some passing event.

It was refreshing to us correspondents, compelled as we were to listen to so much that was prosy and tedious, to hear this bright specimen of Western genius tell his inimitable stories, especially his reminiscences of the Black Hawk War, in which he had commanded a company, which was mustered into the United States service by Jefferson Davis, then second lieutenant of dragoons.

I remember his narrating his first experience in drilling his company. He was marching with a front of over twenty men across a field, when he desired to pass through a gateway into the next inclosure.

"I could not for the life of me," said he, "remember the proper word of command for getting my company endwise so that it could get through the gate, so as we came near the gate I shouted : ' This company is dismissed for two minutes, when it will fall in again on the other side of the gate ! ' "

When the laugh which the description of these novel tactics caused had subsided, Mr. Lincoln added :

" And I sometimes think here, that gentlemen in yonder who get into a tight place in debate, would like to dismiss the House until the next day and then take a fair start."

Mr. Lincoln used to narrate his exploits in wrestling during this campaign, when he was regarded as the champion of Northern Illinois. One day the champion of the Southern companies in the expedition challenged him.

" He was at least two inches taller than I was," said Mr. Lincoln, " and somewhat heavier, but I reckoned that I was the most wiry, and soon after I had tackled him I gave him a hug, lifted him off the ground, and threw him flat on his back. That settled his hash."

Soon after the Presidential campaign of 1848 was opened, Alfred Iverson, a Democratic Representative from Georgia, made a political speech, in which he accused the Whigs of having deserted their financial and tariff principles, and of having " taken shelter under the military coat-tails of General Taylor," then their Presidential candidate.   This gave Mr. Lincoln as a text for his reply, "Military coat-tails."   He had written the heads of what he had intended to say on a few pages of foolscap paper, which he placed on a friend's desk, bordering on an alley-way, which he had obtained permission to speak from.   At first he followed his notes, but, as he warmed up, he left his desk and his notes, to stride down the alley toward the Speaker's chair, holding his left hand behind him so that he could now and then shake the tails of his own rusty, black broadcloth dress-coat, while he earnestly gesticulated with his long right arm, shaking the bony index finger at the Democrats on the other side of the chamber.   Occasionally, as he would complete a sentence amid shouts of laughter, he would return up the alley to his desk, consult his notes, take a sip of water, and start off again.

Toward the close of his speech, Mr. Lincoln poured a torrent of ridicule upon the military reputation of General Cass, and then alluded to his own exploits as a soldier in the Black Hawk War, "where," he continued, "I fought, bled, and came away.   If General Cass saw any live, fighting Indians at the battle of the Thames, where he served as aide-de-camp to General Harrison, it was more than I did; but I had a good many bloody struggles with the mosquitoes, and although I never fainted from the loss of blood,

I can truly say I was often very hungry. Mr. Speaker," added Mr. Lincoln, "if I should ever conclude to doff whatever our Democratic friends may suppose there is of black-cockade Federalism about me, and thereupon they shall take me up as their candidate for the Presidency, I protest they shall not make fun of me as they have of General Cass by attempting to write me into a military hero."

Mr. Lincoln received hearty congratulations at the close, many Democrats joining the Whigs in their complimentary comments. The speech was pronounced by the older members of the House almost equal to the celebrated defence of General Harrison by Tom Corwin, in reply to an attack made on him by a Mr. Crary of Ohio. The two speeches are equally characterized by vigorous argument, mirth-provoking irony and original wit. One Democrat, however (who had been nicknamed "Sausage" Sawyer, from having moved the expulsion of "Richelieu" Robinson from the reporter's gallery for a facetious account of his lunching behind the Speaker's chair on bologna sausage), didn't enthuse at all.

"Sawyer," asked an Eastern Representative, "how did you like the lanky Illinoisian's speech? Very able, wasn't it?"

"Well," replied Sawyer, "the speech was pretty good, but I hope he won't charge mileage on his travels while delivering it."

Mr. Lincoln boarded at Mrs. Spriggs, on Capitol Hill, where he had as his messmates the veteran Joshua R. Giddings, of Ohio ; John Blanchard, John Dickey, A. R. McIlvaine, John Strohm, and James Pollock, of Pennsylvania; Elisha Embree, of Indiana; and P. W. Tompkins, of Mississippi—all Whigs.

Daniel Webster, who was then in the Senate, used occasionally to have Mr. Lincoln at one of his pleasant Saturday breakfasts, where the Western Congressman's humorous illustrations of the events of the day, sparkling with spontaneous and unpremeditated wit, would give great delight to "the solid men of Boston" assembled around the festive board. At one time Mr. Lincoln had transacted some legal business for Mr. Webster connected with an embryo city laid out where Rock River empties into the Mississippi. Mr. Fletcher Webster had gone there for a while, but Rock Island City was not a pecuniary success, and much of the land on which but one payment had been made reverted to the original owners. Mr. Lincoln had charged Mr. Webster for his legal services $10, which the Great Expounder of the Constitution regarded as too small a fee, and he would frequently declare that he was still Mr. Lincoln's debtor.

With these pleasant recollections of Mr. Lincoln, it was not strange that the older correspondents at Washington were glad to learn that he had been

elected President; nor did they agree with Mr.
Stanton, who indulged in tirades against Mr. Lincoln, saying on one occasion he "had met him at
the bar, and found him a low, cunning clown."
They remembered their genial, story-telling friend,
and felt confident that he would be somewhat com-
municative about public affairs, which President Buchanan was not.

When Mr. Seward had Mr. Lincoln smuggled
through Baltimore by night to avoid assassination,
there was some indignation manifested at Washington, for but very few credited the rumors afloat.
Senator Sumner was one of those who believed
that the President-elect was in danger of assassination, and he wrote him after his arrival, cautioning
him about going out at night.

"Sumner," said Mr. Lincoln, "declined to stand
up with me, back to back, to see which was the
tallest man, and made a fine speech about this
being the time for uniting our fronts against the
enemy and not our backs. But I guess he was
afraid to measure, though he is a good piece of a
man. I have never had much to do with bishops
where I live, but, do you know, Sumner is my idea
of a bishop."

Mr. Lincoln gave a cordial greeting to me when I
called on him after his arrival at Willard's Hotel,
and he indulged in some pleasant reminiscences of

his Congressional career. Of course I talked with him about his forthcoming message, and after having made me promise that what he told me should not get into print, he gave me an account of it. He had written it at his Springfield home, and had had it put in type by his friend, the local printer. A number of sentences had been reconstructed several times before they were entirely satisfactory, and then four copies had been printed on foolscap paper. These copies had been locked up in what Mr. Lincoln called a "gripsack," and intrusted to his eldest son Robert.

"When we reached Harrisburg," said Mr. Lincoln, "and had washed up, I asked Bob where the message was, and was taken aback by his confession that in the excitement caused by the enthusiastic reception he believed he had let a waiter take the gripsack. My heart went up into my mouth, and I started down-stairs, where I was told that if a waiter had taken the gripsack I should probably find it in the baggage-room. Going there I saw a large pile of gripsacks and other baggage, and thought that I discovered mine. My key fitted it, but on opening there was nothing inside but a few paper collars and a flask of whiskey. A few moments afterward I came across my gripsack, with the document in it all right, and now I will show it to you—on your honor, mind!"

The inaugural was printed in clear-sized type, and wherever Mr. Lincoln had thought that a paragraph would make an impression upon his audience, he had preceded it with a typographical fist, thus : ☞.

One copy of this printed draft of the inaugural message was given to Mr. Seward, and another to the venerable Francis P. Blair, with request that they would read and criticise; and Mr. Nicolay, who was to be the President's private secretary, made the corrected copy in a fair hand, which Mr. Lincoln was to read. Mr. Nicolay corrected another copy, which was furnished to the press for publication, and which I now own.

At the inauguration, when Mr. Lincoln came out on the platform in front of the eastern portico of the Capitol, his tall, gaunt figure rose above those around him. His personal friend, Senator Baker, of Oregon, introduced him to the assemblage, and as he bowed acknowledgments of the somewhat faint cheers which greeted him, the usual genial smile lit up his angular countenance. He was evidently perplexed, just then, to know what to do with his new silk hat and a large, gold-headed cane. The cane he put under the table, but the hat appeared to be too good to place on the rough boards. Senator Douglas saw the embarrassment of his old friend, and, rising, took the shining hat from its bothered owner

and held it during the delivery of the inaugural address.

Mr. Lincoln was listened to with great earnestness,
and evidently desired to convince the multitude before him rather than to bewilder or dazzle them. It
was plain that he honestly believed every word that
he spoke, especially the concluding paragraphs, one
of which I copy from the original print :

"☞ I am loath to close. We are not enemies,
but friends. We must not be enemies. Though
passion may be strained, it must not break our
bonds of affection. ☞ The mystic chords of memory, which stretch from every battle-field and patriot
grave to every loved heart and hearthstone all over
our broad land, will yet swell the chorus of the
Union when again touched, as they surely will be,
by the better angels of our nature."

The White House, while Mr. Lincoln occupied it,
was a fertile field for news, which he was always
ready to give those correspondents in whom he had
confidence, but the surveillance of the press—first
by Secretary Seward and then by Secretary Stanton—was as annoying as it was inefficient. A censorship of all matter filed at the Washington office
of the telegraph, for transmission to different Northern cities, was exercised by a succession of ignorant
individuals, some of whom had to be hunted up at
whiskey shops when their signature of approval was

desired. A Congressional investigation showed how stupidly the censors performed their duty. Innocent sentences which were supposed to have a hidden meaning were stricken from paragraphs which were thus rendered nonsensical, and information was rejected that was clipped in print from the Washington papers, which it was known regularly found their way into " Dixie."

When irate correspondents appealed to Mr. Lincoln, he would good-naturedly declare that he had no control over his secretaries, and would endeavor to mollify their wrath by telling them a story. One morning in the winter of 1862, when two angry journalists had undertaken to explain the annoyances of the censorship, Mr. Lincoln, who had listened in his dreamy way, finally said :

" I don't know much about this censorship, but come down-stairs and I will show you the origin of one of the pet phrases of you newspaper fellows."

Leading the way down into the basement, he opened the door of a larder, and solemnly pointed to the hanging carcass of a gigantic sheep.

" There," said he, " now you know what *'Revenons à nos moutons'* means. It was raised by Deacon Buffum at Manchester, up in New Hampshire. Who can say, after looking at it, that New Hampshire's only product is granite ? "

Often when Mr. Lincoln was engaged, correspondents would send in their cards, bearing requests for some desired item of news, or for the verification of some rumor. He would either come out and give the coveted information, or he would write it on the back of the card, and send it to the owner. He wrote a legible hand, slowly and laboriously perfecting his sentences before he placed them on paper. The long epistles that he wrote to his generals he copied himself, not wishing any one else to see them, and these copies were kept in pigeon-holes for reference. His remarks at Gettysburg, which have been compared to the Sermon on the Mount, were written in the car on his way from Washington to the battle-field, upon a piece of pasteboard held on his knee, with persons talking all around him; yet when a few hours afterward he read them, Edward Everett said :

"I would rather be the author of those twenty lines than to have all the fame my oration of to-day will give me."

The foreign war correspondents who came to Washington quite outshone us resident scribes by their pretensions and the style in which they lived. The most agreeable of them was Mr. Edward Dyce, who had written a readable book on Count Cavour; the most versatile was George Augustus Sala, and the most brilliant was Vizetelly, whose clever pencil-sketches were in great demand. Anthony Trollope, who visited Washington on postal business and corresponded with a London weekly, was "English, you know;" and, overtopping all the others—in his own estimation at least—was Dr. Russell, of the London *Times*. He organized private theatricals at the British Legation, appearing himself as *Bombastes Furioso;* and he gave pleasant breakfast and supper parties. When the Army of the Potomac was at last ready to move, he obtained a head-quarter pass for himself and his well-stocked ambulance. But when he drove down to the steamer *Canonicus*, on which transportation had been given him, the provost guard refused, by orders from the War Department, to permit him to embark. He hastened to enlist the intercession of Senator Sumner and Lord Lyons, the British Minister, who appealed to Secretary Stanton, but found him inexorable. Secretary Seward said that he was powerless, and Mr. Lincoln refused to interfere, saying grimly :

"This fellow Russell's Bull Run letter was not so complimentary as to entitle him to much favor."

Unable to accompany the army, Dr. Russell sold his expensive ambulance and horses, shook the dust from his feet, and returned to London.

Requests for his autograph signature were a source of annoyance to Mr. Lincoln, who often had to sign his name twenty-five or thirty times a day. When Dr. R. Shelton Mackenzie, of Philadelphia, called at the White House and asked for the President's autograph, Mr. Lincoln said :

"Will you have it on a card or on a sheet of paper?"

"If the choice rested with myself," said the jovial doctor, "I should prefer it at the foot of a commission."

Mr. Lincoln smiled, and shook his head as if he did not see it in that light, but he sat down and wrote a few pleasant lines, adding his legible signature, "A. Lincoln."

After having signed the famous Emancipation Proclamation on the 1st of January, 1863, Mr. Lincoln carefully put away the pen which he had used, for Mr. Sumner, who had promised it to his friend George Livermore, of Cambridge, the author of an interesting work on slavery. It was a steel pen with a wooden handle, the end of which had been gnawed by Mr. Lincoln—a habit that he had when composing anything that required thought.

Mr. Lincoln used to wear at the White House, in the morning and after dinner, a long-skirted, faded dressing-gown, belted around his waist, and slippers. His favorite attitude when listening—and he was a good listener—was to lean forward and clasp his left knee with both hands, as if fondling it, and his face would then wear a sad, wearied look. But when the time came for him to give an opinion on what he had heard, or to tell a story, which something said "re-minded him of," his face would lighten up with its homely, rugged smile, and he would run his fingers through his bristly black hair, which would stand out in every direction like that of an electric experiment doll.

Mr. Lincoln's part in subduing the rebellion will be better appreciated as time clears away the mists of race prejudice and the fogs of political intrigue. He was surrounded by able men, widely differing in opinion on the negro, but each one hoping that he would be President of the United States. To curb their ambitions, to humor their prejudices, and to make them, as he once expressed it, "pull in the traces," was no easy task, and required such a self-sacrificing man, of large brain and heart, to direct public affairs, as was Abraham Lincoln.

BENJAMIN PERLEY POORE.

XVII

LINCOLN THE MAN

NO greater truth found expression in poetic
words than that which Sir Henry Taylor
puts in the speech of Philip Van Artevelde, when
he says, "the world knows not its greatest men."
The poet restricted his meaning to

> "The kings of thought,
> Who wage contention with their time's decay,
> And of the past are all that will not pass away.

But it extends, as well, to those men of affairs who
earn the admiration of the crowd they control.
This ignorance comes of the fact that great men
have enemies while alive, and friends when dead;
and, between the two, the objects of hate and love
pass into historical phantoms far more unreal than
their ghosts are supposed to be. With us, when a
leader dies, all good men go to lying about him, and
from the monument that covers his remains to the
last echo of the rural press, in speeches, sermons,
eulogies and reminiscences, we have naught but
pious lies. There is no tyranny so despotic as that
of public opinion among a free people. The rule

of the majority is to the last extent exacting and brutal. When brought to bear upon our eminent men, it is also senseless. Poor Garfield, with his sensitive temperament, was almost driven to suicide by abuse while alive. He fell by the shot of an assassin, and passed in an instant to the roll of popular saints. One day it was contempt to say a word in his favor, the next it was dangerous to repeat any of the old abuse.

History is, after all, the crystallization of popular beliefs. As a pleasant fiction is more acceptable than a naked fact, and as the historian shapes his wares, like any other dealer, to suit his customers, one can readily see that our chronicles are only a duller sort of fiction than the popular novels so eagerly read; not that they are true, but they deal in what we long to have—the truth. Popular beliefs, in time, come to be superstitions, and create gods and devils. Thus Washington is deified into an impossible man, and Aaron Burr has passed into a like impossible human monster. Through the same process Abraham Lincoln, one of our truly great, has almost gone from human knowledge. I hear of him, read of him in eulogies and biographies, and fail to recognize the man I encountered, for the first time, in the canvass that called him from private life to be President of the then disuniting United States.

General Robert E. Schenck and I had been

selected to canvass Southern Illinois in behalf of free soil and Abraham Lincoln. That part of Illinois was then known as Egypt, and in our missionary labors we learned there that the American eagle sometimes lays rotten eggs. Our labors on the stump were closed in the wigwam at Springfield a few nights previous to the election. Mr. Lincoln was present, and listened, with intense interest, to General Schenck's able argument. I followed in a cheerful review of the situation, that seemed to amuse the crowd, and none more so than our candidate for the Presidency. We were both invited to return to Springfield, at the jubilee, should success make such rejoicing proper. We did return, for this homely son of toil was elected, and we found Springfield drunk with delight. On the day of our arrival we were invited to a supper at the house of the President-elect. It was a plain, comfortable frame structure, and the supper was an old-fashioned mess of indigestion, composed mainly of cake, pies and chickens, the last evidently killed in the morning, to be eaten, as best they might, that evening.

After the supper, we sat, far into the night, talking over the situation. Mr. Lincoln was the homeliest man I ever saw. His body seemed to me a huge skeleton in clothes. Tall as he was, his hands and feet looked out of proportion, so long and clumsy were they. Every movement was awkward in the extreme. He sat with one leg thrown over the other, and the pendent foot swung almost to the floor. And all the while, two little boys, his sons, clambered over those legs, patted his cheeks, pulled his nose, and poked their fingers in his eyes, without causing reprimand or even notice. He had a face that defied artistic skill to soften or idealize. The multiplicity of photographs and engravings makes it familiar to the public. It was capable of few expressions, but those were extremely striking. When in repose, his face was dull, heavy and repellent. It brightened, like a lit lantern, when animated. His dull eyes would fairly sparkle with fun, or express as kindly a look as I ever saw, when moved by some matter of human interest.

I soon discovered that this strange and strangely gifted man, while not at all cynical, was a sceptic. His view of human nature was low, but good-natured. I could not call it suspicious, but he believed only what he saw. This low estimate of humanity blinded him to the South. He could not understand that men would get up in their wrath and fight for an idea. He considered the movement South as a sort of political game of bluff, gotten up by politicians, and meant solely to frighten the North. He believed that, when the leaders saw their efforts in that direction were unavailing, the tumult would subside. "They won't give up the offices," I remember he said, and added, "were it believed that vacant places could be had at the North Pole, the road there would be lined with dead Virginians." He unconsciously accepted, for himself and party, the same low line that he awarded the South. Expressing no sympathy for the slave, he laughed at the Abolitionists as a disturbing element easily controlled, and without showing any dislike to the slave-holders, said only that their ambition was to be restrained.

I gathered more of this from what Mrs. Lincoln said than from the utterances of our host. This good lady injected remarks into the conversation with more force than logic, and was treated by her husband with about the same good-natured indifference with which he regarded the troublesome boys. In the wife's talk of the coming administration there was an amusing assumption that struck me as very womanly, but somewhat ludicrous. For instance, she said, "The country will find how we regard that abolition sneak, Seward!" Mr. Lincoln put the remarks aside, very much as he did the hand of one of his boys when that hand invaded his capacious mouth.

We were not at a loss to get at the fact, and the reason for it, in the man before us. Descended from the poor whites of a slave State, through many generations, he inherited the contempt, if not the hatred, held by that class for the negro. A self-made man, with scarcely a winter's schooling from books, his strong nature was built on what he inherited, and he could no more feel a sympathy for that wretched race than he could for the horse he worked or the hog he killed. In this he exhibited the marked trait that governed his public life. He never rose above the mass he influenced, and was strong with the people from the fact that he accompanied the commons without any attempt to lead, save in the direction they sought to follow. He knew, and saw clearly, that the people of the free States had, not only, no sympathy with the abolition of slavery, but held fanatics, as Abolitionists were called, in utter abhorrence. While it seemed a cheap philanthropy, and therefore popular, to free another man's slave, the fact was that it was not another man's slave. The unrequited toil of the slave was more valuable to the North than to the South. With our keen business instincts, we of the free States utilized the brutal work of the masters. They made, without saving, all that we accumulated. The Abolitionist was hunted and imprisoned under the shadow of the Bunker Hill Monument as keenly as he was tracked by bloodhounds at the South. Wendell Phillips, the silver-tongued advocate of human rights, was, while Mr. Lincoln talked to us, being ostracized at Boston and rotten-egged at Cincinnati. A keen knowledge of human nature in a jury, more than a knowledge of law, in his case, had put our President-elect at the head of his profession, and this same knowledge made him master of the situation when he came to mold into action the stirred impulses of the people.

I felt myself studying this strange, quaint, great man with keen interest. A newly fashioned individuality had come within the circle of my observation. I saw a man of coarse, rough fiber, without culture, and yet of such force that every observation was original, incisive and striking, while his illustrations were as quaint as Æsop's fables. He had little taste for, and less knowledge of, literature, and while well up in what we call history, limited his acquaintance with fiction to that somber poem known as "Why should the spirit of mortal be proud?"

It was well for us that our President proved to be what I then recognized. He was equal to the awful strain put upon him in the four years of terrible strife that followed. A man of delicate mold and sympathetic nature, such as Chase or Seward, would have broken down, not from overwork, although that was terrible, but from the over-anxiety that kills. Lincoln had none of this. He faced and lived through the awful responsibility of the situation with the high courage and comfort that came of indiffer-

23

ence.   At the darkest period, for us, of the war, when the enemy's cannon were throbbing in its roar along the walls of our Capitol, I heard him say to General Schenck, " I enjoy my rations, and sleep the sleep of the innocent."

Mr. Lincoln did not believe, could not be made to believe, that the South meant secession and war. When I told him, subsequently to this conversation, at a dinner-table in Chicago, where the Hon. Hannibal Hamlin, General Schenck, and others were guests, that the Southern people were in dead earnest, meant war, and I doubted whether he would be inaugurated at Washington, he laughed and said the fall of pork at Cincinnati had affected me.   I became somewhat irritated, and told him that in ninety days the land would be whitened with tents.   He said in reply, " Well, we won't jump that ditch until we come to it," and then, after a pause, he added, " I must run the machine as I find it."   I take no credit to myself for this power of prophecy.   I only said what every one acquainted with the Southern people knew, and the wonder is that Mr. Lincoln should have been so blind to the coming storm.

The epigrammatic force of his expressions was remarkable for the singular purity of his words. What he said was so original that I reduced much of it to writing at the time.   One of these was this, on secession : " If our Southern friends are right in their claim, the framers of the government carefully planned the rot that now threatens their work with destruction. If one State has the right, at will, to withdraw, certainly a majority have the right, and we have the result given us of the States being able to force out one State. That is logical."

We remained at Springfield several days, and then accompanied the President-elect, on his invitation, to Chicago. The invitation was so pressing that I believed Mr. Lincoln intended calling General Schenck to his Cabinet. I am still of this opinion, and attribute the change to certain low intrigues hatched at Chicago by the newly created politicians of that locality, who saw in the coming administration opportunities for plunder that Robert E. Schenck's known probity would have blasted.

Subsequent to the supper we had gatherings at Mr. Lincoln's old law office, and at the political head-quarters, at which men only formed the company ; and before those good honest citizens, who fairly worshiped their distinguished neighbor, Mr. Lincoln gave way to his natural bent for fun, and told very amusing stories, always in quaint illustration of the subject under discussion, no one of which will bear printing. They were coarse, and were saved from vulgarity only by being so strangely in point, and told not for the sake of the telling, as if he enjoyed the stories themselves, but that they were, as I have said, so quaintly illustrative.

The man who could open a Cabinet meeting called to discuss the Emancipation Proclamation by reading Artemus Ward, who called for a comic song on the bloody battle-field, was the same man who could guide with clear mind and iron hand the diplomacy that kept off the fatal interference of Europe, while conducting at home the most horrible of all civil wars that ever afflicted a people. He reached with ease the highest and the lowest level, and on the very field that he shamed with a ribald song he left a record of eloquence never reached by human lips before.

There is a popular belief that Abraham Lincoln was of so kind and forgiving a nature that his gentler impulses interfered with his duty. In proof of this, attention is called to the fact that through all the war he never permitted a man to be shot for desertion. The belief is erroneous. There never lived a man who could say "no" with easier facility, and abide by his saying with more firmness, than President Lincoln. His good-natured manner misled the common mind. It covered as firm a character as nature ever clad with human flesh, and I doubt whether Mr. Lincoln had at all a kind, forgiving nature. Such traits are not common to successful leaders. They, like Hannibal, melt their way through rocks with hot vinegar, not honey. And that good-natured way more generally covers a selfish than a generous disposition. Men instinctively find it easier to glide comfortably through life with a round, oily, elastic exterior, than in an angular, hard one. Such give way in trifles and hold their own adversely in all the more serious sacrifices of self to the good or comfort of others. If one doubts what I here assert, let such turn and study the hard, angular, coarse face of this great man. Nature never gave that as an indication of a tender, yielding disposition. Nor had his habits of life in any respect softened its hard lines. Hazlitt tells us, with truth, that while we may control the voice, and discipline the manner, the face is beyond command. Day and night, waking and sleeping, our character is being traced there, to be read by all men who care to make the face a study. It is common, for example, for the President to be in continual trouble over supposed promises to office-seekers. Mr. Lincoln had none of this. He would refuse so clearly and positively that it left no doubt and no hope, and yet in such a pleasant manner that the applicant left with no ill feeling in his disappointment. I heard Secretary Seward say, in this connection, that President Lincoln "had a cunning that was genius." As for his steady refusal to sanction the death penalty in cases of desertion, there was far more policy in the course than kind feeling. To assert the contrary is to detract from Lincoln's force of character as well as intellect. As Secretary Chase said at the time, "such kindness to the criminal is cruelty to the army, for it encourages the bad to leave the brave and patriotic unsupported." The fact is that our war President was not lost in his high admiration of brigadiers and major-generals, and had a positive dislike for their methods and the despotism on which an army is based. He knew that he was dependent on volunteers for soldiers, and to force on such the stern discipline of the regular army was to render the service unpopular. And it pleased him to be the source of mercy, as well as the fountain of honor, in this direction.

I was sitting with General Dan Tyler, of Connecticut, in the antechamber of the War Department, shortly after the adjournment of the Buell court of inquiry, of which we had been members, when President Lincoln came in from the room of Secretary Stanton. Seeing us, he said : "Well, gentlemen, you did not survive the war, and now have you any matter worth reporting, after such a protracted investigation?" "I think so, Mr. President," replied General Tyler. "We had it proven that Bragg, with less than ten thousand men, drove your eighty-three thousand under Buell back from before Chattanooga, down to the Ohio at Louisville, marched round us twice, then doubled us up at Perryville, and finally got out of Kentucky with all his plunder." " Now, Tyler," said the President, "what is the meaning of all this ; what is the lesson ? Don't our men march as well, and fight as well, as these rebels ? If not, there is a fault somewhere. We are all of the same family—same sort." " Yes, there is a lesson," replied General Tyler. " We are of the same sort, but subject to a different handling. Bragg's little force was superior to our larger number, because he had it under control. If a man left his ranks, he was punished ; if he deserted, he was shot. We had nothing of that sort. If we attempt to shoot a deserter, you pardon him, and our army is without discipline." The President looked perplexed. " Why do you interfere ?" General Tyler continued. " Congress has taken from you all responsibility." " Yes," answered the President impatiently, " Congress has taken the responsibility, and left the women to howl about me ; " and so he strode away, and General Tyler remarked that, as it was not necessary for the President to see one of these women, to jeopard an army on such grounds was very feeble. The fact was, however, as I have said, the President had other and stronger motives for his conduct.

Of President Lincoln's high sense of justice, or rather fair play, I have a vivid recollection. Previous to Lee's invasion of Pennsylvania, rumors of which

reached Washington in advance of that suicidal movement on the part of the Confederates, General Halleck issued one of his non-committal orders to General Schenck, then in command at Baltimore, advising
the concentration of our troops at Harper's Ferry.
This referred especially to General Milroy's 10,000
men at Winchester. I was sent, as chief of staff, to
look into Milroy's condition, and empowered to let
him remain or order him back, as I might see fit.
Winchester, as a fortified place, was a military blun-
der. It covered nothing, while a force there was in
constant peril. I had learned enough in the service
to know that a subordinate should take no chances,
and I ordered Milroy back to Harper's Ferry. General Schenck, at Milroy's earnest request, counter-
manded my order, and three days after Milroy found
himself surrounded by Lee's entire army. The gallant old soldier cut his way out, with his entire command. Of course there was a heavy loss of material.
For this Milroy was put under arrest by Secretary
Stanton, and court-martialed by Halleck. Milroy
shielded himself behind Schenck's order, so that the
court convened was really trying my general without
the advantages given him, as defendant, of being
heard in his defense. General Schenck was summoned to appear, and instead of appearing drew up
a protest, that he directed me not only to take to the
President, but read to him, fearing the protest would

be pigeon-holed for consideration when consideration would be too late. It was late in the afternoon, and riding to the White House, I was told the President could be found at the War Department. I met him coming out, and delivered my message. " Let me see the protest," said the President as we walked toward the Executive Mansion. " General Schenck ordered me, Mr. President, to read it to you." " Well, I can read," he responded sharply, and as he was General Schenck's superior officer I handed him the paper. He read as he strode along. Arriving at the entrance to the White House, we found the carriage awaiting to carry him to the Soldiers' Home, where he was then spending the summer, and the guard detailed to escort him drawn up in front. The President sat down upon the steps of the porch, and continued his study of the protest. I have him photographed on my mind, as he sat there, and a strange picture he presented. His long, slender legs were drawn up until his knees were level with his chin, while his long arms held the paper, which he studied regardless of the crowd before him. He read on to the end, then, looking up, said: " Piatt, don't you think that you and Schenck are squealing, like pigs, before you're hurt?" " No, Mr. President." " Why, I am the Court of Appeal," he continued, " and do you think I am going to have an injustice done Schenck?" " Before the appeal can be heard, a soldier's reputation will be blasted by a packed court," I responded. "Come, now," he exclaimed, an ugly look shading his face, "you and I are lawyers, and know the meaning of the word 'packed.' I don't want to hear it from your lips again. What's the matter with the court?" "It is illegally organized by General Halleck." "Halleck's act is mine." "I beg your pardon, Mr. President, the Rules and Regulations direct that in cases of this sort you shall select the court; you cannot delegate that to a subordinate any more than you can the pardoning power," and opening the book I pointed to the article. "That *is* a point," he said, slowly rising. "Do you know, Colonel, that I have been so busy with this war I have never read the Regulations. Give me that book, and I'll study them to-night." "I beg your pardon, Mr. President," I said, giving him the book, "but in the mean time my general will be put under arrest for disobedience, and the mischief will be done." "That's so," he replied. "Here, give me a pencil," and tearing off a corner of the paper General Schenck had sent him, he wrote: "All proceedings before the court convened to try General Milroy are suspended until further orders.—A. LINCOLN." The next morning I clanked into the courtroom with my triangular order, and had the grim satisfaction of seeing the owls in epaulets file out, never to be called again.

With all his awkwardness of manner, and utter dis-
regard of social conventionalities that seemed to invite familiarity, there was something about Abraham
Lincoln that enforced respect. No man presumed
on the apparent invitation to be other than respectful. I was told at Springfield that this accompanied
him through life. Among his rough associates, when
young, he was leader, looked up to and obeyed, because they felt of his muscle and his readiness in its
use. Among his associates at the bar, it was attributed to his ready wit, which kept his duller associates at a distance. The fact was, however, that this
power came from a sense of a reserve force of intellectual ability that no one took account of, save in
its results. Through one of those freaks of nature
that produce a Shakespeare at long intervals, a
giant had been born to the poor whites of Kentucky,
and the sense of superiority possessed President
Lincoln at all times. Unobtruding and even unas-
suming as he was, he was not modest in his assertion, and he as quietly directed Seward in shaping
our delicate and difficult foreign policy as he controlled Chase in the Treasury and Edwin M. Stanton in the War Department. These men, great as
they were, felt their inferiority to their master, and
while all three were eaten into and weakened by
anxiety, he ate and slept and jested as if his shoulders did not carry, Atlas-like, the fate of an empire.

I never saw him angry but once, and I had no wish to see a second exhibition of his wrath. We were in command of what was called the Middle Department, with head-quarters at Baltimore. General Schenck, with that intense loyalty which distinguished this eminent soldier, shifted the military sympathy from the aristocracy of Maryland to the Union men, and made the eloquent Henry Winter Davis and the well-known jurist Judge Bond our associates and advisers. These gentlemen could not understand why, having such entire command of Maryland, the government did not make it a free State, and so, taking the property from the disloyal, render them weak and harmless, and bring the border of free States to the capital of the Union. The fortifications about Baltimore, used heretofore to threaten that city, now, under the influence of Davis, Bond, Wallace, and others, had their guns turned outward for the protection of the place, and it seemed only necessary to inspire the negroes with a faith in us as liberators to perfect the work. The first intimation I received that this policy of freeing Maryland was distasteful to the administration came from Secretary Stanton. I had told him what we thought, and what we hoped to accomplish. I noticed an amused expression on the face of the War Secretary, and when I ended he said dryly, " You and Schenck had better attend to your own business." I asked him what he meant by "our business." He said, "Obeying orders, that's all."

Not long after this talk with Mr. Stanton, the gallant General William Birney, son of the eminent James G. Birney, came into Maryland to recruit for a negro brigade, then first authorized. I directed Birney to recruit slaves only. He said he would be glad to do so, but wanted authority in writing from General Schenck. I tried my general, and he refused, saying that such authority could come only from the War Department, as Birney was acting directly under its instructions. I could not move him, and knowing that he had a leave of absence for a few days, to transact some business at Boston, I waited patiently until he was fairly off, and then issued the order to General Birney. The General took an idle government steamer, and left for the part of Maryland where slaves were most abundant. Birney was scarcely out of sight before I awakened to the opposition I had excited. The Hon. Reverdy Johnson appeared at head-quarters, heading a delegation of solid citizens who wanted the Union and slavery saved, one and inseparable. I gave them scant comfort, and they left for Washington. That afternoon came a telegram from the War Department, asking who was in command at Baltimore. I responded that General Schenck, being absent for a few days only, had left affairs in control of his

chief of staff. Then came a curt summons, order-
ing me to appear at the War Department. I obeyed,
arriving in the evening at the old, somber building. Being informed that the Secretary was at the
Executive Mansion, I repaired there, sent in my
card, and was at once shown into the presence, not
of Mr. Stanton, but of the President. I do not care
to recall the words of Mr. Lincoln. I wrote them
out that night, for I was threatened a shameful dismissal from the service, and I intended appealing to
the public. They were exceedingly severe, for the
President was in a rage. I was not allowed a word
in my own defense, and was only permitted to say
that I would countermand my order as well as I
could. I was saved cashiering through the interference of Stanton and Chase, and the further fact that
a row over such a transaction at that time would
have been extremely awkward.

My one act made Maryland a free State. Word
went out, and spread like wildfire, that "Mr. Linkum was a callin' on de slaves to fight foh freedum,"
and the hoe-handle was dropped, never again to be
taken up by unrequited toil. The poor creatures
poured into Baltimore with their families, on foot,
on horseback, in old wagons, and even on sleds
stolen from their masters. The late masters became
clamorous for compensation, and Mr. Lincoln ordered a commission to assess damages. Secretary

Stanton put in a proviso that those cases only should be considered where the claimant could take the iron-bound oath of allegiance. Of course no slaves were paid for.

The President never forgave me. Subsequently, when General Schenck resigned command to take his seat in Congress, the Union men of Maryland and Delaware, headed by Judge Bond, waited on the President with a request that I be promoted to brigadier-general and put in command of the Middle Department. Mr. Lincoln heard them patiently, and then refused, saying, "Schenck and Piatt are good fellows, and if there were any rotten apples in the barrel they'd be sure to hook 'em out. But they run their machine on too high a level for me. They never could understand that I was boss." Edwin M. Stanton told me, after he left the War Department, that when he sent a list of officers to the President, my name included, as worthy promotion, Lincoln would quietly draw his pen through my name. I do not blame him. His great, thoughtful brain saw at the time what has taken years for us to discover and appreciate. He understood the people he held to a death struggle in behalf of the great Republic, and knew that, while the masses would fight to the bitter end in behalf of the Union, they would not kill their own brothers, and spread mourning over the entire land, in behalf of the negro. He therefore kept the cause of the Union to the front, and wrote to Horace Greeley the memorable words : "If to preserve the Union it is necessary to destroy slavery, slavery will be destroyed; and if to preserve the Union slavery is to be maintained, slavery will be maintained." He well knew that the North was not fighting to liberate slaves, nor the South to preserve slavery. The people of the slave States plunged into a bloody war to build a Southern empire of their own, and the people of the North fought to preserve the government of the fathers on all the land the fathers left us. In that awful conflict slavery went to pieces.

We are quick to forget the facts and slow to recognize the truths that knock from us our pretentious claims to a high philanthropy. As I have said, abolitionism was not only unpopular when the war broke out, but it was detested. The minority that elected Mr. Lincoln had fallen heir to the Whig votes of the North, and while pledging itself, in platforms and speeches, to a solemn resolve to keep slavery under the Constitution in the States, restricted its antislavery purpose to the prevention of its spread into the Territories. I remember when the Hutchinsons were driven from the camps of the Potomac Army by the soldiers for singing their abolition songs, and I remember well that for two years nearly of our service as soldiers we were engaged in returning slaves to their masters, when the poor creatures sought shelter in our lines.

President Lincoln's patriotism and wisdom rose above impulse, or his positive temperament and intellect kept him free of mere sentiment. Looking back now at this grand man, and the grave situation at the time, I am ashamed of my act of insubordination, and although it freed Maryland it now lowers me in my own estimation. Had the President carried his threat of punishment into execution, it would have been just.

The popular mind is slow of study, and I fear it will be long ere it learns that, while an eminent man wins our admiration through his great qualities, he can hold our love only from his human weaknesses that make him one of ourselves. We are told that, with the multitude, nothing is so successful as success, yet there is often more heroism in failure than in triumph. The one is frequently the result of accident, while the other holds in itself all that endears the martyr to the human heart. The unfortunate Hector is, after all, the hero of the Iliad, and not the invulnerable Achilles, and by our popular process of eliminating all human weakness from our great men we weaken, and in a measure destroy, their immortality, for we destroy them. As we accept the sad, rugged, homely face, and love it for what it is, we should accept it as it was, the grandest figure loom-

24

ing up in our history as a nation. Washington taught the world to know us, Lincoln taught us to know ourselves. The first won for us our independence, the last wrought out our manhood and self-respect.

DONN PIATT.

XVIII

LINCOLN'S PERSONALITY

MY acquaintance with Lincoln could hardly be called an acquaintance. I was rather an observer. I followed him as I did every public character during the antislavery conflict. The first thing that really awakened my interest in him was his speeches parallel with Douglas in Illinois, and indeed it was that manifestation of ability that secured his nomination to the Presidency. It was a matter of great importance that the new Presidential election should have another candidate than Fremont, and Lincoln's speech at the Cooper Union, after his controversy with Douglas, settled it.

Seward expected the nomination, but overhopeful nature would, I think, have gone far to damage the whole country if he had been President, and the nomination of Lincoln was, to begin with, the revelation of the hand of God.

He was, in the most significant way, a man that embodied all the best qualities of unspoiled, middle-class men. He had the homely common sense; he had honesty with sagacity; and he had sympathetic nature that prepared him to accept any stormy times. The colored people were the helpless wards; the Southern people, our fellow-citizens.

The weakness of human nature is such that when a man is born he is helpless ; and he can never stand up against the public sentiment of the age in which he lives. Lincoln was able to deal with all classes of men, from his very nature. When he first went to Washington, the general opinion was that he was an honest man but lacked in sagacity ; but a friend told me he was the best judge of men in the country.

Thus far in a general way.

I was editor of the *Independent* in 1861–2, and of course my duty compelled me to keep the run of things, and know what was going on behind and outside.

The first visit I ever made to Washington was before the war. The organization of the church was controlled by the South, and I walked the streets and was regarded by the people there as a sort of dangerous animal. They stood and looked at me as they would a bull-dog or bear. I did not go to Washington again until 1862.

In 1862, the great delay, the want of any success, the masterly inactivity of our leading generals, roused my indignation, and I wrote a series of editorials addressed to the President (three or four), and as near as I can recollect they were in the nature of a mowing machine—they cut at every revolution—and I was told one day that the President had received them and read them through with very serious countenance, and that his only criticism was : " Is thy servant a dog ? " They bore down on him very hard.

I went to England in 1863, not directly or indirectly by request of Mr. Lincoln or of Mr. Seward, and was opposed to speaking there until I was dragged into it by things over there.

On my return from England I fell in with Stanton, and I consider him to be head and shoulders above all others in that conflict.

There was some talk, early in 1864, of a sort of compromise with the South. Blair had told the President that he was satisfied if he could be put in communication with some of the leading men of the South in some way or other, that some benefit would accrue. Lincoln had sent a delegation to meet Alexander Stephens, and that was all the North knew. We were all very much excited over that. The war lasted so long, and I was afraid Lincoln would be so anxious for peace, and I was afraid he would accept something that would be of advantage to the South, so I went to Washington and called upon him. We were alone in his receiving-room. His hair was " every way for Sunday." It looked as though it was an abandoned stubble field. He had on slippers, and his vest was what was called "going free." He looked wearied, and when he sat down in a chair, looked as though every limb wanted to drop off his body. And I said to him, "Mr. Lincoln, I come to you to know whether the public interest will permit you to explain to me what this Southern commission means? I am in a position as editor, not wont to step in the dark." Well, he listened very patiently, and looked up to the ceiling for a few moments, and said : "Well, I am almost of a mind to show you all the documents."

"Well, Mr. Lincoln, I should like to see them if it is proper." He went to his little secretary, and came out and handed me a little card as long as my finger and an inch wide, and on that was written—

"You will pass the bearer through the lines" (or something to that effect).

"A. LINCOLN."

"There," he said, "is all there is of it. Now Blair thinks something can be done, but I don't, but I have no objection to have him try his hand. He has no authority whatever but to go and see what he can do."

"Well," said I, "you have lifted a great burden off my mind."

Well, that being all safely over, we talked a little

about other things, and some one came in and said to him that a deputation had just arrived and wanted to see him.

"Well," said he, "you come along with me." I said I did not want to make any remarks, but he said, "Come along."

We went to a balcony window, and Mr. Lincoln made a few courteous remarks, and then he said, "Now Mr. Beecher will talk to you." I do not remember what I said—a few words.

I do not know that I ever met him after that.

John Dufrees was Public Printer, and was my old friend and chum. He was intimately acquainted with him, and he gave me a good many things which would come more properly from him than me.

When Mrs. Stowe called to see Lincoln towards the close of the war, she says that she spoke of the great relief he must feel at the prospect of an early close of the war and the establishment of peace. And he said, in a sad way, "No, Mrs. Stowe, I shall never live to see peace; this war is killing me;" and he had a presentiment that he would not live long, that he had put his whole life into the war, and that when it was over he would then collapse.

Nobody will ever understand Lincoln who is not acquainted with Western character and habit of thirty or forty years ago.

I have heard of these stories from Stanton. Stanton was as tender as a woman—he was as tender as a lover.   I had great admiration for him.

I came up Wall Street one day and met a friend who said: "I just came back from Washington. Stanton is breaking down; he won't hold out much longer."

Well, it just struck me all in a heap.   I walked into one of those offices in Wall Street and said, "Will you allow me pen and ink?" and wrote to him just what I had heard—that he was sick and broken down and desponding.   I wrote that he need not despond, that the country was saved, and, if he did not do another thing, he had done enough.   I sent the letter, and in the course of a few days I got back a letter, and if it had been a woman writing in answer to a proposal it could not have been more tender.   And when I went to Washington he treated me with great tenderness, as if I had been his son.

When Johnson had come to the Presidency, and Stanton and every one was anxious that he should be kept in Northern influence, I went down to Washington to preach the funeral sermon.   The President was there, and he asked me to call and see him—that he would be happy to see me.

Stanton said, "Go."   I afterward went to see the President.   I returned to Stanton's and went into his study, and he got a box of cigars, and I thought that if I did not smoke he would not like it, and I took a smoke, although it made me sick—puffing occasionally—and when he threw away his, I did mine.

Stanton, evidently, got rest from his great cares through literature; but Lincoln, from the humorists. I understood them both perfectly. Stanton had poetry for his relaxation. Everybody must have somewhere to blow off.

HENRY WARD BEECHER.

XIX

LINCOLN IN HISTORY

WHEN Anson Burlingame was in this country the last time he gave me an account of his life in China, his relations with the principal personages there, and said, finally, " When I die they will erect monuments and temples to my memory. However much I may now protest, they will do that." This, we are told, the people and government of China have done.

Gratitude to public benefactors is the common sentiment of mankind. It has found expression in every age ; it finds expression in every condition of society. Monuments and temples seem to belong to the age of art rather than to the age of letters, but reflection teaches us that letters cannot fully express the obligations of the learned, even to their chief benefactors, and only in a less degree can epitaphs, essays and histories satisfy those who have not the opportunity and culture to read and understand them. Moreover, monuments and temples in honor of the dead express the sentiments of their

contemporaries who survive ; and the sentiments of
contemporaries, when freed from passion, crystallize,
usually, into opinion—the fixed, continuing opinion of
mankind.   Napoleon must ever remain great ; Washington, good and great; Burke, the first of English
orators ; the younger Pitt, the chief of English statesmen ; and Henry the Eighth, a dark character in
British history.   Time and reflection, the competing
fame of new and illustrious men, the antiquarian
and the critic, may modify the first-formed opinion,
but seldom or never is it changed.   The judgment
rendered at the grave is a just judgment usually,
but whether so or not it is not often disturbed.

The fame of noble men is at once the most en-
dearing and the most valuable public possession.
Of the distant past it is all of value that remains ;
and of the recent past, the verdant fields, the vil-
lages, cities and institutions of culture and government are only monuments which men of that past
have reared to their own fame.   History is but the
account of men : the earth, even, is but a mighty
theater on which human actors, great and small,
have played their parts.   Superior talents and favoring circumstances have secured for a few persons
that special recognition called immortality ; that is,
a knowledge of qualities and actions attributed to
an individual whose name is preserved and transmitted, with that knowledge, from one generation to

another. This immortality may be nothing to the dead, but the record furnishes examples and inspiring facts, especially for the young, by which they are encouraged and stimulated to lead lives worthy of the illustrious men of the past. Herein is the value, and the chief value, of monuments, temples, histories and panegyrics. If the highest use of sinners is, by their evil lives and bad examples, to keep saints to their duty, so it is also that the immortality accorded to those who were scourges rather than benefactors serves as a warning to men who strive to write their names upon the page of history. But the world really cherishes only the memory of those who were good as well as great, and hence it is the effort of panegyrists and hero-worshipers to place their idols in that attitude before mankind. The immortal few are those who have identified themselves with contests and principles in which men of all times are interested; or who have so expressed the wish or thought or purpose of mankind, that their words both enlighten and satisfy the thoughtful of every age. When we consider how much is demanded of aspirants for lasting fame, we can understand the statement that that century is rich which adds more than one name to the short list of persons who in an historical sense are immortal. In that sense those only are immortal whose fame passes beyond the country, beyond the race, beyond the language, beyond the century, and far outspreads all knowledge of the details of local and national history.

The empire of Japan sent accredited to the United States as its first minister resident, Ari Nori Mori, a young man of extraordinary ability, and then only twenty-four years of age. A few months before Japan was opened to intercourse with other nations an elder brother of Mori lived for a time as a student at Jeddo, the capital of the empire. Upon his return to his home in the country he informed the family that he had heard of a new and distant nation of which Washington, the greatest and best of men, was the founder, savior and father. Beyond this he had heard little of the country or the man, but this brief statement so inspired the younger brother to know more of the man and of the country, that he resolved to leave his native land without delay, and in disobedience both to parental rule and public law. In this single fact we see what fame is in its largest sense, and we realize also the power of a single character to influence others even where there is no tie of country, of language, of race, or any except that which gives unity to the whole family of man. If, then, the acquisition of fame in a large sense be so difficult, is it wise thus to present the subject to the young? May they not be deterred from those manly efforts which are the prerequisites to success?

I answer, Fame is not a proper object of human effort, and its pursuit is the most unwise of human undertakings. I am not now moralizing; I am trying to state the account as a worldly transaction. Moreover, there is a distinction between the fame of which I have spoken and contemporaneous recognition of one's capacity and fitness to perform important private or public service. This is reputation rather than fame, and it well may be sought by honorable effort, and it should be prized by every one as an object of virtuous ambition. Success, however, is not so often gained by direct effort as by careful, systematic, thorough preparation for duty. The world is not so loaded with genius, nor even with talent, that opportunities are wanting for all those who have capacity for public service.

Mr. Bancroft gave voice to the considerate judgment of mankind when, in conversation, he said, "Beyond question, General Washington, intellectually, is the first of Americans." If this statement be open to question, the question springs from the limitation, for beyond doubt Washington is the first of Americans. His pre-eminence, his greatness, appear in the fact that his faculties and powers were so fully developed, so evenly adjusted and nicely balanced, that in all the various and difficult duties of military and civil life he never for an instant failed to meet the demand which his position and the attendant circumstances made upon him. This was the opinion of his contemporaries. His pre-eminence was felt and recognized by the leaders of the savage tribes of America, by the most sagacious statesmen and wisest observers in foreign lands, and by all of his countrymen who were able to escape the influence of passion and to consider passing events in the light of pure reason.

It is the glory of Washington that he was the first great military chief who did not exhibit the military spirit; and in this he has given to his country an example and a rule of the highest value. The problem of republics is to develop military capacity without fostering the military spirit. This Washington did in himself, and this also his country has done. The zeal of the young men of the Republic to enter the military service for the defense of the Union, and the satisfaction with which they accepted peace and returned to the employments of peace, all in obedience to the example of Washington, are his highest praise.

Washington was also an illustration of the axiom in government, that the faculties and qualities essential to a military leader are the highest endowments of a ruler in time of peace; and the instincts of men are in harmony with this historic and philosophic truth. The time that has passed, since the public career and natural life of Washington ended, has

not dimmed the luster of his fame, nor qualified in the least that general judgment on which he was raised to an equality with the most renowned personages of ancient and modern times.

With this estimate, not an unusual nor an exaggerated estimate, I venture to claim for Abraham Lincoln the place next to Washington, whether we have regard to private character, to intellectual qualities, to public services, or to the weight of obligation laid upon the country and upon mankind. Between Washington and Lincoln there were two full generations of men ; but, of them all, I see not one who can be compared with either.

Submitting this opinion, in advance of all evidence, I proceed to deal with those qualities, opportunities, characteristics and services on which Lincoln's claim rests for the broad and most enduring fame of which I have spoken. We are attracted naturally by the career of a man who has passed from the humblest condition in early life to stations of honor and fame in maturer years. With Lincoln this space was the broadest possible in civilized life. His childhood was spent in a cabin upon a mud floor, and his youth and early manhood were checkered with more than the usual share of vicissitudes and disappointments. The chief blessing of his early life was his step-mother, Sally Bush, who, by her affectionate treatment and wise conduct, did much to elevate the character of the

class of women to which she belonged.   His opportunities for training in the schools were few, and his
hours of study were limited.   The books that he
could obtain were read and re-read, and a grammar
and geometry were his constant companions for a
time; but his means of education bore no logical
relation to the position he finally reached as a
thinker, writer and speaker.   Lincoln is a witness,
for the man William Shakespeare, against those hostile and illogical critics who deny to him the author-
ship of the plays that bear his name because they
cannot comprehend the way of reaching such results
without the aid of books, teachers and universities.
When they show similar results reached by the aid
of books, teachers and universities, or even by their
aid chiefly, they will then have one fact tending
to prove that such results cannot be reached without such aids; but in the absence of the proof we
must accept Shakespeare and Lincoln, and confess
our ignorance of the processes by which their greatness was attained.

Books, schools and universities are helps to all,
and they are needed by each and all in the ratio of
the absence of natural capacity.   By the processes of
reason employed to show that Shakespeare did not
write *Hamlet*, it may be proved that Lincoln did not
compose the speech which he pronounced at Gettysburg.   The parallel between Shakespeare and Lin-

coln is good to this extent. The products of the pen of Lincoln imply a degree of culture in schools which he never had, and a process of reasoning upon that implication leads to the conclusion that he was not the author of what bears his name. We know that this conclusion would be false, and we may therefore question the soundness of a similar process of reasoning in the case of Shakespeare.

The world gives too much credit to self-made men. Not much is due to those who are so largely endowed by nature that they at once outrun their contemporaries who are always on the crutches of books and authorities, and but a little more is due to the larger class who in isolation and privation acquire the knowledge that is gained, usually, only in the schools. In the end, however, we judge the man as a whole and as a result, for there is no trustworthy analysis by which we can decide how much is due to nature, how much to personal effort, and how much to circumstances. Of all the self-made men of America, Lincoln owed least to books, schools, and society. Washington owed much to these, and all his self-assertion, which was considerable, in society, in the army, and in civil affairs, was the assertion of a trained man. Lincoln asserted nothing but his capacity, when it was his duty to decide what was wise and what was right. He claimed nothing for himself, in his personal character, in the nature of deference from others, and too little, perhaps, for the great office he held. The schools create nothing; they only bring out what is; but as long as the mass of mankind think otherwise, an untrained person like Lincoln has an immense advantage over the scholar in the contest for immortality. In this particular, however, the instincts of men have a large share of wisdom in them. When we speak of human greatness we mean natural, innate faculty and power. We distinguish the gift of God from the culture of the schools. The unlearned give the schools too much credit in the work of developing power and forming character; the learned, perhaps, give them too little. But whether judged by the learned or the unlearned, Lincoln is the most commanding figure in the ranks of self-made men which America has yet produced.

Mr. Lincoln possessed the almost divine faculty of interpreting the will of the people without any expression by them. We often hear of the influence of the atmosphere of Washington upon the public men residing there. It never affected him. He was of all men most independent of locality and social influences. He was wholly self-contained in all that concerned his opinions upon public questions and in all his judgments of the popular will. Conditions being given, he could anticipate the popular will and conduct. When the proceedings of the convention of dissenting Republicans, which assembled at Cleveland in 1864, were mentioned to him and his opinion sought, he told the story of two fresh Irishmen who attempted to find a tree-toad that they heard in the forest, and how, after a fruitless hunt, one of them consoled himself and his companion with the expression, "An' faith it was nothing but a noise."

Mr. Lincoln's goodness of nature was boundless. In childhood it showed itself in unfeigned aversion to every form of cruelty to animal life. When he was President it found expression in that memorable letter to Mrs. Bixby of Boston, who had given, irrevocably given, as was then supposed, five sons to the country. The letter was dated November 21, 1864, before the excitement of his second election was over :

" DEAR MADAM :—I have been shown, in the files of the War Department, a statement, of the Adjutant-General of Massachusetts, that you are the mother of five sons who have died gloriously on the field of battle. I feel how weak and fruitless must be any words of mine which should attempt to beguile you from a loss so overwhelming. But I cannot refrain from tendering to you the consolation that may be found in the thanks of the Republic they died to save. I pray that our Heavenly Father may assuage the anguish of your bereavement, and leave you only the cherished memory of the loved and lost, and the solemn pride that must be yours to have laid so costly a sacrifice upon the altar of freedom.

"Yours, very sincerely and respectfully,
"ABRAHAM LINCOLN.
" To Mrs. Bixby, Boston, Massachusetts."

I imagine that all history and all literature may be searched, and in vain, for a funeral tribute so touching, so comprehensive, so fortunate in expression as this.

If we have been moved to laughter by a simple story and to tears by a pathetic strain, we can understand what Lincoln was to all, and especially to the common people who were his fellows in everything except his greatness, when he moved, spoke, and acted among them. It would be a reflection upon the human race if men did not recognize something worthy of enduring fame in one whose kindness and sympathy were so comprehensive as to include the insect on the one side and the noble, but bereaved, mother on the other. To the soldier, General Thomas was " Old Holdfast," General Hooker was " Fighting Joe," and Mr. Lincoln was " Father Abraham." These names were due to personal qualities which the soldiers observed, admired and applauded. Mr. Lincoln was a mirth-making, genial, melancholy man. By these characteristics he enlisted sympathy for himself at once, while his moral qualities and intellectual pre-eminence commanded respect. Mr.

Lincoln's wit and mirth will give him a passport to
the thoughts and hearts of millions who would take
no interest in the sterner and more practical parts of
his character. He used his faculties for mirth and
wit to relieve the melancholy of his life, to parry
unwelcome inquiries, and, in the debates of politics
and the bar, to worry his opponents. In debate he
often so combined wit, satire and statement that his
opponent at once appeared ridiculous and illogical.
Mr. Douglas was often the victim of these sallies in
the great debate for the Senate before the people of
Illinois, and before the people of the country, in the
year 1858. Douglas constantly asserted that abolition
would be followed by amalgamation, and that the
Republican party designed to repeal the laws of
Illinois which prohibited the marriage of blacks and
whites. This was a formidable appeal, to the prejudices of the people of Southern Illinois especially.
"I protest now and forever," said Lincoln, "against
that counterfeit logic which presumes that because I
did not want a negro woman for a slave, I do, necessarily, want her for a wife. I have never had the least
apprehension that I or my friends would marry
negroes if there were no law to keep them from it,
but as Judge Douglas and his friends seem to be in
great apprehension that they might, if there were
no law to keep them from it, I give him the most solemn pledge that I will to the very last stand by the

law of this State, which forbids the marrying of white people with negroes."

Thus in two sentences did Mr. Lincoln overthrow Douglas in his logic and render him ridiculous in his position. Douglas claimed special credit for the defeat of the Lecompton bill, although five-sixths of the votes were given by the Republican Party. Said Lincoln : "Why is he entitled to more credit than others for the performance of that good act, unless there was something in the antecedents of the Republicans that might induce every one to expect them to join in that good work, and, at the same time, leading them to doubt that he would. Does he place his superior claim to credit on the ground that he performed a good act which was never expected of him?" He then gave Mr. Douglas the benefit of a specific application of the parable of the lost sheep.

In the last debate at Alton, October 15, 1858, Mr. Douglas proceeded to show that Buchanan was guilty of gross inconsistencies of position. Lincoln did not defend Buchanan, but after he had stated the fact that Douglas had been on both sides of the Missouri Compromise, he added: "I want to know if Buchanan has not as much right to be inconsistent as Douglas has? Has Douglas the exclusive right in this country of being *on all sides of all questions?* Is nobody allowed that high privilege but himself? Is he to have an entire monopoly on that subject?"

There are three methods in debate of sustaining and enforcing opinions, and the faculty and facility of using these several methods are the tests of intellectual quality in writers and speakers. First and lowest intellectually, are those who rely upon authority. They gather and marshal the sayings of their predecessors, and ask their hearers and readers to indorse the positions taken, not because they are reasonable and right under the process of demonstration, but because many persons in other times have thought them to be right and reasonable. As this is the work of the mere student, and does not imply either philosophy or the faculty of reasoning, those who rely exclusively upon authority are in the third class of intellectual men. Next, and of a much higher order, are the writers and speakers who state the facts of a case, apply settled principles to them, and by sound processes of reasoning maintain the position taken. But high above all are the men who by statement pure and simple, or by statement argumentative, carry conviction to thoughtful minds. Unquestionably Mr. Lincoln belongs to this class. Those who remember Douglas's theory in regard to "squatter sovereignty," which he sometimes dignified by calling it the "sacred right of self-government," will appreciate the force of Lincoln's statement of the scheme in these words: "The phrase, 'sacred right of self-government,' though expressive of the only rightful basis of any government, was so perverted in the attempted use of it as to amount to just this : *That if any one man choose to enslave another, no third man shall be allowed to object.*"

In the field of argumentative statement, Mr. Webster, at the time of his death, had had no rival in America; but he has left nothing more exact, explicit, and convincing than this extract from Lincoln's first speech of the great debate. Here is a statement in less than twenty words, *If any one man choose to enslave another, no third man shall be allowed to object*, which embodies the substance of the opinion of the Supreme Court of the United States in the case of Dred Scott, the theory of the Kansas-Nebraska bill, and exposes the sophistry which Douglas had woven into his arguments on " squatter sovereignty."

Douglas constantly appealed to the prejudices of the people, and arrayed them against the doctrine of negro equality. Lincoln, in reply, after asserting their equality under the Declaration of Independence, added : " In the right to eat the bread, without the leave of anybody else, which his own hand earns, he is my equal, and the equal of Judge Douglas, and the equal of every living man." Douglas often said—and he commanded the cheers of his supporters when he said it—" I do not care

whether slavery is voted up or voted down." In his
final speech at Alton, Lincoln reviewed the history
of the churches and of the government in connection
with slavery, and he then asked : "Is it not a false
statesmanship that undertakes to build up a system
of policy upon the basis of caring nothing about the
very thing that everybody does care the most
about?" He then, in the same speech, assailed
Douglas's position in an argument, which is but a
series of statements, and, as a whole, it is, in its logic
and moral sentiment, the equal of anything in the
language: "He may say he doesn't care whether an
indifferent thing is voted up or down, but he must
logically have a choice between a right thing and a
wrong thing. He contends that whatever commu-
nity wants slaves has a right to have them. So they
have, if it is not a wrong. But if it is a wrong, he
cannot say people have a right to do wrong. He
says that, upon the score of equality, slaves should
be allowed to go into a new territory like other
property. This is strictly logical, if there is no difference between it and other property. If it and
other property are equal, his argument is entirely
logical. But if you insist that one is wrong and the
other right, there is no use to institute a comparison between right and wrong. You may turn
over everything in the Democratic policy from beginning to end—whether in the shape it takes on

the statute-book, in the shape it takes in the Dred Scott decision, in the shape it takes in conversation, or in the shape it takes in short maxim-like arguments—it everywhere carefully excludes the idea that there is anything wrong in it. That is the real issue. That is the issue that will continue in this country when these poor tongues of Judge Douglas and myself shall be silent. It is the eternal struggle between these two principles, right and wrong, throughout the world. They are the two principles that have stood face to face from the beginning of time, and will ever continue to struggle. The one is the common right of humanity; and the other, the divine right of kings. It is the same principle in whatever shape it develops itself. It is the same spirit that says, ' You work and toil and earn bread, and I'll eat it.' No matter in what shape it comes, whether from the mouth of a king who seeks to bestride the people of his own nation and live by the fruit of their labor, or from one race of men as an apology for enslaving another race, it is the same tyrannical principle."

To the Democrat who admitted that slavery was a wrong, Mr. Lincoln addressed himself thus: "You never treat it as a wrong. You must not say anything about it in the free States, because *it is not here*. You must not say anything about in the slave States, because *it is there*. You must not say anything about it in the pulpit, because that is religion, and has nothing to do with it. You must not say anything about it in politics, because that will disturb the security of my place. There is no place to talk about it as being wrong, although you say yourself it is a wrong."

Among the rude people with whom Lincoln passed his youth and early manhood, his personal courage was often tested, and usually in support of the rights or pretensions of others, or in behalf of the weak, the wronged, or the dependent. In later years his moral characteristics were subjected to tests equally severe. Mr. Lincoln was not an agitator like Garrison, Phillips, and O'Connell, and as a Reformer he belonged to the class of moderate men, such as Peel and Gladstone; but in no condition did he ever confound right with wrong, or speak of injustice with bated breath. His first printed paper was a plea for temperance; and his second, a eulogy upon the Union. His positive, personal hostility to slavery goes back to the year 1831, when he arrived at New Orleans as a laborer upon a flatboat. "There it was," says Hanks, his companion; "we saw negroes chained, maltreated, whipped and scourged. Lincoln saw it, said nothing much, was silent from feeling, was sad, looked bad, felt bad, was thoughtful and abstracted. I can say, knowing it, that it was on this trip that he formed his opinion of slavery.   It run its iron in him then and there, May, 1831.   I have heard him say so often and often." In 1850, he said to his partner, Mr. Stuart: "The time will come when we must all be Democrats or Abolitionists.   When that time comes my mind is made up.   The slavery question can't be compromised."   In 1855, he said : "Our progress in degeneracy appears to me to be pretty rapid.   As a nation we began by declaring that *all men are created equal.* We now practically read it *all men are created equal except negroes.*"   In his Ottawa speech of 1858, he read an extract from his speech at Peoria, made in 1854, in these words : "This declared indifference, but as I must think *real* zeal for the spread of slavery, I cannot but hate.   I hate it because of the monstrous injustice of slavery itself.   I hate it because it deprives our Republican example of its just influence in the world, enables the enemies of free institutions with plausibility to taunt us as hypocrites, causes the real friends of freedom to doubt our sincerity, and, especially, because it forces so many really good men among ourselves into an open war with the very fundamental principles of civil liberty, criticising the Declaration of Independence, and insisting that there is no right principle of action but self-interest."

These extracts prepare the reader for the most important utterance by Mr. Lincoln previous to his elevation to the Presidency.

The Republican Convention of the State of Illinois met at Springfield, June 17, 1858, and nominated Mr. Lincoln for the seat in the Senate of the United States then held by Stephen A. Douglas. This action was expected, and Mr. Lincoln had prepared himself to accept the nomination in a speech which he foresaw would be the pivot of debate with Judge Douglas. That speech he submitted to a council of at least twelve of his personal and political friends, all of whom advised him to omit or to change materially the first paragraph. This Mr. Lincoln refused to do, even when challenged by the opinion that it would cost him his seat in the Senate. It did cost him his seat in the Senate, but the speech would have been delivered had he foreseen that it would cost him much more. After its delivery, and while the canvass was going on, he said to his friends: "You may think that speech was a mistake, but I never have believed it was, and you will see the day when you will consider it was the wisest thing I ever said. If I had to draw a pen across and erase my whole life from existence, and I had one poor gift or choice left as to what I should save from the wreck, I should choose that speech, and leave it to the world unerased." These are the words that he prized so highly, and which, for the time, cost him so much: "If we could first know where we are and whither we are tending, we could better judge what to do and how to do it. We are now far into the fifth year since a policy was initiated with the avowed object and confident promise of putting an end to slavery agitation. Under the operation of that policy, that agitation has not only not ceased, but has constantly augmented. In my opinion it will not cease until a crisis shall have been reached and passed. 'A house divided against itself cannot stand.' I believe this government cannot endure permanently, half slave and half free. I do not expect the Union to be dissolved; I do not expect the house to fall; but I do expect it will cease to be divided. It will become all one thing or all the other; either the opponents of slavery will arrest the further spread of it, and place it where the public mind shall rest in the belief that it is in the course of ultimate extinction, or its advocates will push it forward, till it shall become alike lawful in all the States, old as well as new, North as well as South." To the pro-slavery, sensitive, prejudiced, Union-saving classes it was not difficult to interpret this paragraph in a highly offensive sense. The phrase, "A house divided against itself cannot stand" was interpreted as a declaration against the Union. It was, in fact, a declaration of the existence of the irrepressible conflict.

Douglas availed himself of the opportunity to excite the prejudices of the people, and thus secured

his re-election to the Senate. Mr. Lincoln had a
higher object: he sought to change public sentiment.
No man ever lived who better understood the means
of affecting public sentiment, or more highly appreciated its power and importance. At Ottawa he said:
"In this and like communities public sentiment is
everything. With public sentiment nothing can fail;
without it nothing can succeed. Consequently, he
who molds public sentiment goes deeper than he
who enacts statutes or pronounces decisions. He
makes statutes and decisions possible or impossible
to be executed."

I have quoted thus freely from Mr. Lincoln that
we may appreciate his moral courage; that we may
rest in the opinion that he was an early, constant,
consistent advocate of human liberty; and that we
might enjoy the charm of his transcendently clear
thought, convincing logic, and power of statement.
When he became President, and was called to bear
the chief burden in the struggle for liberty and the
Union, he was never dismayed by the condition of
public affairs, nor disturbed by apprehensions for his
personal safety. He was like a soldier in the field,
enlisted for duty, and danger was, of course, incident
to it. I was alone with Mr. Lincoln more than two
hours of the Sunday next after Pope's defeat in
August, 1862. That was the darkest day of the sad
years of the war. McClellan had failed upon the

26

Peninsula. Pope's army, reinforced by the remains of the Army of the Peninsula, had been driven within the fortification of Washington. Our losses of men had been enormous, but most serious of all was the loss of confidence in commanders. The army did not confide in Pope, and the authorities did not confide in McClellan. In that crisis Lincoln surrendered his own judgment to the opinion of the army, and re-established McClellan in command. When the business to which I had been summoned by the President was over—strange business for the time: the appointment of assessors and collectors of internal revenue—he was kind enough to ask my opinion as to the command of the army. The way was thus opened for conversation, and for me to say at the end that I thought our success depended upon the emancipation of the slaves. To this he said : " You would not have it done now, would you ? Must we not wait for something like a victory?" This was the second and most explicit intimation to me of his purpose in regard to slavery. In the preceding July or early in August, at an interview upon business connected with my official duties, he said, " Let me read two letters," and taking them from a pigeon-hole over his table he proceeded at once to do what he had proposed. I have not seen the letters in print. His correspondent was a gentleman in Louisiana, who claimed to be a Union man. He tendered

his advice to the President in regard to the reorganization of that State, and he labored zealously to
impress upon him the dangers and evils of emancipation. The reply of the President is only important from the fact that when he came to that part of
his correspondent's letter he used this expression:
" You must not expect me to give up this government without playing my last card." Emancipation
was his last card. He waited for the time when two
facts or events should coincide. Mr. Lincoln was as
devoted to the Constitution as was ever Mr. Webster. In his view, a military necessity was the only
ground on which the overthrow of slavery in the
States could be justified. Next he waited for a public sentiment in the loyal States not only demanding
emancipation but giving full assurance that the act
would be sustained to the end. As for himself, I
cannot doubt that he had contemplated the policy
of emancipation for many months, and anticipated
the time when he should adopt it. At his interview
with the Chicago clergy he stated the reasons
against emancipation, and stated them so forcibly
that the clergy were not prepared to answer them;
but the accredited account of the interview contains
conclusive proof that Mr. Lincoln then contemplated
issuing the proclamation. It may be remembered by
the reader that in the political campaign of 1862,
a prominent leader of the People's Party, the late

Judge Joel Parker, of Cambridge, Massachusetts, said in public that Mr. Lincoln issued the proclamation under the influence of the loyal governors who met at Altoona in September of that year. As I was about to leave Washington in the month of October to take part in the canvass, I mentioned to the President the fact that such a statement had been made. He at once said : "I never thought of the meeting of the governors. The truth is just this : When Lee came over the river, I made a resolution that if McClellan drove him back I would send the proclamation after him. The battle of Antietam was fought Wednesday, and until Saturday I could not find out whether we had gained a victory or lost a battle. It was then too late to issue the proclamation that day, and the fact is I fixed it up a little Sunday, and Monday I let them have it."

Men will probably entertain different opinions of one part of Lincoln's character. He not only possessed the apparently innate faculty of comprehending the tendency, purposes and opinions of masses of men, but he observed and measured with accuracy the peculiarities of individuals who were about him, and made those individuals, sometimes through their peculiarities and sometimes in spite of them, the instruments or agents of his own views. Of the three chief men in his Cabinet, Seward, Chase and Stanton, Mr. Stanton was the only one who never thus yielded to this power of the President. The reason was creditable alike to the President and to Mr. Stanton. Mr. Stanton was frank and fearless in his office, devoted to duty, destitute of ambition, and uncompromising in his views touching emancipation and the suppression of the rebellion. The popular sentiment of the day made no impression upon him. He was always ready for every forward movement, and he could never be reconciled to a backward step, either in the field or the Cabinet. It is no injustice to Mr. Seward and Mr. Chase to say that they had ambitions which under some circumstances might disturb the judgment. These ambitions and their tendencies could not escape the notice of the President.

Mr. Lincoln was indifferent to those matters of government that were relatively unimportant; but he devoted himself with conscientious diligence to the graver questions and topics of official duty, and in the first months of his administration, at a moment of supreme peril, by his pre-eminent wisdom, of which there remains indubitable proof, he saved the country from a foreign war. I refer to the letter of instruction to Mr. Adams, written in May, 1861, and relating to the proclamation of the Government of Great Britain recognizing the belligerent character of the Confederate States.

In the greatest exigencies his power of judging

402 REMINISCENCES OF ABRAHAM LINCOLN

immediately and wisely did not desert him. On the eve of the battle of Gettysburg, General Hooker resigned the command of the army. This act was a painful, a terrible surprise to Mr. Stanton and the President. Mr. Stanton's account to me was this: "When I received the dispatch my heart sank within me, and I was more depressed than at any other moment of the war. I could not say that any other officer knew General Hooker's plans, or the position even of the various divisions of the army. I sent for the President to come to the War Office at once. It was in the evening, but the President soon appeared. I handed him the dispatch. As he read it his face became like lead. I said, 'What shall be done?' He replied instantly, 'Accept his resignation.'" In secret, and without consulting any one else, the President and Secretary of War canvassed the merits of the various officers of the army, and decided to place General Meade in command. Of this decision General Meade was informed by a dispatch sent by a special messenger, who reached his quarters before the break of day the next morning. It may be interesting to know the grounds on which the President decided to promote General Meade.

First—That he was a good soldier, if not a brilliant one.

Second—That he was a native of Pennsylvania,

and that State at that moment was the battle-field of the Union.

Third—The President apprehended that a demand would be made for the restoration of General McClellan, and this he desired to prevent by the selection of a man who represented the same political opinions in the army and in the country.

Mr. Lincoln entertained advanced thoughts and opinions upon all worthy topics of public concern; indeed, his opinions were in advance, usually, of his acts as a public man. This is but another mode of stating the truth, that he possessed the faculty of foreseeing the course of public opinion—a faculty essential to statesmen in popular governments.

In 1853, in a campaign letter, he said : " I go for all sharing the privileges of government who assist in bearing its burdens. Consequently, I go for admitting all whites to the right of suffrage who pay taxes or bear arms, by no means excluding females." In 1854, he said : " Labor is prior to and independent of capital. Capital is only the fruit of labor, and could never have existed if labor had not first existed. Labor is the support of capital, and deserves much the higher consideration." In April of the same year, he said : " I am naturally antislavery. If slavery is not wrong, nothing is wrong. I cannot remember when I did not so think and feel." In his last public utterance he declared himself in favor of extending the elective franchise to colored men.

Thus he died without one limitation in his expressed opinions of the rights of men which the historian or eulogist will desire to suppress or to qualify. It is to be said further of this many-sided man, and most opulent in natural resources, that he takes rank with the first logicians and orators of every age. His mastery over Douglas in the debate of 1858 was complete. While President, and by successive letters, he effectually repelled the attacks and silenced the criticisms of the New York Committee, of which Erastus Corning was the head, that condemned illegal arrests and the suspension of the writ of habeas corpus; of the Union Committee of the State of Illinois, that proposed to save the Union if slavery could be saved with it; of the Democratic Convention of the State of Ohio, that denounced the arrest of Vallandingham; and of Horace Greeley himself, when he complained of the policy the President seemed to be pursuing on the subject of emancipation.

As I approach my conclusion, I ask a judgment upon Mr. Lincoln, not as a competitor with Mr. Douglas for a seat in the Senate of the United States, but as a competitor for fame with the first orators of this and other countries, of this and other ages.

In support of this view I quote the closing paragraph of his first speech in the canvass of 1858. "Our cause, then, must be intrusted to, and conducted by its own undoubted friends, those whose hands are free, whose hearts are in the work, who do care for the result. Two years ago the Republicans of the nation mustered over thirteen hundred thousand strong. We did this under the single impulse of resistance to a common danger, with every external circumstance against us. Of strange, discordant, and even hostile elements, we gathered from the four winds, and formed and fought the battle through, under the constant, hot fire of a disciplined, proud and pampered enemy. Did we brave all then to falter now? Now, when that same enemy is wavering, dissevered and belligerent? The result is not doubtful. We shall not fail; if we stand firm we shall *not fail*. Wise counsels may accelerate, or mistakes delay it, but sooner or later the victory is sure to come." We all remember his simple, earnest, persuasive appeals to the South, in his first inaugural address. At the end he says : " I am loath to close. We are not enemies, but friends. We must not be enemies. Though passion may have strained, it must not break our bonds of affection. The mystic cords of memory, stretching from every battle-field and patriot grave to every living heart and hearthstone all over this broad land, will yet swell the chorus of the Union when again touched, as surely they will be, by the better angels of our nature." There is nothing elsewhere in our literature of plaintive entreaty to be compared with this. It combines the eloquence of the orator with the imagery and inspiration of the poet. But the three great papers on which Lincoln's fame will be carried along the ages are the proclamation of emancipation, his oration at Gettysburg, and his second inaugural address. The oration ranks with the noblest productions of antiquity, with the works of Pericles, of Demosthenes, of Cicero, and rivals the finest passages of Grattan, Burke or Webster. This is not the opinion of Americans only, but of the cultivated in other countries, whose judgment anticipates the judgment of posterity.

When we consider the place, the occasion, the man, and, more than all, when we consider the oration itself, can we doubt that it ranks with the first of American classics? That literature is immortal which commands a permanent place in the schools of a country, and is there any composition more certain of that destiny than Lincoln's oration at Gettysburg? "Fourscore and seven years ago, our fathers brought forth upon this continent a new nation, conceived in liberty and dedicated to the proposition that all men are created equal. Now, we are engaged in a great civil war, testing whether that nation, or any nation so conceived and so dedicated, can long endure. We are met on a great battle-field of that war. We are met to dedicate a portion of it as the final resting-place of those who have given their lives that that nation might live. It is altogether fitting and proper that we should do this. But in a larger sense we cannot dedicate, we cannot consecrate, we cannot hallow this ground. The brave men, living and dead, who struggled here, have consecrated it far above our power to add or detract. The world will little note nor long remember what we say here, but it can never forget what they did here. It is for us, the living, rather to be dedicated here to the unfinished work that they have thus far so nobly carried on. It is rather for us to be here dedicated to the great task remaining before us; that from these honored dead we take increased devotion to the cause for which they here gave the last full measure of devotion; that we here highly resolve that these dead shall not have died in vain; that the nation shall, under God, have a new birth of freedom, and that government of the people, by the people, for the people, shall not perish from the earth." But if all that Lincoln said and was should fail to carry his name and character to future ages, the emancipation of four million human beings by his single official act is a passport to all of immortality that earth can give. There is no other individual act performed by any person on this continent that can be compared with it. The Declaration of Independence, the Constitution, were each the work of bodies of men. The Proclamation of Emancipation in this respect stands alone. The responsibility was wholly upon Lincoln; the glory is chiefly his. No one can now say whether the Declaration of Independence, or the Constitution of the United States, or the Proclamation of Emancipation was the highest, best gift to the country and to mankind. With the curse of slavery in America there was no hope for republican institutions in other countries. In the presence of slavery the Declaration of Independence had lost its power; practically, it had become a lie. In the presence of slavery we were to the rest of mankind and to ourselves a nation of hypocrites. The gift of freedom to four million negroes was not more valuable to them than to us; and not more valuable to us than to the friends of liberty in other parts of the world.

In these days, when politicians and parties are odious to many thoughtful and earnest-minded persons, it may not be amiss to look at Mr. Lincoln as a politician and partisan. These he was, first of all and always. He had political convictions that were ineradicable, and they were wholly partisan. As the rebellion became formidable, the Republican party became the party of the Union; and as the party of the Union, with Mr. Lincoln at its head, it was from first to last the only political organization in the country that consistently, persistently, and without qualification of purpose, met, and in the end successfully met, every demand of the enemies of the government, whether proffered in diplomatic notes or on the field of battle. He struggled first for the Union, and then for the overthrow of slavery as the only formidable enemy of the Union. These were his tests of political fellowship, and he carefully excluded from place every man who could not bear them. He accepted the great and most manifest lesson of free government, that every wise and vigorous administration represents the majority party, and that the best days of every free country are those days when a party takes and wields power by a popular verdict, and guards itself at every step against the assaults of a scrutinizing and vigorous opposition. He accepted the essential truths that a free government is a political organization, and that the political opinions of those intrusted with its administration, as to what the government should be and do, are of more consequence to the country than even their knowledge of orthography and etymology. As a consequence, he accepted the proposition that every place of executive discretion or of eminent administrative power should be occupied by the friends of the government. This, not because the spoils belong to the victors, but for the elevated and sufficient reason that the chief offices of state are instrumentalities and agencies by

which the majority carry out their principles, perfect
their measures, and render their policy acceptable to
the country.   And also for the further reason that
in case of failure the administration is without excuse.
The entire public policy of Mr. Lincoln was the natural outgrowth of his political principles as a Republican.   Through the influence of experience and the
exercise of power the politician ripened into the
statesman, but the ideas, principles, and purposes of
the statesman were the ideas, principles, and purposes
of the partisan politician.   In prosecuting the war
for the Union, in the steps taken for the emancipation of the slaves, Mr. Lincoln appeared to follow
rather than to lead the Republican party.   But his
own views were more advanced usually than those of
his party, and he waited patiently and confidently for
the healthy movements of public sentiment which he
well knew were in the right direction.   No man was
ever more firmly or consistently the representative
of a party than was Mr. Lincoln, and his acknowledged greatness is due, first, to the wisdom and justice of the principles and measures of the political
party that he represented, and, secondly, to his fidelity in every hour of his administration, and in every
crisis of public affairs, to the principles, ideas and
measures of the party with which he was identified.

Having seen Mr. Lincoln as frontiersman, politician,
lawyer, stump-speaker, orator, statesman and patriot,
it only remains for us to contemplate him as an his-

torical personage. First of all, it is to be said that Mr. Lincoln is next in fame to Washington, and it is by no means certain that history will not assign to Lincoln an equal place, and this without any qualification of the claims or disparagement in any way of the virtues of the Father of this country. The measure of Washington's fame is full, but for many centuries, and over vast spaces of the globe and among all peoples passing from barbarism or semi-servitude to civilization and freedom, Mr. Lincoln will be hailed as the Liberator. In all governments struggling for existence, his example will be a guide and a help. Neither the gift of prophecy nor the quality of imagination is needed to forecast the steady growth of Lincoln's fame. At the close of the twentieth century the United States will contain one hundred and fifty or two hundred million inhabitants, and from one-fourth to one-third of the population of the globe will then use the English language. To all these and to all their descendants Mr. Lincoln will be one of the three great characters of American history, while to the unnumbered millions of the negro race in the United States, in Africa, in South America, and in the islands of the sea, he will be the great figure of all ages and of every nation. His fame will increase and spread with the knowledge of Republican institutions, with the expansion and power of the English-speaking race, and with the deeper respect which civilization will create for whatever is attractive in personal character, wise in the administration of public affairs, just in policy, or liberal and comprehensive in the exercise of constitutional and extra-constitutional powers.

It was but an inadequate recognition of the character and services of Mr. Lincoln that was made by the patriots of Rome when they chose a fragment from the wall of Servius Tullius and sent it to the President with this inscription: "To Abraham Lincoln, President for the second time of the American Republic, citizens of Rome present this stone, from the wall of Servius Tullius, by which the memory of each of those brave asserters of Liberty may be associated. Anno 1865." The final and nobler tribute to Mr. Lincoln is yet to be rendered, not by a single city nor by the patriots of a single country. A knowledge of his life and character is to be carried by civilization into every nation and to every people. Under him and largely through his acts and influence justice became the vital force of the Republic. The war established our power. The policy of Mr. Lincoln and those who acted with him secured the reign of justice ultimately in our domestic affairs. Possessing power and exhibiting justice, the nation should pursue a policy of peace.

Power, Justice and Peace; in them is the glory of the regenerated Republic.

GEORGE S. BOUTWELL.

XX

"DEAR TO DEMOCRACY"

GLAD am I to give even the most brief and shorn testimony in memory of Abraham Lincoln. Everything I heard about him authentically, and every time I saw him (and it was my fortune through 1862 to '65 to see, or pass a word with, or watch him, personally, perhaps twenty or thirty times*), added to and annealed my respect and love

---

* From my Note-book in 1864, at Washington City, I find this memorandum, under date of August 12 :

I see the President almost every day, as I happen to live where he passes to or from his lodgings out of town. He never sleeps at the White House during the hot season, but has quarters at a healthy location, some three miles north of the city, the Soldiers' Home, a United States military establishment. I saw him this morning about 8.30 coming in to business, riding on Vermont Avenue, near L Street. He always has a company of twenty-five or thirty cavalry, with sabres drawn, and held upright over their shoulders. The party makes no great show in uniforms or horses. Mr. Lincoln, on the saddle, generally rides a good-sized, easy-going gray horse, is dress'd in plain black, somewhat rusty and dusty ; wears a black stiff hat, and looks about as ordinary in attire, &c., as the commonest man. A lieutenant, with yellow straps, rides at his left, and following behind, two by two, come the cavalry men in their yellow-striped jackets. They are generally going at a slow trot, as that is the pace set them by the One they wait upon. The sabres and accoutrements clank, and the entirely unornamental *cortege* as it trots toward Lafayette Square arouses no sensation, only some curious stranger stops and gazes. I see very plainly ABRAHAM

27

at the passing moment.   And as I dwell on what I myself heard or saw of the mighty Westerner, and blend it with the history and literature of my age, and of what I can get of all ages, and conclude it with his death, it seems like some tragic play, superior to all else I know—vaster and fierier and more convulsionary, for this America of ours, than Eschylus or Shakspeare ever drew for Athens or for England.   And then the Moral permeating, underlying all ! the Lesson that none so remote, none so illiterate—no age, no class—but may directly or indirectly read !

LINCOLN's dark brown face, with the deep cut lines, the eyes, &c., always to me with a latent sadness in the expression.   We have got so that we always exchange bows, and very cordial ones.

Sometimes the President goes and comes in an open barouche.   The cavalry always accompany him, with drawn sabres.   Often I notice as he goes out evenings—and sometimes in the morning, when he returns early—he turns off and halts at the large and handsome residence of the Secretary of War on K Street, and holds conference there.   If in his barouche, I can see from my window he does not alight, but sits in the vehicle, and Mr. Stanton comes out to attend him.   Sometimes one of his sons, a boy of ten or twelve, accompanies him, riding at his right on a pony.

Earlier in the summer I occasionally saw the President and his wife, toward the latter part of the afternoon, out in a barouche, on a pleasure ride through the city.   Mrs. Lincoln was dressed in complete black, with a long crape veil. The equipage is of the plainest kind, only two horses, and they nothing extra. They pass'd me once very close, and I saw the President in the face fully, as they were moving slow, and his look, though abstracted, happen'd to be directed steadily in my eye.   He bow'd and smiled, but far beneath his smile I noticed well the expression I have alluded to.   None of the artists or pictures have caught the subtle and indirect expression of this man's face.   One of the great portrait painters of two or three centuries ago is needed.

Abraham Lincoln's was really one of those characters, the best of which is the result of long trains
of cause and effect—needing a certain spaciousness
of time, and perhaps even remoteness, to properly
enclose them—having unequaled influence on the
shaping of this Republic (and therefore the world)
as to-day, and then far more important in the future.
Thus the time has by no means yet come for a thorough measurement of him. Nevertheless, we who live
in his era—who have seen him, and heard him, face
to face, and are in the midst of, or just parting from,
the strong and strange events which he and we have
had to do with, can in some respects bear valuable,
perhaps indispensable testimony concerning him.

I should first like to give what I call a very fair
and characteristic likeness of Lincoln, as I saw him
and watched him one afternoon in Washington, for
nearly half an hour, not long before his death. It
was as he stood on the balcony of the National
Hotel, Pennsylvania Avenue, making a short speech
to the crowd in front, on the occasion either of a set
of new colors presented to a famous Illinois regiment,
or of the daring capture, by the Western men, of
some flags from "the enemy," (which latter phrase,
by the by, was not used by him at all in his remarks.)
How the picture happened to be made I do not
know, but I bought it a few days afterward in
Washington, and it was endorsed by every one

to whom I showed it.   Though hundreds of por-
traits have been made, by painters and photogra-
phers (many to pass on, by copies, to future times),
I have never seen one yet that in my opinion de-
served to be called a perfectly *good likeness;* nor do
I believe there is really such a one in existence.
May I not say too, that, as there is no entirely competent and emblematic likeness of Abraham Lincoln
in picture or statue, there is not—perhaps cannot
be—any fully appropriate literary statement or sum-
ming-up of him, yet in existence.

The best way to estimate the value of Lincoln is
to think what the condition of America would be to-
day, if he had never lived—never been President.
His nomination and first election were mainly accidents, experiments.   Severely viewed, one cannot
think very much of American Political Parties, from
the beginning, after the Revolutionary War, down
to the present time.   Doubtless, while they have had
their uses—have been and are " the grass on which
the cow feeds "—and indispensable economies of
growth—it is undeniable that under flippant names
they have merely identified temporary passions, or
freaks, or sometimes prejudice, ignorance, or hatred.
The only thing like a great and worthy idea vitaliz-
ing a party and making it heroic was the enthusiasm
in '64 for re-electing Abraham Lincoln, and the reason behind that enthusiasm.

How does this man compare with the acknowledged " Father of his country?" Washington was
modeled on the best Saxon and Franklin of the age
of the Stuarts (rooted in the Elizabethan period)—
was essentially a noble Englishman, and just the
kind needed for the occasions and the times of 1776–
'83. Lincoln, underneath his practicality, was far
less European, far more Western, original, essentially non-conventional, and had a certain sort of
out-door or prairie stamp. One of the best of
the late commentators on Shakespeare (Professor
Dowden), makes the height and aggregate of
his quality as a poet to be, that he thoroughly
blended the ideal with the practical or realistic. If
this be so, I should say that what Shakespeare did
in poetic expression, Abraham Lincoln essentially
did in his personal and official life. I should say
the invisible foundations and vertebra of his character, more than any man's in history, were mystical,
abstract, moral and spiritual—while upon all of them
was built, and out of all of them radiated, under the
control of the average of circumstances, what the vulgar call *horse-sense*, and a life often bent by temporary
but most urgent materialistic and political reasons.

He seems to have been a man of indomitable
firmness (even obstinacy) on rare occasions, involving great points ; but he was generally very easy,
flexible, tolerant, respecting minor matters. I note

that even those reports and anecdotes intended to level him down, all leave the tinge of a favorable impression of him. As to his religious nature, it seems to me to have certainly been of the amplest, deepest-rooted kind.

But I do not care to dwell on the features presented so many times, and that will readily occur to every one in recalling Abraham Lincoln and his era. It is more from the wish—and it no doubt actuates others—to bring for our own sake, some record, however incompetent—some leaf or little wreath to place, as on a grave.

Already a new generation begins to tread the stage, since the persons and events of the Secession War. I have more than once fancied to myself the time when the present century has closed and a new one opened, and the men and deeds of that contest have become vague and mythical—fancied perhaps in some great Western city, or group collected together, or public festival, where the days of old, of 1863 and '4 and '5 are discussed—some ancient soldier sitting in the background as the talk goes on, and betraying himself by his emotion and moist eyes —like the journeying Ithacan at the banquet of King Alcinoüs, when the bard sings the contending warriors, and their battles on the plains of Troy:

"So from the sluices of Ulysses' eyes,
Fast fell the tears, and sighs succeeded sighs."

I have fancied, I say, some such venerable relic of this time of ours, preserved to the next or still the next generation of America. I have fancied on such occasion, the young men gathering around ; the awe, the eager questions. "What! have you seen Abraham Lincoln — and heard him speak — and touched his hand ? Have you, with your own eyes, looked on Grant, and Lee and Sherman?"

Dear to Democracy, to the very last! And among the paradoxes generated by America not the least curious, was that spectacle of all the kings and queens and emperors of the earth, many from remote distances, sending tributes of condolence and sorrow in memory of one raised through the commonest average of life—a rail-splitter and flat-boatman !

Considered from contemporary points of view— who knows what the future may decide ?—and from the points of view of current Democracy and The Union (the only thing like passion or infatuation in the man was the passion for the Union of These States), Abraham Lincoln seems to me the grandest figure yet, on all the crowded canvas of the Nineteenth Century.

WALT WHITMAN.

XXI

"THE GENTLEST MEMORY OF OUR WORLD"

STRANGE mingling of mirth and tears, of the tragic and grotesque, of cap and crown, of Socrates and Rabelais, of Æsop and Marcus Aurelius, of all that is gentle and just, humorous and honest, merciful, wise, laughable, lovable and divine, and all consecrated to the use of man ; while through all, and over all, an overwhelming sense of obligation, of chivalric loyalty to truth, and upon all the shadow of the tragic end.

Nearly all the great historic characters are impossible monsters, disproportioned by flattery, or by calumny deformed. We know nothing of their peculiarities, or nothing but their peculiarities. About the roots of these oaks there clings none of the earth of humanity. Washington is now only a steel engraving. About the real man who lived and loved and hated and schemed we know but little. The glass through which we look at him is of such high magnifying power that the features are exceedingly indistinct. Hundreds of people are now engaged in smoothing out the lines of Lincoln's face

—forcing all features to the common mold—so that he may be known, not as he really was, but, according to their poor standard, as he should have been.

Lincoln was not a type. He stands alone—no ancestors, no fellows, and no successors. He had the advantage of living in a new country, of social equality, of personal freedom, of seeing in the horizon of his future the perpetual star of hope. He preserved his individuality and his self-respect. He knew and mingled with men of every kind; and, after all, men are the best books. He became acquainted with the ambitions and hopes of the heart, the means used to accomplish ends, the springs of action and the seeds of thought. He was familiar with nature, with actual things, with common facts. He loved and appreciated the poem of the year, the drama of the seasons.

In a new country, a man must possess at least three virtues—honesty, courage and generosity. In cultivated society, cultivation is often more important than soil. A well executed counterfeit passes more readily than a blurred genuine. It is necessary only to observe the unwritten laws of society—to be honest enough to keep out of prison, and generous enough to subscribe in public—where the subscription can be defended as an investment. In a new country, character is essential; in the old, reputation is sufficient. In the new, they find what a man really is;

in the old, he generally passes for what he resembles,
People separated only by distance are much nearer
together than those divided by the walls of caste.

It is no advantage to live in a great city, where
poverty degrades and failure brings despair. The
fields are lovelier than paved streets, and the great
forests than walls of brick. Oaks and elms are
more poetic than steeples and chimneys. In the
country is the idea of home. There you see the
rising and setting sun ; you become acquainted with
the stars and clouds. The constellations are your
friends. You hear the rain on the roof and listen
to the rhythmic sighing of the winds. You are
thrilled by the resurrection called Spring, touched
and saddened by Autumn, the grace and poetry of
death. Every field is a picture, a landscape ; every
landscape, a poem ; every flower, a tender thought ;
and every forest, a fairy-land. In the country you
preserve your identity—your personality. There
you are an aggregation of atoms, but in the city
you are only an atom of an aggregation,

Lincoln never finished his education. To the
night of his death he was a pupil, a learner, an in-
quirer, a seeker after knowledge. You have no idea
how many men are spoiled by what is called education. For the most part, colleges are places where
pebbles are polished and diamonds are dimmed. If
Shakespeare had graduated at Oxford, he might

have been a quibbling attorney or a hypocritical parson.

Lincoln was a many-sided man, acquainted with smiles and tears, complex in brain, single in heart, direct as light; and his words, candid as mirrors, gave the perfect image of his thought. He was never afraid to ask—never too dignified to admit that he did not know. No man had keener wit or kinder humor. He was not solemn. Solemnity is a mask worn by ignorance and hypocrisy—it is the preface, prologue, and index to the cunning or the stupid. He was natural in his life and thought— master of the story-teller's art, in illustration apt, in application perfect, liberal in speech, shocking Pharisees and prudes, using any word that wit could disinfect.

He was a logician. Logic is the necessary product of intelligence and sincerity. It cannot be learned. It is the child of a clear head and a good heart. He was candid, and with candor often deceived the deceitful. He had intellect without arrogance, genius without pride, and religion without cant—that is to say, without bigotry and without deceit.

He was an orator—clear, sincere, natural. He did not pretend. He did not say what he thought others thought, but what he thought. If you wish to be sublime you must be natural—you must keep close to the grass. You must sit by the fireside of the heart: above the clouds it is too cold. You must be simple in your speech: too much polish suggests insincerity. The great orator idealizes the real, transfigures the common, makes even the inanimate throb and thrill, fills the gallery of the imagination with statues and pictures perfect in form and color, brings to light the gold hoarded by memory, the miser—shows the glittering coin to the spendthrift, hope—enriches the brain, ennobles the heart, and quickens the conscience. Between his lips, words bud and blossom.

If you wish to know the difference between an orator and an elocutionist—between what is felt and what is said—between what the heart and brain can do together and what the brain can do alone—read Lincoln's wondrous words at Gettysburg, and then the speech of Edward Everett. The oration of Lincoln will never be forgotten. It will live until languages are dead and lips are dust. The speech of Everett will never be read. The elocutionists believe in the virtue of voice, the sublimity of syntax, the majesty of long sentences, and the genius of gesture. The orator loves the real, the simple, the natural. He places the thought above all. He knows that the greatest ideas should be expressed in the shortest words—that the greatest statues need the least drapery.

Lincoln was an immense personality—firm but not obstinate. Obstinacy is egotism—firmness, heroism. He influenced others without effort, unconsciously; and they submitted to him as men submit to nature, unconsciously. He was severe with himself, and for that reason lenient with others. He appeared to apologize for being kinder than his fellows. He did merciful things as stealthily as others committed crimes. Almost ashamed of tenderness, he said and did the noblest words and deeds with that charming confusion—that awkwardness—that is the perfect grace of modesty. As a noble man, wishing to pay a small debt to a poor neighbor, reluctantly offers a hundred-dollar bill and asks for change, fearing that he may be suspected either of making a display of wealth or a pretense of payment, so Lincoln hesitated to show his wealth of goodness, even to the best he knew.

A great man stooping, not wishing to make his fellows feel that they were small or mean.

He knew others, because perfectly acquainted with himself. He cared nothing for place, but everything for principle; nothing for money, but everything for independence. Where no principle was involved, easily swayed—willing to go slowly, if in the right direction—sometimes willing to stop, but he would not go back, and he would not go wrong. He was willing to wait. He knew that the event was not waiting, and that fate was not the fool of chance. He knew that slavery had defenders, but no defense, and that they who attack the right must wound themselves. He was neither tyrant nor slave. He neither knelt nor scorned. With him, men were neither great nor small,—they were right or wrong. Through manners, clothes, titles, rags and race he saw the real—that which is. Beyond accident, policy, compromise and war he saw the end. He was patient as Destiny, whose undecipherable hieroglyphs were so deeply graven on his sad and tragic face.

Nothing discloses real character like the use of power. It is easy for the weak to be gentle. Most people can bear adversity. But if you wish to know what a man really is, give him power. This is the supreme test. It is the glory of Lincoln that, having almost absolute power, he never abused it, except upon the side of mercy.

Wealth could not purchase, power could not awe this divine, this loving man. He knew no fear except the fear of doing wrong. Hating slavery, pitying the master—seeking to conquer, not persons, but prejudices—he was the embodiment of the self-denial, the courage, the hope, and the nobility of a nation. He spoke, not to inflame, not to upbraid, but to convince. He raised his hands, not to strike, but in benediction. He longed to pardon.

He loved to see the pearls of joy on the cheeks of a wife whose husband he had rescued from death.

Lincoln was the grandest figure of the fiercest civil war.   He is the gentlest memory of our world.

ROBERT G. INGERSOLL.

THE END